LATIN AMERICA'S CHRISTIAN DEMOCRATIC PARTIES

LATIN AMERICA'S CHRISTIAN DEMOCRATIC PARTIES

A Political Economy

Edward A. Lynch

PRAEGER

Westport, Connecticut
London

Library of Congress Cataloging-in-Publication Data

Lynch, Edward A.
    Latin America's Christian democratic parties : a political economy /
Edward A. Lynch.
       p. cm.
    Includes bibliographical references and index.
    ISBN 0-275-94464-6 (alk. paper)
    1. Christian democratic parties — Latin America 2. Christian
democracy — Latin America.   3. Latin America — Economic policy.
I. Title.
JL969.A45L96 1993
324.28'082 — dc20   92-23069

British Library Cataloguing in Publication Data is available.

Library of Congress Catalog Card Number: 92-23069
ISBN: 0-275-94464-6

First published in 1993

Praeger Publishers, 88 Post Road West, Westport, CT 06881
An imprint of Greenwood Publishing Group, Inc.

Printed in the United States of America

∞™

The paper used in this book complies with the
Permanent Paper Standard issued by the National
Information Standards Organization (Z39.48 — 1984).

10 9 8 7 6 5 4 3 2 1

Contents

» «
———————————

Acknowledgments

My interest in the relationship between politics and economics is a longstanding one. My interest in the progress and activities of Latin American political parties is even older. Thus, it is impossible to highlight, or even to mention, all the people who have contributed to my thinking on these important issues. Some individuals, however, have had a direct impact on this particular book and thus deserve my thanks.

David Jordan suggested concentrating on the policies of particular political parties as a way of managing some of my initial studies of Latin America. Jack Schrems at Villanova University helped to stimulate my interest in papal encyclicals and also provided friendly guidance and correction to my considerations of neoliberalism. Alfred G. Cuzán, from the University of West Florida, heard me deliver some of the thoughts contained here at a Southern Political Science Association Conference and offered helpful suggestions.

Both Villanova's Department of Political Science and Hollins College provided word processing, research, and other support, without which this project would have been considerably delayed. Villanova's most valuable contribution was assigning me Richard Gibbons and John Kreeger as research assistants. Rich and John spent countless hours in library stacks and microform rooms finding me the raw material for this book. Their imagination, efficiency, and intelligence were invaluable. I am, of course, solely responsible for everything that appears here.

Finally, for providing just the right combination of intellectual guidance and friendly encouragement, for asking some of those basic questions that I did not think to ask, for reading each incarnation of this idea, and for just putting up with it all, I thank you, Jacquie.

» «
———————

Introduction

In 1964, Eduardo Frei Montalva won the Chilean presidential election for the Chilean Christian Democratic Party. Four years later, Rafael Caldera brought the Venezuelan Christian Democrats to power. These two victories, in two of the only Latin American countries that were democratic during that period, seemed to presage a major shift in Latin American politics. Dominated for decades by violent clashes between the polarized forces of the right and left, the continent's politics seemed to have finally found its center.

The Christian Democrats were, on the surface, an attractive political movement that seemed to offer something to both poles. They were staunchly anti-Communist, yet they were not trapped in a hopeless reactionary mode. They accepted the need for radical economic and social change in Latin America, yet they pledged to achieve this change through peaceful means. Where they promised land reform, they also promised compensation for displaced owners. Where they promised nationalization of basic resources, compensation for foreign multinational corporations was part of the policy. The Christian Democrats seemed to offer a society in which laborers and capitalists could coexist without struggle and with mutual respect. Private property and social responsibility, they believed, could be similarly juxtaposed.

By 1973, however, Christian Democrats had been voted out of power in both Chile and Venezuela, in both cases by large margins. In the few Latin American countries in which democracy still existed in the 1970s, Christian Democracy was weak. Even as Latin American states restored democracy in the 1980s, Christian Democratic parties did poorly. On the few occasions when they were elected, they were not effective, and they were always replaced after one term. Christian Democracy, which had begun the 1960s with realistic hopes of dominating the continent's politics, ended the 1980s with its future in doubt.

This book attempts to answer the question of how and why this decline took place. My hypothesis, based on extensive examination of the evidence, is that Christian Democracy has failed to reach its potential because it has forgotten its ideological roots. This has caused Christian Democratic parties to veer unpredictably to the political left and right, to attempt to imitate their rivals, and to fail to present a coherent alternative to these rivals. Most significantly, Christian Democrats have embraced the Latin American state too closely, particularly in their economic policies. They have been far too anxious to involve the state in economic decisions.

STATISM, CORPORATISM, AND THE CHRISTIAN DEMOCRATS

Alfred Stepan, in his seminal work on the state-society relationship, argued that the Catholic tradition in Latin America has contributed significantly to the continent's high degree of state economic intervention. The political and social thought of the Catholic Church, he says, is profoundly statist and has always supported the notion of a dominant state. The Catholic Church teaches its members to be obedient, even subservient, to any legitimate authority.[1]

This understanding of Catholic political thought is simply incorrect. Although in its social writings the Catholic Church acknowledges the necessity of the state to make up for the shortcomings of society, it fears the state and seeks to limit its powers. Catholic political thinkers prefer that civil society look after itself, with minimal help from the state. The mechanisms for self-government are independent social groups.

These groups, which include families, labor unions, professional organizations, churches, private schools, chambers of commerce, charitable organizations, and others, act to restrict radical individualism by inducing people to put the interests of the group before their own selfish interests. In doing so, independent social groups also protect individuals from the power of the state. An atomized society, in which individualism has destroyed independent social groups or warped their political function, is an invitation to overbearing state power.

Of equal importance to a genuine understanding of Catholic political thought is the relationship between independent social groups and the state. In this regard, Stepan draws too close a connection between the Catholic Church's political theory and that of Aristotle. Although they have much in common, there is an important difference. For Aristotle, the state is anterior to independent social groups, just as the whole is prior to the parts. The latter receive their authority from the state, and the state grants this authority for its own purposes.

For Catholic political thinkers, the relationship is just the opposite. Families, private schools, churches, unions, professional organizations, and even substate political entities, all are anterior to the state in authority, even if they are created after a particular state is established. While all such groups have duties to a legitimate state, just as citizens have the duty to obey the just commands of a legitimate state, the state has duties also. It owes recognition to independent social groups and it cannot destroy them. If the state attempts to do so, it has exercised authority illegitimately and forfeited its right to be obeyed.

There are various ways to attack independent social groups, and Catholic social thought condemns them all. The most direct method of attack is persecution, especially suppression of independent groups, prohibitions against their formation, or prohibitions against their activities. More subtle, but no less dangerous, is for the state to make independent social groups part of the state apparatus, thus destroying the independence that is central to their contribution to a healthy society.

To speak favorably of the political function of social groups is to suggest support for some form of corporatism. This can be defined as a method of organizing society into cohesive social groups that serve as organs of political representation and that exercise some control over persons and activities within their jurisdiction. The Catholic Church distinguishes between acceptable and unacceptable forms of corporatism.

If this term means the state's recognition that its authority and its freedom of action are limited by the existence of social groups that it does not control and cannot easily coerce, this is acceptable. If corporatism means that the state will take the wishes of independent social groups into account when making its decisions, this is also acceptable.

Catholic political thinkers believe that corporatism is illegitimate, however, when the corporatist state wishes to create its own social groups, tie them closely to the state, turn them into the agents of state power, and use them to give the impression that society as a whole is represented. Thus, for example, it is entirely consistent for the Church to insist on the right of labor unions, families, and private schools to have the state pay particular attention to their needs, as the Church did in Benito Mussolini's early days, but then to condemn the creation and official recognition of groups wedded to the Fascist Party, which purported to represent segments of society. This sort of Fascist corporatism has nothing to do with the Catholic concept of the same name. The distinction is a vital one.

Stepan rightly points out that corporatism can be misused to restructure domination. An elite group, accustomed to control of the state and committed to excluding newcomers, can create "official" labor unions, peasant groups, professional organizations, women and youth groups, and numerous other recognized interest groups to give the impression that a political system is open and representative. Groups demanding additional outputs from the state, or perhaps demanding to be left alone, can be co-opted into accepting less, while the real structure of domination continues undisturbed.

Catholic political thinkers agree with Stepan about the danger of such misuse. Thus, Catholic social thought insists on the genuine independence of social groups and warns against close ties to either a state or a political party. This warning includes ties to Christian Democratic parties.

The Church's strong stand in favor of independent social groups, like its insistence on ecclesiastical autonomy, is part of its deeper belief that while state power is indispensable, it must be limited, divided, checked, and even frustrated at times. When the state performs its legitimate functions, citizens owe the state obedience. There will be many times, however, that the state will overstep these bounds. Using Thomas Aquinas's principle of *lex mala, lex nulla,* or "Unjust law is no law," the Catholic Church upholds the right to legitimate civil disobedience and even legitimate revolt.[2] The existence of independent social groups will make this civil disobedience far more effective and perhaps forestall the use of coercive power.

My conclusion, therefore, is that the political, economic, and social thought of the Catholic Church is antistatist in its essentials. If Catholic social thought can be called statist because it also upholds obedience to the just commands of legitimate authority, then only the most extreme forms of libertarianism are not statist. Compared to both the theory and the practice of most Latin American political parties, Catholic social thought is antistatist.

The Bases for Comparison

This book will show that Latin America's Christian Democratic parties have failed to gain greater popularity in Latin America because they have abandoned the principles of Catholic social thought that animated the Christian Democratic movement. This thesis requires some basis for comparing political parties that, after all, came to power and exercised political power in vastly different circumstances. A few words on the reasons for comparison, and the methodology, are in order.

I will compare the political behavior of political parties with certain important shared characteristics. These include similar philosophical antecedents as well as operation under similar political conditions. These similar political conditions include at least a partially established democratic system, with genuinely free elections that are meaningful. By meaningful, I mean that the results accurately reflect the choices that the electorate has made, that the electorate's choices were not unduly restricted, and that the electorate has made its choice on a rational basis.

The Christian Democratic politicians included in this study, therefore, are for the most part elected officials who must face the electorate after being given political power. This book does not include any examination of dictatorial regimes that claim some form of Catholicism as their basis of legitimacy.

Other important points of similarity among Latin American Christian Democratic parties exist that make a comparative study worthwhile. The parties operate within a common cultural heritage and, to a large degree, within a common political culture. The parties operate in countries in which the vast majority of the population is at least nominally Catholic and in which a party that is outwardly committed to the Catholic faith may reasonably expect some support on that basis alone. Almost all Latin American Christian Democratic parties exist in fragile democratic systems and interact with important groups, such as the armed forces, that have not accepted democracy as the most desirable form of government.

In the realm of economic policy, which is the central focus of this book, there are other important points of comparison. All Latin American countries face difficult economic challenges. These include achieving faster and more equitable economic development, although there are vast differences between Latin American countries in this regard. Nevertheless, all Latin American countries face poverty, economic stagnation, poor distribution, currency softness, and foreign economic interference. Put differently, the Latin American Christian Democrats operate in systems with similar social and economic inputs to the political system.

In this regard, it is also appropriate to include the experiences of Christian Democratic parties in the Latin European countries, including Italy, France, and Belgium. These countries, which share a cultural affinity with Latin America, faced many similar economic problems at the time their Christian Democratic parties vied for political power. Italy and Belgium, like the Latin American states, are relatively new to the international scene and must deal with serious ethnic differences within their borders. This common experience also makes it appropriate to exclude consideration of the German Christian Democrats. In their case, the basis for comparison is inadequate. (Were they included, however, their experience would confirm my thesis.)

The most important basis for comparison of Christian Democratic parties is their common ideological heritage. Without exception, Latin America's Christian Democratic parties claim a connection with a common body of political philosophy, namely, Catholic social thought. Whatever differences in emphasis, or differences in actual performance, came about later on, the Christian Democrats maintain that their ideologies are derived from the social thought of the Church. Indeed, the parties' leaders themselves were convinced enough of their common characteristics and concerns to create the International Christian Democratic Union in the 1950s, to which all the Latin European and Latin American Christian Democratic parties belonged.

Since the Christian Democrats themselves profess that they have much in common, and since they all claim descendence from the same political and social philosophy, it is entirely appropriate to compare their performance based on this root philosophy. How well have the Christian Democrats retained their relationship to Catholic social thought?

The evidence shows that Christian Democrats do not gain political support, or even much respect, from jettisoning their first principles. Christian Democrats gain little when they try to achieve greater ideological flexibility, either to broaden their political support or to ease the formation of political coalitions. Whatever benefits such purported pragmatism brings to other political parties, for the Christian Democrats it usually backfires.

This book specifically compares Christian Democratic economic policy outputs. I am not comparing the ways in which these outputs were formed in various Christian Democratic regimes but, rather, the Christian Democrats' economic policies, their effects, their consistency with Catholic social thought, and finally, the costs of any inconsistency.

A Summary of the Hypothesis

Catholic social thought, the acknowledged forerunner of Christian Democracy, provides a coherent, consistent, and comprehensive basis for creating and implementing economic and social policy. Although it is short on specific policy prescriptions, its basic outlines provide more than adequate guidance for a political party seeking to address serious economic and social questions. With some changes in emphasis over the years, the most important elements of Catholic social thought have remained unchanged.

These include an emphasis on the moral and spiritual nature of human beings, with an acknowledgment that their political and economic natures are also important. Catholic social thought holds that neither capitalism nor socialism, in its pure form, is an adequate base for a just society. While suspicious of the radical individualism of capitalism, the authors of Catholic social thought also condemn excessive state power, even in the name of controlling capitalism's excesses. They condemn both philosophies as materialistic.

Catholic social thought supports some of the elements of a free economy, such as private property, free exchange of goods and services, investment for profit, and limited state intervention in the economy. At the same time, it supports a relatively high level of state social spending, while warning that government social programs should not replace existing private programs. At base, Catholic social thought supports a free economic system in which people are induced to act morally with the fruits of their labor and investment. The use of state power to ensure an equitable society should be a last resort.

Christian Democracy appeared in Europe at the beginning of the twentieth century. Christian Democracy in Catholic Europe emerged from World War II in a strong position. Although Catholic parties had existed in Italy and Belgium before, the postwar parties were more firmly committed to independence from the Catholic Church but less committed to Catholic social thought.

In Italy, France, and Belgium, Christian Democratic parties made statements during their formative years that coincided with the most important elements of Catholic social thought. All the parties wished to place limits on the economic power of the state, for example. After World War II, however, the European Christian Democrats all found themselves in positions of political power even while their ideological formation was still proceeding. Almost immediately, they became convinced that economic power, in the hands of a state run by Christian Democrats, was not so fearsome. All the Latin European Christian Democrats attempted to increase state economic power. Party leaders frequently defended these departures from Catholic social thought by insisting that the pressures of governing, and the requirement that they be reelected to continue governing, forced them to be pragmatic and not to insist on such a close fidelity to ideology.

Christian Democratic pragmatism, however, has not been pragmatic. If it was supposed to make it easier for Christian Democrats to govern, it failed. Having accepted the proposition that the state should provide economic benefits, Christian Democrats find it difficult to continue without bankruptcy and to stop without disappointing their clients. If embracing state economic power was supposed to enhance their electoral chances, it failed here too. Only in Italy, where the influence of the Catholic Church is strongest and where the only united statist party is the Communist Party, has Christian Democracy had a continuous run in office.

The French party, for its part, embraced the state even more wholeheartedly than the Italian, ceasing to exist by 1969. The Belgians, in contrast, returned to a closer identification with Catholic social thought, after a brief flirtation with state power, and have seen their electoral fortunes improve.

The European experience proved to be a harbinger for the Latin American Christian Democratic parties. Most of these appeared in the 1950s, sometimes at direct papal initiative, but usually as the result of middle-class students studying the social documents of the Catholic Church and determining to apply them to their countries. In these formative days, Latin America's Christian Democrats retained their fidelity to Catholic social thought, although they were far less concerned with protecting private property and limiting state intervention in such macroeconomic areas as foreign exchange, foreign investment, or rules of ownership.

Latin America's Christian Democrats did retain a strong commitment to the health and autonomy of independent social groups. Once they came to power themselves, however, the party leaders came to believe that the government should create or subsidize independent social groups, including the family, private schools, and labor unions. In doing so, they threatened the independence of these groups and seriously violated the ideological principles they claimed. Like the Europeans, Latin America's Christian Democrats decided that state power in friendly hands was not a threat.

Having made this decision with regard to independent social groups, to which their founders had made strong commitments, Christian Democrats found it relatively easy to pursue land reform policies and nationalize basic resources in violation of Catholic social thought. Without exception, the continent's Christian Democratic parties have supported or enacted land reform and nationalization programs that have vastly increased the economic power of the state.

They have repeated this process in a number of other economic areas, including regulation of foreign and domestic capital investment, taxes, exchange rate policies, and even laws regarding labor unions. In every case, Christian Democrats ignored Catholic social thought's warning against increasing state economic power.

Like the Europeans, the Latin American Christian Democrats have perceived their breaches of Catholic social thought to be merely pragmatic responses to the pressures of governing. This defense is inadequate for two reasons. First, there is no convincing evidence that most Christian Democratic leaders made any real search for economic solutions that adhered more strictly to Catholic social thought. Increasing state power was not a last resort but a first resort. Second, Christian Democrats claim, and base a large part of their appeal upon, their connection with the social thought of the Catholic Church. They are not, in other words, supposed to be just another political party, primarily concerned with gaining power and constantly eyeing the next election.

This loss of commitment to their own ideological roots has not helped the Christian Democrats gain supporters, in spite of their leaders' insistence that they are only being pragmatic. It is virtually impossible to find an instance where departing from Catholic social thought has resulted in greater support for a Christian Democratic party. The party leaders themselves have tacitly acknowledged this, first by insisting that they are not straying from Catholic social thought and, second, by insisting with equal fervor that if they are, they are doing so moderately.

Such moderation has frequently been the undoing of Latin American Christian Democratic parties. By accepting a higher degree of state power but arguing that it should grow only moderately or slowly, the Christian Democrats have taken a position that often makes them seem like less coherent and less-committed imitators of Social Democratic parties. Where Christian Democrats have competed with Social Democrats or the more radical Socialists, they have done poorly.

In the process, Christian Democrats have contributed mightily to the statist legacy that confronted Latin American reformers at the beginning of the 1980s. This decade saw a continentwide desire to reduce state economic power and to substitute some form of economic liberalism for the statism that had been a political fact of life in most of Latin America under both leftist and rightist regimes. Political parties espousing liberal economic and political principles appeared in most Latin American countries, providing yet another challenge to Christian Democrats.

It was a challenge to which they were ill equipped to respond. Having spent most of the 1960s and 1970s finding one reason after another to increase state economic power, Christian Democrats faced the new challenges of 1980s liberalism without any coherent ideological basis for response. Squeezed between more radical statists and the rising liberals, the movement threatened to disappear altogether.

Had they retained their roots in Catholic social thought, or returned to them in the 1980s, the Christian Democrats would have been able to gain the votes of Latin Americans weary of statism but still wary of unbridled capitalism. Evidence from recent elections in El Salvador, Guatemala, Chile, and Peru suggests that this is a sizable electoral bloc. Whereas staunchly liberal parties have failed, parties with the platforms closest to Catholic social thought have prospered. If Christian Democracy has a future, it lies in rediscovering the potency of the philosophy that gave it birth.

NOTES

1. Alfred Stepan, *The State and Society: Peru in Comparative Perspective* (Princeton, N.J.: Princeton University Press, 1977).

2. For a fuller discussion of Catholic thought on this issue, see my *Religion and Politics in Latin America: Liberation Theology and Christian Democracy* (New York: Praeger, 1991).

I

Roots of Christian Democratic Theory

1

Roots in Catholic Social Thought

Christian Democracy did not exist before the late nineteenth century. Prior to the reign of Pope Leo XIII (1878–1903), the Catholic Church had grave doubts about the morality of political democracy. To decide pressing questions related to the welfare of all the people based on counting heads seemed improper. Closer to home, for half a century after the unification of Italy, the Church held that "it is not expedient" for Catholics to take part in the Masonic-influenced, anti-Catholic Italian regime.

With the reign of Leo, however, came a revival of Catholic interest in the writings of St. Thomas Aquinas. Writing during the High Middle Ages, Aquinas had asserted that the Law of God was written in the hearts of all redeemed men, and that man's *natural* tendency was toward the Good. Because of obstacles in front of this tendency, including the passions, emotions, and sin, men require a Church to guide their moral decisions.

With the Church's gentle shepherding, however, individual human beings could be trusted with political suffrage. Leo, drawing from the religious humanism of Aquinas, decided that the Catholic Church should view democracy as morally neutral and accept that there are both good and bad democracies, depending on the morality of the people involved.

Since the Church could see that the secular state was an important current reality, it focused on the hope that a Catholic presence could "infuse, as it were, into all the veins of the state the healthy sap and blood of Christian wisdom and virtue."[1] Catholics in public office would bring with them a "firm and constant resolution of promoting by every means the social and economic welfare of the people."[2]

Catholics began to wonder how a Church that was supposed to be aloof from politics could, while retaining its independence, still be a benign influence on the political system. The determination to exert such an influence formed the basis of Catholic social thought, which would become the basis for every Christian Democratic party in Europe and Latin America. The founders of Christian Democratic parties were determined to adhere closely to Catholic social thought.

I will show, however, that almost all Christian Democratic parties have abandoned the principles of Catholic social thought upon coming to power. Nevertheless, Christian Democratic parties have maintained an outward commitment to these principles. Christian Democratic parties have only very rarely gained any political success from distancing themselves from Catholic social thought. In fact, close adherence to Catholic political and social principles has brought greater rewards.

Catholic social thought comes from what are usually called the "social encyclicals" of several Roman Catholic popes. Encyclicals are official papal letters to the Church body, formally addressed to a bishop or a group of bishops in an area the Pope wishes to reach. Because they are public, encyclicals are, in effect, addressed to the whole world.

Papal encyclicals apply the Catholic faith to a particular question that has arisen among the faithful. They do not merely present the opinion of one pope but carry the entire tradition of the Church since the time of Christ. Encyclicals are not statements with papal infallibility and they lack the force of such a pronouncement. They do, however, represent the Church's last word on the treated subject. No opinion at variance with an encyclical can rightly claim to be "Catholic" opinion.

Most commentators consider *Rerum Novarum*, published in 1891, to be the first social encyclical. While this was the first in a series of papal documents treating economic issues, Leo XIII had worked toward this watershed piece with a series of more general treatments of Catholic political morality. Moreover, he drew much of *Rerum Novarum* from the thought of Thomas Aquinas, whose works were already 600 years old.[3]

Nevertheless, Leo's pontificate does mark a turning point in Catholic thought on politics and economics, so his writings make a convenient starting point. Virtually every pope after him continued the discussion in one form or another. Pope Pius XI (1922–1939), Pope Paul VI (1963–1978), and Pope John Paul II (1978–date), have written extensively on social themes.

The most important social encyclicals are *Rerum Novarum*, *Quadragessimo Anno* (1931), *Divini Redemptoris* (1937), *Mater et Magistra* (1961), *Pacem in Terris* (1963), *Populorum Progressio* (1967), *Laborem Exercens* (1981), *Sollicitudo Rei Socialis* (1987), and the latest, written to commemorate the centennial of *Rerum, Centesimus Annus*.

THEMES OF CATHOLIC SOCIAL THOUGHT

My concern is with the political economy of Latin America's Christian Democratic parties. Catholic social thought does not, however, divide itself into such discreet categories. To know the economic thought of the Church, it is necessary to begin with a more general consideration of Catholic thought on the nature of human beings, on morality, and on society. Only then can we progress to specifically economic concerns.

The Nature of Man

Considering that they were written over the course of a century, the social encyclicals contain a remarkable consistency, although with obvious differences in emphasis. As noted above, the Catholic Church was not immediately friendly to political democracy. This system errs in treating all political opinions as inherently equal, judging them only according to their attractiveness to voters. In doing so, democrats "renounc[ed] the infinitely wise and paternal laws of God, and the unifying and elevating doctrine of Christ's love, [and] resign[ed] themselves to the whim of a poor, fickle human wisdom."[4]

This is not to say that persons have no role in their own government. Catholic thought takes a middle position between the extreme humanism of the Enlightenment and the extreme pessimism about human beings that some Protestant churches express. For Aquinas, man had three possible natures. He might be totally depraved and thus unable to do any good on his own. Salvation for most men is thus impossible, but for a few, due to God's gratuitous action, it may be attainable.

On the other hand, human nature may already be perfect, or at least perfectible, here in this life. Rather than totally depraved, man may be totally good, and able to do good without guidance from God. A variation of this belief is that only some people are so blessed, and it is their duty to guide the benighted remainder of society. Whether earthly perfection is given to few or many, however, the confidence of Enlightenment thinkers that perfection was achievable is unmistakable.

The danger of this belief in the perfectibility of man is the accompanying belief in the efficacy of all means to achieve this perfection. As John Paul II put it, "When people think that they possess the secret of a perfect social organization that makes evil impossible, they also think that they can use any means, including violence and deceit, in order to bring it into being."[5]

The Catholic position, defined not only by Aquinas but by Catholic thinkers during the Counter-Reformation, is that man is neither fully good nor fully evil. He was perfect before Original Sin, depraved afterward, but lifted to a "natural" state by Christ's redemptive sacrifice. Catholics do not believe, however, that Christ's work relieved man of the need to work for his own redemption. Persons must accept and participate in redemption by living morally. The extent to which this work is unfinished is the extent to which man remains imperfect.

These theological statements have political implications. Man is only imperfectly capable of knowing or finding the Good on his own. He needs the help of a loving God. This God, according to the Catholic Church, reveals himself through that Church. Man's primary duty in life is to open himself to those revelations and to respond to them. This means living a moral life. Thus, the political priority of the popes has always been maintaining a moral society, as opposed to a richer or more egalitarian society.

Church teaching on the nature of man suggests conclusions about the nature of a just society. Man must be allowed to fulfill his spiritual destiny. No political regime may interfere with that. Individuals, guided by Church teachings, are capable of judging human laws to see if they are consistent with the Law of God. Pius XI wrote to German Catholics in 1937, advising them to beware the anti-Christian strictures of the Nazi regime: "Human laws in flagrant contradiction with the Natural Law are vitiated with a taint that no force, no power can mend."[6] Such laws, according to Aquinas, should not be obeyed.

In the same vein, Pius XII (1939–1958) wrote that it was a "pernicious error" to "divorce civil authority from every kind of dependence upon the Supreme Being . . . and from every restraint of a Higher Law derived from God as from its First Source." He continued, "Goods, or blood [the state] can demand; but the soul redeemed by God, never."

The state, while necessary in this fallen world, is still a construct of men, intended to serve men. It is subordinate to civil society. The popes have a deep suspicion of state power, especially of state economic power. Most of their recommendations for changes in social structures are designed to protect and promote the economic independence of individuals.

The social institutions that perform this function are independent social groups such as families, private schools, labor unions, professional organizations, charitable organizations, and clubs. Such institutions protect individuals from the coercive power of the state, since united groups of people are always more difficult to coerce. Labor unions and professional organizations protect individuals from overbearing private economic power. At the same time, independent social groups nurture a feeling of social solidarity, blunting the edges of selfish individualism. Catholic social thought demands the autonomy and promotes the growth and proliferation of independent social groups.

Catholic social thought teaches that human beings can accomplish great things through the use of reason. These powers and abilities, however, require from humanity a certain humility. Because of Original Sin, man cannot achieve perfection in this life. His choices, therefore, are between degrees of imperfection. Men must realize that there are questions their reason cannot answer, and that in creating social and economic systems they should be cautious and deliberate, taking proper care to ensure that the cure is not worse than the targeted disease.

Rejection of Materialism

Catholic social thought does concern itself with this life and does consider the question of material progress. Its authors differ from conventional politicians (and economists) in their refusal to sacrifice morality to any purely material end. Some of the evils affecting modern society, according to Leo, include "the insatiable craving for things perishable, with complete forgetfulness of things eternal."[7] More recently, John Paul II has warned that consumerism represents "a direct appeal to human instincts — while ignoring in various ways the reality of the person as intelligent and free."[8]

Secular states promised material progress, and sometimes delivered, according to Pius XII. This "superficial success," however, did not justify making material prosperity the primary standard for a society. Of particular danger were the promises of the Socialists and Communists, who were the most candid in their demand that society concern itself with purely material progress. By renouncing God and heaven, Socialists and Communists ignored the only true source of peace and tranquility.

The Church recognizes the difficulty of pursuing salvation while starving, however. Catholic social thought expresses a deep concern for the basic material interests of people, especially those of poor people.[9] People must be allowed to have what they need, but they must be induced to be satisfied with a reasonably comfortable life. The demand for luxuries is to be avoided. Much more important to John Paul II was the necessity "to create lifestyles in which the quest for truth, beauty, goodness and communion with others for the sake of the common growth are the factors which determine consumer choices, savings and investments."

Since material progress, while important, is secondary to the life of the spirit, the means to achieve material progress must be moral and proportionate to the desired end. Catholic social thought recommends gradual and incremental solutions, consistent with their moderate aspirations for this world. In the latter half of the twentieth century, Catholic popes have been vociferous in their demand that the rich nations of the world accept a lower level of material prosperity to provide a better life for people in poorer countries.

It is important to keep in mind that for the authors of the social encyclicals, the "laws" of economics are not unbreakable. An economist, looking at a recommendation that the developed world do with fewer material goods so that poorer countries may have more would unhesitatingly point out that the popes are removing the incentive for producing material goods. The Church responds that self-interest is not enough to run a society. People in developed nations should use their enormous productive power to create goods that can be given to poor people.

Prohibition against Political Expediency

The confidence of the Catholic popes in humanity's ability is considerable, but it is not absolute. Thus, they often found themselves at odds with the "naturalists," who had as their doctrine that human nature and reason ought in all things to be mistress and guide. Reason, for the popes, must be molded and guided by higher authority. Human action, even in the realm of politics, must always be guided by moral precepts, not by the perceived needs of political expediency.

Even when referring specifically to Catholic Action, a lay political movement that was precursor to Christian Democracy, the popes forbade compromise of moral principles to achieve political ends. Pius XI (1922–1939) stipulated that Catholic Action must only foster political ends that are praiseworthy, must approach these ends with solid Christian principles, and must adopt means that are just and proportionate. To do otherwise is to reject higher morality.

This guiding morality must have constant reference to God. Leo criticized a number of natural philosophies because of their purported commitment to earthly morality. Pius XII wrote, "National and international life must rest no longer on the quicksands of changeable and ephemeral standards that depend only on the selfish interests of groups and individuals."[10] Such a moral system, without absolutes, the popes believe, merely masks the worst kind of moral relativism and opportunism and could be used to justify anything.

It is the decline of obedience to higher moral authority that destroys "the indispensable foundation of the stability and quiet of that internal and external, private and public, order, which alone can support or safeguard the prosperity of states."[11] States and governments use the resulting instability, a natural outgrowth of strictly earthly morality, to justify their frequent resorts to coercion.

This coercion, however, cannot work. John XXIII, writing in 1963, warned, "A civil authority which uses as its only or its chief means either threats and fear of punishment or promises of rewards cannot effectively move men to promote the common good of all."[12] Any political arrangement that fails to appeal to man's highest nature is doomed to fail.

Here we see one of the bases for Catholic social thought's suspicion of state power. In the absence of recognized higher authority, state officials are tempted to elevate their own thoughts and philosophies to the level of infallible truths. This threatens individual freedom. Writing to German Catholics in 1937, Pius XI sought to undercut the basic theory of Nazism: "He who [makes] the race, the people or the state, or the form of Government . . .

the ultimate norm of all, even of religious values and deifies them with an idolatrous worship, perverts and falsifies the order of things created and commanded by God."[13]

Man, as a created person, possesses rights he holds from God, which the state not only cannot infringe but must also protect against denial, suppression, or neglect. The most effective way to protect these rights is to limit the power of the state by forcing it to share power with independent social groups.

Man is an imperfect creature, prone to error and to failure and in need of guidance. Given his limited ability to govern himself, his power to govern others must be limited. Catholic social thought applies this principle consistently in the realm of economics.

ECONOMIC ELEMENTS OF CATHOLIC SOCIAL THOUGHT

Private Property

Central to Catholic economic and social theory is the Church's attitude toward private property. For the popes, in an ideal world there would be no such thing. In the real world, however, property allows human beings to earn a living independent of the state and of potentially ruthless employers. As such, it is an institution worth protecting.

It is also an institution open to scandalous abuse. The Catholic pontiffs are not hesitant to condemn misuse, underuse, or dangerous use of property. The complexity of their position, however, is in their insistence that attacks on abuses of private property should not lead to a general prohibition on ownership. Such a prohibition would only lead to greater state power, which is even more fearsome than uncontrolled private economic power. Land reform proposals, therefore, must promote private ownership and must avoid state control of land.

Property, according to Leo's *Rerum Novarum*, is acquired by saving money and purchasing it. Since the money for land comes from remuneration for labor, it is as inviolate as the labor itself. Taking a person's land is the same as taking his legitimate wages. Even the fact that some people use their wages immorally does not automatically give their neighbors the right to deprive them of these wages.

Thus the popes condemn socialism and communism because they seek to destroy the legitimate ownership of property that came about because of "lawful inheritance, intellectual or manual labor, or economy in living."[14] Any political movement based on Catholic social thought must recognize the right of acquiring and possessing property. Addressing the regulations of the Italian Popular Christian Action movement in 1905, Pius X stressed that man has the right of permanent ownership of the goods of this earth, both consumable and nonconsumable.

The state by no means may suppress this right. According to John XXIII (1958–1963), "Private ownership of material goods helps to safeguard and develop family life. Such goods are an apt means to secure for the father of a family the healthy liberty he needs to fulfill the duties assigned to him by the Creator."[15]

John continued later in *Mater et Magistra*, "The right of private individuals to act freely in economic affairs is recognized in vain, unless they are at the same time given an opportunity of freely selecting and using things necessary for the exercise of this right." One function of private property is the protection of individuals from state power. Therefore, increasing the power of the state, by allowing it to impose more than minimal regulations on land use, or to suppress property rights altogether is a cure worse than any disease.

The Church warns against allowing the state to take over providing the social security that individually owned property conveys. Even in 1963, when government-provided social security was an accepted fact of modern economic life, John XXIII insisted that the traditional Catholic preference for property was not outmoded but, rather, underlined by the difficulties of various government plans.

Central to the Catholic position on private property is the insistence that it be available, in modest quantities, to everyone. Where socialism and communism promise no proprietors, and capitalist consolidation inevitably leads to few proprietors, Catholic social thought seeks to create a society wherein all are proprietors. Only then will workers of all classes feel they are working for themselves and therefore work to the best of their ability.

In industrial societies, land is no longer the most important form of property, so the principle of "all proprietors" is even more important. Catholic social thought encourages the formation of profit-sharing schemes in which workers receive part of their salary in the form of shares of stock. Such schemes provide greater economic security to workers while increasing their productivity, preventing envy and covetousness, encouraging the marriage of ownership and management, even in the largest firms, and creating a feeling of common enterprise.

This last is a vitally important ingredient of Catholic social thought on property. The right to private property is subordinate to the duty to use material goods for the good of all. It is a right that carries responsibilities. Leo XIII stated this most baldly in *Rerum Novarum:* "Whoever has received from the divine bounty a large share of temporal blessings, whether they be external or corporeal, or gifts of the mind, has received them for the perfecting of his own nature and . . . for the benefit of others."

Paul VI was more suspicious of private economic power than was any other twentieth-century pontiff. He emphasized more strongly than the others that no one has a right to what he does not need when others lack necessities. The documents of the Second Vatican Council also reflect this pontiff's insistence that the world's wealthy have a special obligation because of their wealth.

John Paul II accepted this point and elaborated: "The characteristic principle of Christian social doctrine [is that] the goods of this world are *originally meant for all.* The right to private property is *valid and necessary,* but it does not nullify the value of this principle."[16] Private property is under a "social mortgage, which means that it has an intrinsically social function, based upon and justified precisely by the principle of the universal destination of goods."

Abuses of the social mortgage, however, must be corrected with extreme care. Although the Church agrees that states have a right to expropriation, it is limited to circumstances where large accumulations of property "impede the general prosperity because they are extensive or unused or poorly used, or because they bring hardship to peoples, or are detrimental to the interests of the country."[17]

Even here, the popes are careful to point out that if the state can expropriate, it is not because the state has gained a right but because an individual property owner has forfeited one. The state merely acts as trustee for the people. Even the Second Vatican Council, frequently reluctant to uphold the rights of property holders, stipulated that "the transfer of goods from private to public ownership may be undertaken only by competent authority in accordance with the demands and within the limits of the common good, and it must be accompanied by adequate compensation."[18] Ideally, the state should immediately sell the property or business to several smaller owners.

Similarly, Catholic social thought allows public ownership of utilities or other public agencies if their importance is "too great to be left in private hands without injury to the community at large." State ownership is a danger too, as John XXIII warned when he wrote, "In the administration of the state itself, there [may] develop an economic imperialism in the hands of a few."[19]

Thus the state, if it must take over property, should do so temporarily and as a trustee of the people. Pius XI warned in *Quadragessimo Anno* that while abuse and nonuse of property could excite envy, even these did not destroy the general right to own property. John Paul reminded his readers 50 years later that nationalization and socialization of property are different. Only the latter means widespread ownership, under intermediate bodies "with real autonomy from the public powers."[20] Here as elsewhere, Catholic social thought takes the side of civil society over the state.

Business Ethics

Undertaken with the proper spirit, capital investment is perfectly all right, and it is necessary to ensure the production of material goods needed for a society to progress. John XXIII acknowledged that private initiative is central to making an economic system work. Where such initiative is lacking or repressed, political tyranny is inevitable.

In *Sollicitudo Rei Socialis,* John Paul II adds a right to "freedom of economic initiative" to the rights enumerated by his predecessors. He adds,

"Experience shows us that the denial of this right, or its limitation in the name of an alleged 'equality,' of everyone in society, diminishes, or in practice absolutely destroys, the spirit of initiative, that is to say *the creative subjectivity of the citizen.*"[21]

Put differently, if men cannot initiate economic activity, they are no longer independent persons. The pontiff warns about what he calls a "special form of poverty," as serious as material poverty, which consists of being denied this very right. The two forms of poverty are related. John Paul contends that it is the lack of the right to economic initiative that has led to so much poverty in underdeveloped countries. In place of encouraging its people to be productive, the pope laments that Third World countries simply demand what they need from the First World.[22]

Nevertheless, productivity and growth are only means to an end. For the Church, salvation of individuals is always paramount. Individual capitalists are eligible for salvation if they "renounce some of their rights so as to place their goods more generously at the service of others."[23] The rich have a Christian duty, Paul VI believed, to pay higher taxes, which public authorities can use for development.

The duty of the rich to give does not presume the right of the poor (or the state) to take if the rich fail to give. The reason that the rich should give in the first place is to acquire the blessings that go with sacrifice. Even John XXIII, who was less concerned with the "rights" of the wealthy, acknowledged that Jesus told the rich to turn their goods into "spiritual treasures" by giving them away. If their wealth is simply taken from them, regardless of the motives, their chance to merit salvation through charity is also taken away. No earthly authority has the right to do this.

Criticism of Capitalism and Socialism

The papal encyclicals use very harsh language to condemn both pure capitalism and pure socialism. Pius XI marked the fortieth anniversary of *Rerum Novarum* by writing, "Just as the unity of society cannot be founded on the opposition of classes, so also the right ordering of economic life cannot be left to a free competition of forces." Individualism and collectivism, for Pius XI, were the "twin rocks of shipwreck, the former denying the social and public character of man, and the latter denying the private and individual character of man."[24]

Six years later, Pius XI wrote in *Divini Redemptoris:* "There would be today neither socialism nor communism if the rulers of the nations had not scorned the teachings of the Church." He added, "Socialism and communism come out of the failures of lay liberalism."[25]

The popes blame unbridled capitalism for an excessive concentration of wealth in few hands. According to Pius XI, this has allowed the appearance of a despotic "economic dictatorship consolidated in the hands of a few, who are often not owners but only trustees and managing directors of invested funds."[26] Catholic social thought deplores the divorce of ownership from management, which is inevitable as properties grow larger and proprietors grow fewer. This process makes Marxism more appealing, even though this system completely divorces management from ownership.

Paul VI made some of the Church's harshest statements about the role of capitalism in the modern world. The growth of large multinational corporations (MNCs), he believed, meant that the "excessive concentration of means and [economic] powers that Pope Pius XI already condemned on the 40th anniversary of *Rerum Novarum*, is taking on a new and very real image."[27]

Such statements prompted *The Wall Street Journal* to call Paul VI's philosophy "warmed over Marxism." Seen against the background of traditional Catholic social thought, however, Paul's seemingly radical statements become much less original than they seemed to many at the time that he issued them. Pope John Paul II, for his part, has softened some of Paul's statements.

Capitalism is an economic system in which man is treated as an instrument of production, rather than the effective subject of work and a true maker and creator. In addition, capitalism rewards competition and profit making without limit and without a corresponding social obligation. In this sense, capitalism reinforces its supposed archenemy, Marxism. According to John Paul II, the affluent consumer society seeks to defeat Marxism by besting it in purely material terms. Capitalism "agrees with Marxism, in the sense that it totally reduces man to the sphere of economics and the satisfaction of material needs."[28]

Writing in the aftermath of communism's fall in Central Europe, John Paul II modified the harshness of traditional Catholic condemnation of capitalism by distinguishing between capitalism's desirable and undesirable features. Asking if Central Europeans should seek capitalism, the pope wrote:

If by "capitalism" is meant an economic system which recognizes the fundamental and positive role of business, the market, private property and the resulting responsibility for the means of production, as well as free human creativity in the economic sector, then the answer is certainly in the affirmative, even though it would perhaps be more appropriate to speak of a "business economy," "market economy," or simply "free economy."[29]

The Catholic popes' anger at the abuses of private business is matched, however, by skepticism about balancing the power of capitalists by extending and consolidating state power. The popes condemn socialism because it proposes a cure far worse than the evils it tries to eliminate. Statist philosophies in general are suspect because they give greater importance to the state than to the society that gives life to political structures.

John XXIII and Paul VI, the popes of the Second Vatican Council, seemed the least enthusiastic about capitalism and private investment. They were also writing at a time of great confidence in the ability of governments to provide economic growth and justice at the same time. John Paul II has tempered their friendliness to the state, drawing both on his own experiences under the powerful Polish Communist state and the general erosion of confidence in state-directed economic development that occurred in the 1980s.

INDEPENDENT SOCIAL GROUPS

Both capitalism and socialism leave the individual without adequate protection from forces he cannot control. According to Catholic social thought, the welfare of individuals is the highest political goal. At the same time, the popes deplore the radically selfish individualism of modern capitalism and seek to counter its corrosive influence on society as well.

The method for achieving these different goals is the promotion of independent social groups. Leo XIII said in the first social encyclical that the family and society are prior to the state, which exists to serve and to protect them. John Paul II added a century later, "The social nature of man is not completely fulfilled in the State, but is realized in various intermediary groups, beginning with the family and including economic, social, political and cultural groups which stem from human nature itself and have their own authority."[30]

A healthy society, according to Catholic social thought, will be made up of thousands of independent social groups. Such associations encourage individuals to think not just of themselves but also of their fellows. In this way, they discourage selfishness. At the same time, they protect individuals from overbearing state power or from excessive private economic power.

Independent social groups must appear naturally, however. If the state starts creating its own social groups, they are not independent and they will fail in their most important function, protecting individuals from the state. The proper role of government is to allow independent social groups to appear and to survive. The state should avoid taking over their functions.

John Paul II, sponsor of the free trade union Solidarity, draws a distinction between the official unions of Poland's Communist regime and the independent unions. Only the latter truly represent the interests of workers before employers, in Poland's case, the government. Official unions largely do just the opposite. They relay the government position to the workers and close off an important channel of dissent and negotiation.

The attitude of Catholic social thought toward state power is that the persons who occupy positions of power are apt to misuse it. Society may protect itself from these intrusions by putting up "No Trespassing" signs in the form of legal or constitutional protections. These signs will work better, however, if society supplements them with a series of strong fences. Independent social groups, by confronting the state with the combined power of many individuals, serve as these fences.[31]

The Rights of the Family

Society for the popes is an organic body that is anterior to any government. It is made up of parts, with the health of each contributing to the health of the whole. The most important of these parts, and the most in need of promotion and protection, is the family. Central to the existence of the family is the sanctity of the marriage contract. For over 100 years the Catholic popes have complained about "impious laws that put at naught the sanctity of this great sacrament, and put it on the same footing with mere civil contracts."[32]

Man and the family are, by nature, anterior to the state. It is they who grant the state power to govern society, but only for the good of the families themselves. Thus families do not request privileges from a master state; they have rights apart from a servant state. Public interference in family life should be limited to the alleviation of extreme want and the prevention of gross violations of rights.

The insistence on a "just" or "family wage" is also part of Catholic social thought's preoccupation with family protection. Such a wage must allow a family to live on the earnings of a single breadwinner (interestingly, there is no insistence that this be the father), so that the children have one parent at home during the day. Such an arrangement not only helps families but also makes society more healthy as well.

The state has an obligation to write laws that favor the family, especially in the matter of housing, working conditions, social security, and taxes. None of this favoritism, however, makes families or their representatives merely another interest group looking for public largess. In favoring families, the state is only recognizing the rights of bodies that created the state, and which owe nothing to the state in return.

Catholic social thought extends this argument to educational policy. Social encyclicals are filled with assertions that the parents possess the primary right to educate their children. That they may entrust state institutions to oversee this education does not imply any cession of rights. Parents should control curriculum and must be allowed to choose schools for their children. The Second Vatican Council insisted: "Every family, in that it is a society with its own basic rights, has the right freely to organize its own religious life in the home under the control of the parents. . . . The civil authority must therefore recognize the rights of parents to choose with genuine freedom schools and other means of education."[33]

Catholic social thought is particularly concerned with what institutions have access to the minds and hearts of young people. This is hardly surprising, since much of Catholic social thought was written as a direct challenge to regimes of the right and left that sought to monopolize the time and loyalty of youth.

Pius XI protested vigorously when Mussolini disbanded the youth wing of Catholic Action. The dictator demanded that Italian youths belong to official Fascist organizations. The pope wrote: "A conception of the state which makes the young generations belong entirely to it without any exception from the tenderest years up to adult life cannot be reconciled . . . with the natural right of the family."[34]

In his attack on Nazism, Pius XI noted that the Nazis directed their first attack on Catholicism through the schools, which were specifically protected in the 1923 Concordat between the Vatican and Berlin. Earlier, Leo had admonished the bishops to "devote the greatest part of your care to [the youth's] instruction; and do not think that any precaution can be great enough in keeping them from masters and schools whence the pestilent breath of the sects is to be feared."[35]

This is not to say that the state must stay out of education altogether. On the contrary, education is an area where Church and state must coexist, but each with its own recognized sphere. While the state can determine minimum standards for biology, mathematics, or history, it cannot claim a monopoly on education or even any particular right to primacy in education.

Churches as Independent Social Groups

After the family the most important social association is the Church. Catholic social thought warns of any political philosophy that seeks to lessen the importance of the office and authority of the Church in the decisions of the civil state. Any state that desires independence from the Church probably also desires independence from any other form of higher authority and will be tempted toward totalitarianism.

To perform its functions properly, the Church must be completely independent of the state. This means, among other things, the recognition that the Church, like the family, is anterior to the state and superior to it. No state can rightly contend, though many secular states attempt it, that the Church possesses no right nor any legal power of action save that which she holds by the concession and favor of the government.

Religious liberty means absolute freedom of action for the Church, without any threat of interference from the state. Even a government as seemingly friendly to the Church as Mussolini's during its early years was the target of harsh criticism when it sought to limit the Church's independence. The Nazis, for their part, created "the impression that infidelity to Christ the King constitutes a signal and meritorious act of loyalty to the modern State," according to Pius XI.[36]

While this unfriendliness is bad, neutrality by the state on the question of religion is little better. The state, according to Catholic social thought, is clearly bound to the public profession of religion. To have a coherent society, states must acknowledge that they too are under authority. Religion, for its part, must be protected, favored, and given the credit and sanction of the law.

It is important to note, however, that papal writings do not insist that states acknowledge the Catholic Church as the one official Church. On the contrary, Catholic social thought insists on independence for the Church, which any official connection with a government would seriously compromise.

The Church must be free and autonomous, according to the popes, "without hindrance, in accordance to her own judgement [to act] in all matters that fall within its competence."[37] The state, on the other hand, must be humble enough to accept spiritual aid from the Church, recognizing that a moral populace serves its legitimate interests as well. Again, this means that the scope of state power is necessarily limited.

Labor Unions

Labor unions are particularly important independent associations. John Paul II, who sponsored and supported the Solidarity trade union in Poland, wrote in 1987:

The denial or the limitation of human rights—as for example the right to religious freedom, the right to share in the building of society, the freedom to organize and to form labor unions, or to take the initiative in economic matters—do these not impoverish the human person as much as, if not more than, the deprivation of material goods?[38]

John Paul's thoughts are in line with Catholic social thought. Pius XI wrote in *Quadragessimo Anno* that workers, far from obtaining the exalted place in human society to which their numbers and efforts entitled them, had become neglected and despised by modern society. Early popes thought that workers could best improve their lot by becoming members of the bourgeoisie. The most virtuous economic goal of any political movement, according to Leo, is to enable working men "to obtain, little by little, those means by which they may provide for the future."[39]

The insistence on a just wage is part of this conviction. The Church believes that ownership of capital assets should be encouraged. A just wage is one that allows for some savings and thus allows workers to progress to the middle class. For John Paul II, the existence of a just wage, perhaps through government allowances or grants, is a concrete means of verifying the justice of an entire socioeconomic system.[40]

Unions, though, must conform to the same moral standards as states and schools. For a union to act morally is more important than to gain shorter hours or higher pay. To this end, the popes insist that workers' unionizing efforts be under religious auspices. In addition, the popes place a considerable burden on employers, insisting on the family wage and warning that God will require an account of how they treated their employees.

Forming unions is a fundamental right. Without some sort of moral guidance, however, union leaders can become shortsighted and overly selfish. Under such misguided leadership, unions might use their ultimate (and legitimate) weapon, a strike, to win settlements harmful to the general economy or to make demands of a directly political nature. In either case, the true interests of workers are ignored.

Consistent with its perception of society as an organic whole, Catholic social thought utterly rejects labor agitation based on class struggle. The ideal labor arrangement is one in which owners and workers unite to create mutual aid societies, many private insurance companies, and private charitable organizations, as well as labor unions.

The challenge of Marxism makes such Catholic workers' guilds all the more important, since the Communists seek to make workers forget the primacy of morality and stress that any means are permissible to bring about revolution.[41] Communist and socialist labor unions are the worst of all, since their demands are designed to destroy the capitalist system and to replace it with one in which free labor unions vanish altogether.

The state can play a limited role in protecting workers' rights. It should ensure that labor-management agreements are entered into according to the norms of justice and equity. States should also make it as easy as possible for new businesses to start and for workers to move from place to place in search of employment. Even better are laws and conditions that allow businesses to move easily so that the workers can stay close to home.[42] A productive economy, with many small employers, offers the widest choice of employment and thus is most friendly to workers. The state cannot, and should not, guarantee employment, since it cannot ensure the right to work without controlling every other aspect of economic life.[43]

In addition to their rights to organize unions and be paid a just wage, more recent popes add that workers deserve partly or completely subsidized medical insurance and a yearly vacation. The Church emphasizes, however, that employers, and not the state, should provide these benefits. Catholic social thought notes the employers' self-interest here in the form of more productive workers.

LEGITIMATE VERSUS ILLEGITIMATE STATE POWER

Families, churches, and labor unions do not form a comprehensive list of independent social groups. The above examples, however, are some of the more important independent social groups that protect individuals from coercion while countering harmful individualism. Catholic social thought does not pretend that every government action is evil, nor does it believe that every act of independent social groups is wise or moral. Rather, the popes attempt to describe the proper balance toward state and society, which must coexist.

This same demand for balance is visible in Catholic social thought on state power. It is based on the Catholic view of humankind and of society. States are staffed by human beings. Human beings are imperfect. Part of this imperfection is the desire to use other people. No institution allows this more easily than the state. Therefore, the state must be constantly viewed with suspicion. As fearful as unbridled capitalism is, an unbridled state is worse. No private enterprise has the same claim of authority, and the same access to tax money, that a state does.

Since people are imperfect, states will sometimes issue unjust commands or pass unjust laws. These, according to the Church, simply have no force. But this is scant comfort without the aforementioned independent social groups to keep the state from enforcing unjust commands. In his 1885 encyclical *Immortale Dei*, Leo boasts that the Catholic Church has always been the "originator, the promoter or the guardian of whatever has been usefully established to curb the license of rulers opposed to the true interests of the people."

Governments can be the agent of the common good or the enemy of the common good, depending on the people in charge. Since men and women cannot achieve the common good as individuals, states per se are legitimate. The popes, especially early in the century, were careful to acknowledge the state's right to allegiance. In fact, early social encyclicals warned state authorities of secret societies like the freemasons, socialists, and communists that sought to overthrow them.

Citizens owe allegiance only to lawful governments that issue just commands. (An independent Church says which commands are just.) Even a democratic system, based on the will of the people, does not destroy the obligation of citizens to submit themselves to just commands. When a state fails to perform its proper functions, the results are "incurable disorders and the exploitation of the weak by the unscrupulous strong."[44]

In the economic realm, the state exists to coordinate the activities of the population. Quoting Leo, John Paul II stipulated that the state "has the task of determining the juridical framework within which economic affairs are to be conducted, and thus of safeguarding the process of a free economy, which presumes a certain equality between the parties."[45] As society grows more complex, this coordinating role will necessarily grow also. In the nineteenth century, Leo acknowledged that states must have wider areas of concern.

The state should provide unemployment benefits and undertake overall planning for economic matters affecting the whole community. Ideally, the state will coordinate and supplement the planning activities of private citizens and organizations. If the state threatens individual initiative, however, it has crossed the line between justified state action and tyranny.

To diminish the threat of any particular state exercising too much economic power, the popes also have an apparent preference for freer trade and lower trade barriers. Only Paul VI warned that these could be detrimental when "the economic conditions between trading partners differ too widely." John

XXIII, for his part, said that the best aid that rich countries can offer to the Third World is "to promote the freer movement of goods, of capital and of men."

John Paul was more enthusiastic about regional free trade arrangements, saying that nations "of the *same geographical area* should establish *forms of cooperation* which will make them less dependent on more powerful producers; they should open their frontiers to the products of the area; . . . they should combine in order to set up those services which each one separately is incapable of providing."

With every acknowledgment of a useful area for government activity, Catholic social thought adds a warning about the danger of overbearing government. Leo listed examples of acceptable state intervention in *Rerum Novarum* but emphasized that they must be limited and undertaken as a last resort. John Paul was particularly eloquent in this regard when he cautioned that where government is too strong, "in the place of creative initiative there appears passivity, dependence and submission to the bureaucratic apparatus . . . which puts everyone in a position of almost absolute dependence, which is similar to the traditional dependence of the worker-proletarian in capitalism."[46]

Thus the state must be imaginative in its economic policies. Although the state legitimately acts to avert mass unemployment or to reduce inequality, it must not do so in a way that compromises individual freedom. Although self-interest is flawed as a basis for human action, "where self-interest is violently suppressed, it is replaced by a burdensome system of bureaucratic control which dries up the wellsprings of initiative and creativity."[47] Since absolute freedom and absolute social equality are incompatible in any society composed of people with different talents, states must seek the best balance they can, recognizing that no earthly arrangement will be perfect.

There can be no doubt that where Catholic social thought allows for more state power, its theorists do so with great reluctance and with the repeated insistence on the importance of societal initiative. To maintain some balance between the power of the state and the power of individuals, Catholic social thought insists on the principle of subsidiarity.

This principle holds that if government is to get involved in economic matters, it should do so through smaller and subordinate government bodies rather than larger and higher authorities. No larger collectivity can morally take over a function that can be performed by a smaller and more local agency. Thus Catholic social thought prefers independent social groups to government, local governments to national governments, and regional arrangements to global ones.[48]

CONCLUSION

Once it became "expedient" for Catholics to participate in politics, the Church had to develop detailed guidelines for this participation. Herein lies the origin of Christian Democratic theory. It would be left to lay Catholics to further develop these tenets into functioning political movements and parties. Latin Europeans, especially in Italy, France, and Belgium, would make the first efforts in this direction.

The political movements they created, to the extent that they were based on the social encyclicals, perceived this world as important but secondary. Similarly, political success, while also important, was also secondary to the duty of upholding Catholic morality.

Thus Christian Democratic parties would have far less room than their wholly secular counterparts to make compromises in doctrine to attain political or electoral success. As the history of Christian Democracy shows, this has been both their greatest strength and their greatest temptation.

NOTES

1. Leo XIII, Pope, *Immortale Dei* (The Christian Constitution of States), 1 November 1885. Official Vatican translation reprinted in Leo XIII, Pope, *The Great Encyclical Letters of Pope Leo XIII* (New York: Benzinger Brothers, 1903), p. 131.

2. Pius X, Pope, *Il Fermo Proposito* (Letter to Italian Bishops), 11 June 1905, paragraph 19. Official Vatican translation in Vincent A. Yzermans, *All Things in Christ: Encyclicals and Selected Documents of Saint Pius X* (Westminster, Md.: Newman Press, 1954).

3. See Alejandro Chaufen, *Christians for Freedom: Late-Scholastic Economics* (San Francisco: Ignatius Press, 1986).

4. Pius XII, Pope, *On the Function of the State in the Modern World*, 20 October 1939, Official Vatican translation (Boston: St. Paul Editions), p. 16.

5. John Paul II, Pope, *Centesimus Annus* (On the Hundredth Anniversary), 15 May 1991, Official Vatican translation (Boston: St. Paul Editions), paragraph 25.

6. Pius XI, Pope, *Mit brennender Sorge* (Letter to the German Bishops), 14 March 1937. Official Vatican translation in Pius XI, Pope, *Sixteen Encyclicals of Pope Pius XI* (Washington, D.C.: National Catholic Welfare Conference, 1938), paragraph 30.

7. Leo XIII, Pope, *Inscrutabili Dei* (On the Evils Affecting Modern Society), 21 April 1878. Official Vatican translation in *Great Encyclical Letters of Leo XIII*, pp. 9–10.

8. John Paul II, *Centesimus Annus*, paragraph 36.

9. Pius XI in *Quadragessimo Anno:* "In protecting private individuals and their rights, chief consideration ought to be given to the weak and the poor." John Paul II repeated this sentiment in paragraph 10 of *Centesimus Annus.*

10. Pius XII, *On the Function of the State*, p. 33.

11. Ibid., p. 16.

12. John XXIII, Pope, *Pacem in Terris* (Peace on Earth), 11 April 1963, Official Vatican translation (Boston: St. Paul Editions, 1963), paragraph 48.

13. Pius XI, *Mit brennender Sorge*, paragraph 12.

14. Leo XIII, Pope, *Quod Apostolici Muneris* (Socialism, Communism, Nihilism), 28 December 1878. Official Vatican translation in *Great Encyclical Letters of Leo XIII*, p. 23.

15. John XXIII, Pope, *Mater et Magistra* (Christianity and Social Progress), 15 May 1961, paragraph 45.

16. John Paul II, Pope, *Sollicitudo Rei Socialis* (Of Social Concerns), 30 December 1987, paragraph 42. (Italics in original.)

17. Paul VI, Pope, *Populorum Progressio* (On the Development of Peoples), 26 March 1967. Official Vatican translation (Boston: St. Paul Editions, 1967), paragraph 24.

18. "Gaudium et Spes" (Pastoral Constitution of the Church in the Modern World), in Austin P. Flannery, ed., *Documents of Vatican II* (Grand Rapids, Mich.: William B. Eerdmans Publishing Co., 1975), pp. 977–78.

19. John XXIII, *Mater et Magistra*, paragraphs 34, 118.

20. John Paul II, *Laborem Exercens* (On Human Labor), 15 May 1981, paragraph 37.

21. John Paul II, *Sollicitudo Rei Socialis*, paragraph 15. (Italics in original.)

22. Ibid., paragraph 44.

23. Ibid., paragraph 23.

24. Pius XI, Pope, *Quadragessimo Anno*. Official Vatican translation in *Sixteen Encyclicals*, paragraph 46.

25. Pius XI, Pope, *Divini Redemptoris* (On Atheistic Communism), 19 March 1937. Official Vatican translation in *Sixteen Encyclicals*, paragraph 38.

26. Pius XI, *Quadragessimo Anno*.

27. Paul VI, Pope, *Octogesima Adveniens* (On the Coming Eightieth), 14 May 1971, Official Vatican translation (Boston: St. Paul Editions, 1971), paragraph 44.

28. John Paul II, *Centesimus Annus*, paragraph 19.

29. Ibid., paragraph 42.

30. Ibid., paragraph 13.

31. Proponents of a stronger state often contend that the increasing complexity of modern life, and especially of modern economic life, makes growth in state power necessary. Catholic social thought replies that this very complexity makes necessary larger and stronger independent social groups, as well as a stronger state. See especially *Mater et Magistra*.

32. Leo XIII, *Inscrutabili Dei*, p. 18.

33. "Dignitatis Humanae" (Declaration on Religious Liberty) in Flannery, p. 803.

34. Pius XI, Pope, *Non abbiamo bisogno* (On Catholic Action), 29 June 1931. Official Vatican translation in *Sixteen Encyclicals*, pp. 7, 24.

35. Leo XIII, *Humanum Genus* (Freemasonry), 20 April 1884. Official Vatican translation in *Great Encyclical Letters of Leo XIII*, p. 104.

36. Pius XI, *Mit brennender Sorge*, paragraph 21.

37. Leo XIII, *Immortale Dei*, p. 113.

38. John Paul II, *Sollicitudo Rei Socialis*, paragraph 15.

39. Leo XIII, Pope, *Graves de Communi* (Christian Democracy), 18 January 1901. Official Vatican translation in *Great Encyclical Letters of Leo XIII*, p. 485.

40. John Paul II, *Laborem Exercens*, paragraph 46.

41. Leo XIII, *Humanum Genus*, p. 103.

42. John XXIII, *Pacem in Terris*, paragraph 102.

43. See John Paul II, *Centesimus Annus*, paragraph 48.

44. John XXIII, *Mater et Magistra*, paragraph 19.

45. John Paul II, *Centesimus Annus*, paragraph 15.

46. John Paul II, *Sollicitudo Rei Socialis*, paragraph 15.

47. John Paul II, *Centesimus Annus*, paragraph 25.

48. For an excellent discussion of subsidiarity, see John Schrems, *Principles of Politics* (Englewood Cliffs, N.J.: Prentice Hall, 1986), Chapters 9–11.

2

European Christian Democracy: Foreshadowing Failure in Latin America

As we saw in Chapter 1, Christian Democracy was born of the determination of the Catholic popes that lay Catholics get involved in the political process. Their presence, the pontiffs hoped, might Christianize this political process. To do this, Catholics would need a coherent and comprehensive political, economic, and social philosophy based upon Church teachings.

The image of seasoned politicians referring to the documents of the Catholic Church before making a policy decision is an unlikely one. Politicians usually make such decisions based on the needs of the moment and how they might best contribute to their long-range goals. The strictures of Catholic social thought seem to throw up substantial obstacles to the kind of political maneuvering required in many real-life situations.

Even a cursory glance at the analyses of political parties undertaken by political scientists shows the importance of interest aggregation to the success of a political party. Most authors use this term to refer to efforts by a political party to widen its appeal to voters or, put differently, to increase the size of its electoral coalition. It is the function of political parties to seek power. In a democratic system, they do this by persuading electors to vote for the party's representatives.

In the multiparty systems that exist in most countries where Christian Democratic parties exist, the obstacles to a strict adherence to party ideology are great. Since it is unusual for a single party to win a majority of votes in a multiparty system, interest aggregation takes place both before and after an election. Before an election, party representatives appeal to as many voters as possible. After the election, those same party leaders must negotiate with their rivals to form a majority coalition and allow government to function.

In some multiparty systems, however, especially in those with a congress or parliament elected by proportional representation, party leaders conclude that gaining a majority of seats is unlikely. They may, under these circumstances, try to simply solidify their base support to better position themselves for the postelection negotiations.

Increasing a party's appeal involves risk. To broaden a party's electoral base, its leaders may decide to ignore parts of their ideology or even abandon them altogether. It may often seem most promising to appeal to voters who have previously been part of a rival's base. A single vote, taken from a rival, is worth two on election day. The risk comes when a party risks confusion, or even disgust, among its own followers by deemphasizing or jettisoning parts of its ideology. Yet party leaders may conclude that no other party will satisfy such disillusioned voters and that their most likely form of protest against party apostasy will be abstention. In this case, the party leadership may conclude that raids on a rival's coalition justify the risk.

Furthermore, even the most committed party leadership will find that actual political power makes demands that an abstract and untested ideology did not consider or does not satisfy. What seemed like a good idea at party congresses may not be feasible once the party gains political power. This may be especially true if the party is part of a broad coalition in a multiparty legislature. Rigid orthodoxy may cost the party its opportunity to help direct the course of government, thus making it fail in a party's other duties, such as interest articulation, representation, or policy making.

The difficulties of strict adherence to party ideology have been considerable for the men and women committed to creating political parties based on Catholic social thought. The papal encyclicals, while long on inspiration and even on the specifics of proper public policy, are short on tactical advice. The very nature of Catholic social thought, moreover, demands greater adherence to first principles, or ideology, than that demanded of other, less ideological parties.

Thus Christian Democratic parties have far less flexibility than their secular rivals to alter their ideology to suit particular circumstances. The following chapters will show that in their efforts to aggregate interests, Christian Democrats in Europe and Latin America have frequently imitated their closest rivals, even where this has meant abandoning Catholic social thought.

The most frequent area of apostasy has been in the acceptance of state power. Where the popes have unswervingly warned against its increase, Christian Democrats have acquiesced to such increases, sometimes out of a belief that with Christian Democrats in charge, state power is not so fearsome, and sometimes because of less idealistic and narrower political considerations. In most cases, Christian Democrats in Europe and Latin America perceive their most serious rivals to be Social Democratic parties, which promise greater state intervention in the economy, purportedly for the common good.

Determined to aggregate interests by raiding the bases of these rival Social Democrats, Christian Democrats have sought increases in state power. At the same time, some Christian Democratic leaders have sought to use state economic power to create clients for even more state intervention, with the hoped-for result of attracting even more voters.

In doing so, the Christian Democrats have overlooked a source of potential support that could have been theirs without sacrificing such an important element of Catholic social thought. Greater economic benefits from the state creates a clientele for such benefits. They may even convince some social democratic voters that the Christian Democrats are just as enthusiastic about state power. However, state economic intervention limits the economic freedom of some citizens. Economic benefits cost money. There is no way to design a government program that can benefit more people than have to pay for it.

Thus a potential constituency for reduced state economic intervention always exists. In Latin America, such constituencies not only exist but often are not represented by any other political party. Thus the Christian Democrats had numerous opportunities to attract new voters without threatening their base support and without having to sacrifice their adherence to Catholic social thought.

The evidence shows that Christian Democratic "pragmatism," in the form of forsaking their first principles for immediate political gain, has rarely paid political dividends to the leaders who embraced it. Attempts to gain support by imitating rivals have been almost uniformly unsuccessful. There are far more examples of Christian Democratic parties winning elections or increasing their strength by mobilizing new voters, especially voters skeptical of state power, through a close adherence to Catholic social thought.[1]

EARLY CHRISTIAN DEMOCRACY IN EUROPE

Christian Democracy per se began in the late nineteenth and early twentieth century. In Catholic countries, Catholic philosophers studied the social encyclicals that formed the basis of Catholic social thought and formed small groups of committed Catholics to explore ways to put them into practice. Functioning political parties eventually came from these humble beginnings.[2]

Early Christian Democratic theory clearly reflected Catholic social thought. The situation just after World War II, however, presented the European movement with an opportunity and a temptation. For the Western allies occupying Europe, the Christian Democrats, especially in Italy, seemed like the perfect carriers of the anti-Communist banner. Pope Pius XII also perceived the danger of Italian communism and sought to strengthen the Italian Christian Democrats to oppose them. Washington and Rome made similar party-building efforts in France and Belgium.

Their efforts were successful. In the 1948 Italian elections, the Democrazia Cristiana (DC) Party swept the balloting. The Allies managed to avoid Communist victories in France and Belgium as well. By 1954, Christian Democrats held 37 percent of the parliamentary seats in West Germany, Austria, Switzerland, Belgium, Luxembourg, France, and Italy. Christian Democrats dominated European parliaments until the mid-1970s.

Christian Democratic political parties in France and Italy attained political power before their ideological development was complete. Under the pressure of perceived political needs, both parties made compromises in the principles of Catholic social thought. The changes that Christian Democratic leaders made in the name of pragmatism, however, did nothing to improve the political fortunes of the parties. They sacrificed their ideological roots, alienating many potential supporters, but gained almost nothing in return.

Christian Democracy in France and Italy declined as a result of their rejection of the tenets of Catholic social thought. In the process, they foreshadowed the fate of Christian Democracy in Latin America. Christian Democracy in Belgium started along the same route, but by returning to the movement's original spirit, Christian Democrats have reversed their decline. Their example provides hope for their Latin American counterparts.

A crucial area of concern for Catholic social thought is the power of the secular state. The social encyclicals of the popes, even those of Paul VI, emphasized their suspicion of the secular state. Early Christian Democratic thought in France, Italy, and Belgium was antistatist, and the parties prospered. Later, hoping to best their Social Democratic opponents in elections, Latin European Christian Democrats imitated their statism. This failed to produce the goal of stronger electoral support. In fact, blurring the lines has been positively harmful.

Of even greater importance to Catholic social thought is the health and autonomy of civil society, and of the independent social groups that make up this society. Families, labor unions, professional organizations, guilds, clubs, and churches combat both the radical individualism of capitalism and the dangers of overbearing statism. Christian Democracy was supposed to protect individuals and increase social solidarity without increasing state power. Only independent social groups can produce this outcome. Yet in France and Italy, Christian Democratic parties weakened such associations. In doing so, they ultimately weakened themselves.

CHRISTIAN DEMOCRACY IN FRANCE

French Catholic Social Thought before Maritain

No single human being dominates the theory of Christian Democracy like Jacques Maritain. His influence on Christian Democracy, both in Europe and in Latin America, exceeds that of all other Christian Democratic theorists. Maritain did not spring from a vacuum, however. The study of Catholic social thought began earlier. Catholics, inspired by the democratic sentiments of Felicite de Lammenais, defended themselves from the anticlerical 1830 revolution by creating independent social groups that could blunt the oppressive hand of the state. Philippe Buchey worked largely among the working class, denying the revolutionary government part of its desired base.

Lammenais also founded *L'Avenir*, an independent Catholic newspaper. Count de Montalembert, Jean Henri Lacordaire, and Charles de Coux, all leaders in the French Christian Democratic movement, joined him as editors of the short-lived journal. Although written before the social encyclicals, *L'Avenir* anticipated Catholic social thought on the rights of workers, the importance of independent social groups, and the need for limitations on state power. *L'Avenir* was particularly adamant about decentralization of power for the benefit of regional and local authorities.[3]

During the Third Republic, French Christian Democracy came under the influence of René de la Tour de Pin. A Thomist scholar, la Tour de Pin founded Working Men's Clubs for skilled workers. Most of these clubs were run, paternalistically, by the employers for the benefit of "their" workers. La Tour de Pin also established and ran hostels for apprentices and conducted evening classes.[4] By 1880 the Working Men's Club movement had 35,000 members.

Early Christian Democracy in France always chose limited social improvements in favor of more grandiose, but less certain, schemes. In the textile mills of northern France, for example, the movement organized employers to provide an impressive list of social services. The Christian Democrats thus distinguished themselves from the Socialists, who insisted on state-regulated, society-wide change and ignored achievable short-term goals.

The publication of *Rerum Novarum* in 1891 spurred Catholic intellectuals to develop a specifically Catholic response to the changes and challenges of the Industrial Revolution and capitalism. Leon Harmel founded the Cercles d'Êtudes, a study group that functioned almost as a Christian Democratic political party. By 1896, there were enough active Cercles in France to hold a national congress. At this gathering, the Christian Democrats insisted on work as a basic human right, demanded that the state refrain from measures that would make family life more difficult, and reaffirmed their commitment to advance social justice by persuasion. The delegates carefully avoided asking that the state enforce Catholic social doctrine.[5]

Gradual change and self-help were the bases of the Christian Democratic Catholic Action movement. Catholic Action aid centers in the slums of Paris, for example, concentrated not so much on helping families as on equipping families to help themselves. The essential aid for this purpose, the Christian Democrats believed, should come from other families in the neighborhood.

Protection of the family, the most important independent social group, was a priority for early French Christian Democracy. At the 1920 Catholic Action Congress in Lille, the delegates issued the Declaration of the Rights of the Family. These consisted of "the right to protection from public immorality and social disorganization, especially unemployment; the right of parents to determine the general character of their children's schooling; the right to earn, save and inherit; and for fair treatment in the matter of taxes and allowances." Families also have the right to weighted political representation through extra votes for heads of households.

During World War I, French Christian Democrats encouraged employers to give higher salaries to workers with large families. During the 1920s and 1930s, after Christian Democratic pressure, employers also provided education and management training for employees.

After the war, the first Christian Democratic political party appeared. Albert de Mun founded the Popular Liberal Action (ALP) party and developed a program calling for the recognition of independent trade unions, a minimum wage, restrictions on speculative or nonproductive investment, the encouragement of family landholding, local political autonomy, and freedom of association.[6] The ALP filled the void left by the papal ban on the right-wing Action Francaise in 1926.

Even at this early stage, French Christian Democracy began to soften its attitude toward state power. De Mun began the trend by suggesting that some of Christian Democracy's social goals, such as job security for workers, could be provided by the use of state power. In 1936, the Christian Democratic Confederation of Christian Trade Unions (CFTC) wrote a plan for the French economy and agreed with the socialist CGT that credit, insurance, fuel, power, transport, tourism, and health services ought to be state run.[7] For the most part, however, French Christian Democrats sought ways to improve society themselves, not trusting the state to do so.

Jacques Maritain

Maritain's first book, *Integral Humanism*, appeared in 1936. His corpus is very large, and differences in emphasis, or even contradictions, appear in Maritain's writings as he considered questions in new surroundings or in the light of new information. Maritain's difficulties in developing a coherent political philosophy are reflected in the actions of European and Latin American Christian Democrats.

Most of Maritain's works are eloquent and forceful on the need to limit state power. The state, he wrote in 1951, receives its authority from the people. The state is not a sovereign entity. The people, for that matter, are not sovereign either; only God is sovereign. The will of the people is not absolute. It must obey the dictates of what Aquinas called the Natural Law. Any unjust law, even if it expresses the will of the people, is no law, according to Maritain.

Maritain believed that the Hegelian concept of the state as a person, a suprahuman person, was a source of great mischief. Maritain conceded that the state is the topmost part of the body politic, but only a part, and merely an instrumental agency for the just will of individuals.[8] The state is subordinate to the body politic and exists only as a means to achieve the common good.

Society must be directed toward the good of individual persons. Such a society is characterized, first and foremost, by its protection of individual autonomy and the individual right to make the goods of nature serve individual human needs. A just society will provide the means for man to live a fully human life and to achieve salvation.

In a healthy society, one in which people are accustomed to freedom and autonomy, all forms of social and economic activity start with the free initiative of individuals and the "mutual tension" of independent social groups. These groups have a right to autonomy from state power. The state exists to make up for the deficiencies of society. An active state, therefore, indicates a weak society and exists only where society has been weakened by laziness or apathy. Even here, the state should seek to return power to independent social groups as soon as possible.[9]

Maritain stipulated that a body politic can give away its right to autonomy if it desires. The right derives from a society's self-sufficiency, which, Maritain warned, some bodies politic are losing. Lack of commitment to maintaining independent social groups, beginning with the family, characterizes such a loss.

Maritain agreed with the popes and early Christian Democrats that the family was anterior to the state and that the family needed an independent source of income (such as property) to be truly independent. State-directed efforts to provide land must, therefore, actually give families full title and not make them dependent on the continued goodwill of the state. Moreover, state land reform efforts should occur only if large landowners cannot be persuaded to share their bounty or if they begin to use their land unproductively or destructively.

Work, according to Maritain, involves the application of reason to material. It is thus reserved for man, the only rational creature. Work is also related to property, since men will apply reason more imaginatively and diligently to material that they own, and from whose improvement they will profit.[10] Each person has a proprietary right over himself and his acts and has a right to own something on which he can "imprint the mark of his rational being."

Neither Aquinas nor Maritain suggests that private property will cure all social or economic ills. In fact, it can cause and exacerbate these ills. In an imperfect world, however, convenience and the need for peaceful use of land dictate that there be property owned by individuals, to the exclusion of all others.[11] This appropriation of property should be individual, to give maximum scope to the individual talents to manage, administer, and use.

Property should serve man's nature. Collective ownership, under state control, frustrates the use of individual talents and so undermines the purpose of ownership. Co-ownership and comanagement are acceptable to Maritain only to the extent that they expand private ownership and free initiative. State-created and directed cooperatives stifle these things and are dangerous.

Since man is imperfect, he will use his rightfully owned land, on occasion, in ways that violate the rights of others and detract from the common good. Land could be left fallow during famine, its ecology could be ignored, or its use could be determined "not by reason [but by] an act of avarice that deprives others of their due."[12] Like the breakdown of independent social groups, this is a sign of a weak society and a harbinger of dangerous state control.

Maritain prefers that greedy individuals change their ways, saying that the question of devoting surplus land to the common good is a matter "for the individual conscience and the confessional, rather than for sociology or legislation."[13] Tragically, this does not always work. Law, backed by state action, can therefore regulate the use of private property, although it cannot destroy the right of ownership.

Maritain draws a very blurry line here, which later Christian Democrats would use to socialize property under their control. He does not indicate at what point state regulation causes property to cease to be private in any real sense. He thus opens a door to comprehensive regulation. His omission indicates misguided confidence in state power to cure the defects of civil society.

Private property, Maritain reminded his readers, must contribute to the full use of man's human abilities. When a regime based on property becomes depersonalized and passes under the sway of what Maritain calls "inorganic collective forces," then property no longer serves man's nature.[14] These "collective forces" are personal holdings so large that the owners have lost touch with their own possessions.

Under these conditions, concentrated private property becomes more dangerous than state power because there is less chance of orientation toward the common good. To have a large percentage of available property in a few hands is "social disorder." It makes a revolution in the social body inevitable. Maritain did not explain why putting property in the hands of one owner, the state, was an improvement.

Maritain's thought on state control of business is also ambiguous. He thought that the state should avoid nationalization, which he said was really "statization." Yet he thought that it might be necessary for those public services "so immediately concerned with the very existence, order and internal peace of the body politic that a risk of bad state management is then a lesser evil than the risk of giving the upper hand to private interests."

State intervention to protect the worker is another example of Maritain's confidence in state power. For the popes, and for early French Christian Democrats, independent unions were the institution through which workers should protect their rights. Maritain believed that the state should play an active role. The right to work became a guarantee of work, even if the state must create the job. The right to dignity in work became the right to relief, to unemployment insurance, to sick benefits, and to retirement funds, all provided by a state somehow endowed with the goodness, and the resources, to do so equitably.

Maritain failed to explain how society automatically eliminates the danger of neglect of the common good simply by having the state intervene. That state bureaucrats might also neglect the common good and serve only certain interest groups seems not to have occurred to him. Nor did he consider that bureaucrats might have a great interest in destroying independent social groups to increase their own power.

For Maritain, it was the failures of industrial capitalism and of autonomous society that made increased state intervention necessary. While he repeatedly professed to dislike state machinery, Maritain saw no alternative to its growth. He tried again and again to establish abstract limits to state power; but having endowed it with a privileged view of the common good, he found this impossible.

The Popular Republican Movement

Maritain's ambiguous thinking about state power is reflected in French Christian Democracy. The movement in France came of age with the creation of the Popular Republican Movement (MRP) in 1944. Favoritism by the Allies thrust the MRP into political power while it was still getting organized. This, plus its still rather vague ideology, would make the MRP unable to resist the pressure toward a very un-Catholic confidence in state power.

Étienne Gilson, a Thomist in Maritain's tradition, played an important role in formulating MRP doctrine. Under his guidance, the new party decided that rather than avoiding the state, as Catholic social thought suggests, they should use state power to achieve the goals of Catholic social thought.[15]

From the beginning, the MRP lacked the traditional Catholic suspicion of state power. Gilson himself believed that while the state could not create social entities, it could systematize, adapt, arbitrate, order, and coordinate them. While the state must not substitute itself for intermediate social structures, it must intervene "for the purpose of helping them to achieve individual goals."[16]

Gilson believed that the state must work through social groups to deal with individuals. The family, the school, the union, and the Church existed to allow individuals to develop to their potential. The state should deal only with these groups, not with individuals directly.

Coming out of World War II, however, the MRP found that the war's devastation, and the years of Nazi occupation, had destroyed or corrupted all the independent social groups. In a crucial decision, however, the party chose not to work for the rejuvenation of these groups right away but, rather, to empower the state to perform some of the same functions.

In the 1945–1946 Constituent Assembly, the MRP worked closely with the Socialist Party to nationalize France's banks, insurance companies, coal mines, and electricity and gas utilities. Since the MRP lacked definite economic ideas, the Socialists were able to convince them that state control was more just than private control. It is possible that the MRP delegates believed that state control would be temporary, just long enough to allow private concerns to reestablish themselves. Such naivete about the tenacity of state control would be typical of the MRP. Having jettisoned the popes' more principled stand against increased state power, they opened the door that Maritain had found so difficult to close.

Like Maritain, the MRP constantly spoke of the dangers of state power and constantly agreed to increase it. A 1947 MRP statement on nationalization said that this policy should be "restricted" to circumstances where the targeted business is in an area "essential to the life of the nation," where private ownership menaces the independence of the state, and where private initiative is "bankrupt."[17]

Not only are these very broad criteria that can be easily extended, but they also display a change in focus. Where Catholic social thought aimed to protect the individual's independence, the MRP by 1947 worried about the independence of the state. Nationalization, they came to believe, was the only way to ensure that industry would be run for the good of all. Like Maritain, the MRP leadership drew the a priori conclusion that the public sector would always act with wisdom and public spiritedness.

MRP members François de Menthon, Pierre Henri Teitgen, and Maurice Bye strongly supported state economic planning. For them, planning meant state control of economic activity, not just coordination. This group became dominant in the MRP, and the party advocated extensive state planning to rebuild the war-shattered economy. Such detailed planning meant a loss of freedom; but this, the MRP said, was preferable to the social injustice caused by economic liberalism. Again, that state planning and social injustice could coexist was, for them, inconceivable.

The Christian Democratic labor wing, the CFTC, also embraced state economic power. It announced in 1945 that it was "no longer afraid of phrases such as 'nationalization' or 'planned economy.'" The CFTC also said, however, that it "defended human personality against the encroachment of the state as well as against the abuses of capital."

Not all MRP members favored nationalization or increased state power. Paul Bacon, part of the MRP left, opposed statist nationalization but thought that the state should require profit sharing in large firms, "to make work more tolerable and human."[18] The state would do better, he thought, to offer tax incentives to firms with profit sharing, rather than to use force. Bacon's proposals went nowhere. Popular Republican members Pierre Pflimlin, Robért Schuman, and Robért Lecourt saw the state as a guide to the efforts of private firms. Its role should consist of providing information and suggestions. The MRP leadership rejected their ideas, too.

Defenders of the MRP claim that its ability to work not only with Socialists but also with Communists brought the latter into the political system in a responsible way and thus prevented civil war in 1946. Similarly, their existence prevented Charles deGaulle from polarizing French politics, which would also have led to civil war.

The MRP may have performed these functions, but neither required that they jettison their principled support of Catholic social thought nor that they embrace the secular state. Indeed, maintaining a Catholic outlook would have established the MRP as a genuine alternative to left-right polarization and increased their political power.

As it was, their alliances with the Socialists only drove their more conservative backers toward deGaulle. This diminished the MRP and weakened their hand in coalition negotiations with the Socialists. In the end, the Gaullist-Socialist split occurred anyway. Facing political irrelevance, the MRP dissolved itself in 1969.

CHRISTIAN DEMOCRACY IN ITALY

Early Christian Democratic Theory

Italian Christian Democratic experience differs from that of France. Its early thinkers adhered closely to Catholic social thought, even when in positions of political power. Only later did Italian Christian Democracy make compromises that destroyed the intellectual basis for opposition to statism. This departure from Catholic social thought failed to produce the desired results. The DC has never matched its immediate postwar success, when it most closely identified with Church social teachings.

The Vatican took an interest in lay Catholic political activity as the threat of a united Italy under a secular, anticlerical regime became more certain. The popes formed Catholic Action groups under hierarchical control in the 1850s to "focus attention on . . . the special responsibility of the clergy and the independence of the Church." Italian Christian Democracy was thus born of the determination to limit state power.

Preventing the Italian state from gaining a monopoly on the time and activities of young people was also a priority. In 1868, the Vatican helped to create the Italian Catholic Youth Movement. Other Catholic clubs also appeared, and the First National Catholic Congress was held in 1874. By 1881, the Congress Movement, which was more overtly political, existed under papal direction.

The next step was to organize labor. In 1894, Father Romulo Murri organized an independent labor union movement and sought to systematize the efforts of existing Catholic worker service organizations. Young workers, the main targets of the Socialist, Communist, and Masonic-Liberal organizations, were the priority.

Catholic priests worked with devout lay people on these projects. Both groups wanted to protect young people from oppressive, unbridled capitalism by "draw[ing] together students and young workers in a common consciousness of the possibility and need, by a united effort, to overcome the capitalist structures of society and to construct a new order."[19]

These initial Christian Democratic efforts were marked by the determination to exclude the state. The 1899 Program of the Young Christian Democrats, written at a conference in Turin called by Murri, sought to limit state power at every turn. Point 1, for example, called upon the state to allow full freedom and legal recognition to independent trade unions and trade associations. Point 3 demanded "extensive decentralization of the administration as a step toward real autonomy for local and regional authorities."

Even where the Turin program seemed to increase state power, it was a negative power, usually consisting in outlawing some specific abuse but without taking on any additional responsibilities itself. The program consistently built up independent social groups. Point 4 insisted on protection for women and child laborers, compulsory Sunday holidays, pensions, and a minimum wage. But it also insisted that the "practical application of these general rules . . . be entrusted to the corporative organizations of the professions."

Point 5 demanded the "serious protection of small property." Point 6 came as close as any to increasing state power by suggesting the development of a merchant navy. Point 7 followed with a demand for sharp and progressive tax reductions, and Point 8 called for the abolition of consumption taxes, the reduction or elimination of tariffs and property taxes, and their replacement with a moderate, progressive income tax.[20]

Luigi Sturzo

The ideas of the Turin program stimulated the Congress movement to find ways to make them more concrete. Meanwhile, Italian Christian Democracy was profoundly influenced by the appearance of Luigi Sturzo, a Catholic priest wholly committed to the practical establishment of Catholic social thought. He founded the Christian Democratic Popular Party (PP) in 1919, taking advantage of the end of the formal Vatican prohibition on Catholic participation in Italian politics in 1918.

Like the MRP, the PP began its career with great political success. In its first electoral test, in 1919, it won 100 Chamber of Deputies seats and a central position in the governing coalition. Unlike the MRP, however, it retained its commitment to Catholic social thought even while in power. The PP proved that instant political power does not have to mean compromising principle.

Sturzo insisted that the basic claims of the Italian state were invalid. Secular politicians, for example, made much of their commitment to grant human rights to the citizens. Sturzo maintained that such rights came from God, and that the state not only did not grant them, but also was required to respect them whether it wanted to or not. The PP did not seek to adapt itself to the state but insisted that the state itself had to adapt. Sturzo wrote in 1945, "The theory that the individual exists for the state and not the state for the individual, that everything must be for the state, within the state and with the state, creates a clear cut division between oppressors and oppressed, who in other words can be called *masters and slaves.*"[21]

Individuals protect themselves by setting up independent social groups that are harder for the state to coerce than individuals. In medieval times, Sturzo wrote in 1938, the nobility, the Church, and independent communes limited the power of kings, and all of these based their independence on the sustenance derived from the ownership of property.[22]

As kings attacked these institutions, and especially the Catholic Church, property and political power became atomized, allowing both large private trusts and powerful governments to emerge. With only weak and isolated individuals to confront it, political power could act without moral scrutiny.

To counterbalance the claims of this rapacious liberal state, Catholics must form independent social groups, beginning with free, pluralist schools. Sturzo feared homogenized education, writing, "The empire of the State over the soul is in continuous progress . . . where the State, while not totalitarian, seeks to give its own imprint to the education and cultural formation of the country."[23] The insistence of the liberal Italian state for a monopoly on education, Sturzo said, made it all the easier for the Fascists to control schooling.

This same liberal elite also ignored the rights of workers and alienated them from society. This provided an opportunity for the Socialists and Communists, whom Catholics had to counter. When workers were prevented from becoming owners, class warfare and societal instability were inevitable. Capitalists, Sturzo believed, tended to consolidate their enterprises and then use the state to prevent the entry of new competitors. This inhibits the welfare of capital and of labor at the same time.

Sturzo shared Maritain's fear of big business, but like John Paul II, he took pains to distinguish destructive forms of capitalism from constructive ones. By capital, he wrote, "we do not mean . . . the fruit of productivity and labor. . . . By capitalism we mean above all the system of the exploitation of work, by which all benefits accrue to those who have brought money into a business. We mean the anonymity and irresponsibility of the money and shares representing the capital of a business."[24]

Thus capitalism is dangerous only when it passes out of the hands of risk takers and into the hands of anonymous managers who are not owners. Sturzo firmly believed in the necessity of small capitalism as an element of freedom. He wrote: "Where there is no fundamental economic liberty, political liberty is lost as well. . . . The abolition of private property strikes a deathblow at individual liberty."[25]

Ownership, far from being taken away, should be extended by removing the various protections that large landowners write into the laws. Small-holders should not be weighed down with debts and taxes but should be given relief by limiting taxes and lowering interest rates through balanced national budgets.

The agrarian reform program of the PP, which Sturzo called the most complete land reform project in Italian history, focused on giving outright ownership to as many people as possible. The state would provide credit and infrastructure but not retain ownership itself. The PP also realized that the reform must be gradual to avoid doing away with property rights altogether. The post–World War I governments failed to act upon these comprehensive proposals, thus opening the countryside to Socialist violence and Fascist reaction. This helped to pave the way for Mussolini's victory. Once in power, the Fascists negated the PP plan.

Sturzo never left any doubt that he feared state power more than unbridled private greed. As selfish and potentially harmful as the latter is, it is easier to recognize and less likely to present itself as something laudable. The state, on the other hand, uses ideology to equate its power with ethics. Once this occurs, the assertive state "cannot but seek to gain complete control of the whole economy of the country, in order to subordinate it to political ends."[26] The state seeks to become Leviathan. In so doing, it creates tension and opposition, which it then uses as an excuse to extend power further.

The Christian Democratic Party

The PP's principled adherence to Catholic social thought won it praise from friends, respect from its democratic rivals, and the special hatred of Mussolini. The postwar Christian Democratic Party (DC), however, followed a very different path. Many Christian Democrats began their rehabilitation of the secular state when they realized the potential to use state power to achieve Christian Democratic social goals. Sturzo rejects this possibility out of hand, saying that not even the lofty goals of *Rerum Novarum* could be imposed by the state from above. Any such attempt would sully those goals.

Almost from the moment of its inception, the DC has had close and intimate ties with the Italian state. Under these circumstances, Christian Democrats could convince themselves that the state was wiser, fairer, and more committed to the common good than individuals. The principled adherence to Catholic social thought that marked the career of Luigi Sturzo would vanish and be replaced with the same counterproductive pragmatism that helped to destroy the French MRP.

Mussolini's Fascist government exiled Sturzo in 1926 as part of its campaign to eliminate political rivals. Alcide deGasperi took his place and oversaw the creation of the DC. Formerly, deGasperi had been a cataloguer in the Vatican library. He had close ties to Popes Pius XI and Pius XII.

The honeymoon in Vatican-Italian relations that followed the Lateran Treaty in 1929 was short lived. By 1931, the Fascists had attacked Catholic youth groups, Catholic free trade unions, and even individual priests and nuns. Pope Pius XI, starting in 1931, used the Christian Democrats who remained in Italy to develop a political resistance to Mussolini. This Vatican blessing was a tremendous boost to party fortunes that had flagged after the Sturzo exile.

With the fall of the Fascist regime in 1943, the DC was able to come above ground again, owing much to the protection and counsel of the Church under Pius XII. While this gave the DC a head start over other parties seeking to gain control of Italy's postwar politics, it also induced many DC members to assert their independence from Vatican control. One oft-chosen method for doing so was rejection of the antistatist elements of Catholic social thought.

DeGasperi's leadership of the DC was marked by his determination to make the party the permanent leader in the Italian parliament. To do so he presented the party as the only realistic alternative to atheistic communism. He supplemented this appeal with the wide use of patronage and state money.

DeGasperi was motivated by the fear that without the DC in the center, Italian politics would polarize between the extreme right and left, leading to civil war. His conception of the role of a center party, however, was to avoid controversy and to avoid making enemies. This tempted him to use state funds to purchase the loyalty of centrist coalition partners such as the Liberal and Republican parties.[27]

In 1945, DC economic policy contained five major points: first, that there is no single answer to the state-versus-private-sector question; second, that the DC accepts the extensive public ownership the Fascists had left behind; third, that government economic planning should be consistent with private initiative; fourth, that central control stifles initiative and creativity; and fifth, that about 75 percent of the Italian economy should be free from state control.[28]

The contradictions within these statements indicate that the DC had a deeper problem than just short-sighted pragmatism. The party could not decide if government economic decision making was a good or bad thing. Forced at times to make a choice, however, the DC has almost invariably chosen to allow the government to grow. In power continuously since 1943, the DC has presided over the creation of one of the largest and most powerful state economic sectors in Western Europe.

From 1943 to 1950, the DC could do little more than draft a new constitution and oversee the physical reconstruction of the country. These tasks resulted in the consolidation and exercise of considerable political and economic power. The bill of rights added to the constitution directs the state to lend its active support and machinery to secure the right to work, to "security," to welfare, and to education.

The document also allowed the state to exact from each citizen "such tasks as will contribute to the material and spiritual progress of society."[29] Italy's constitution also empowers the state to coordinate and direct private economic activity toward social ends.

One the DC's most immediate postwar aims was the revival of economic activity in the south. To stimulate this, the party created a public corporation to promote economic growth. The DC, according to one author, was anxious "to gain control over this exceedingly important instrument of economic policy."

The Institute of Industrial Reconstruction (IRI) also had enormous political possibilities. Since 1945, it has allowed the survival of autarchic and bankrupt industries that should have been reformed. Their survival, however, allowed the DC to control, or at least to partly control, the endemic corruption in southern Italy while using the bureaucracy of the IRI to reward party faithful with jobs and government contracts.

Thus the IRI allowed the DC to increase its influence in an area hitherto uncontrolled. Once the DC leadership saw the ease with which this could be done, they established hundreds, then thousands, of public industries, establishing at the same time a strong tradition of government intervention in industry. By 1979, Italy had 60,000 public and quasi-public corporations.[30]

In spite of this record, much of the party's political success is dependent on support from the Italian business community. Most businesspeople know they depend upon friendly relations with government agencies to prosper.[31] Large businesses have used these relations to persuade the DC to violate another principle of Catholic social thought by introducing measures to protect Italy from the free movement of goods and capital promised by the European Community.

On the mass level, DC support rests largely on clientism, itself based upon the availability of massive amounts of government resources to recruit and satisfy clients. The 60,000 public corporations mentioned above are an integral part of this effort. In almost every case, DC members occupy decision-making positions in the firms. Patronage keeps the system operating. The DC has neglected the fact that patronage, by definition, benefits fewer people than it deprives.

During the 1960s, the DC moved further to the left. DeGasperi was attracted by the Socialist Party's (PSI) offer of a coalition, even though the Church firmly rejected it. For deGasperi, however, it was a question of pragmatism. "For well-defined purposes of parliamentary government," he explained, "[the Christian Democrats] have sought or accepted participation in governments in which Socialists were represented."[32]

In the 1970s, a new DC secretary sought a coalition with the Communists. He wanted to attract Italians who had been offended by the party's opposition to a referendum on the legalization of divorce. Benigno Zaccagnini targeted the young, the intellectuals, and unions in particular. He was motivated by the growth of the PCI's popularity. Yet Zaccagnini hampered the renovation the DC sorely needed by taking what one author calls a "basically defensive motive vis à vis the growing appeal and legitimacy of the PCI."[33]

This begs the question of why the PCI was surging in the first place. After years of anti-Communist rhetoric from the DC, coupled with actions indicating that statist policies were not all that fearsome, part of the Italian electorate evidently concluded that committed statism might be preferable to the watered-down version the DC offered.

The DC did nothing to counter this belief. Aldo Moro, the DC parliamentary chief in 1978, cited what he called the "profound" ideological differences between the DC and the PCI and then, incongruously, called for pragmatic cooperation with them. The Communist success in the 1975 elections convinced the DC to make an opening to the left. Since the Christian Democrats depended so heavily on patronage, they were vulnerable to a party that promised to increase the state sector even more, thus permitting even greater economic rewards.

The Christian Democrats responded by expanding the state sector themselves, especially in rural areas, which had unexpectedly gone PCI in 1975. The DC has increased its colonization of some of the most parasitic sectors of the Italian economy by allowing government funds to flow to public corporations that are notoriously unproductive. The DC had become so divorced from its own principles that by the 1970s it perceived that the only way to fight its long-time enemies was to imitate them. In doing so, they succeeded only in legitimizing their opponents while blunting their own appeal.

As this process has continued, the DC has largely lost the dedicated following that marked the Sturzo years. Those who give their time and energy to the DC today, for the most part, do so not out of ideological commitment but, rather, in return for, or in anticipation of, economic favors based on machine politics. A large percentage of the DC membership are either public employees or housewives who still connect the DC with Catholicism.

Christian Democratic losses have been particularly heavy among young people. Disgusted with the insider, nonideological nature of Italian politics, the country's youth has largely opted out of politics and out of the DC. This is an almost complete turnaround from the Sturzo years, when PP youth groups flourished.

The DC may have been saved from annihilation by the murder of Aldo Moro by the Communist Red Brigade in 1978. This halted the potentially disastrous PCI coalition effort and allowed younger DC members to question the policy of accommodation. Since 1978, the most vigorous trend in the DC has been the rediscovery of the party's roots in Catholic social thought.

However, DC policy is still primarily directed toward accommodation and imitation. Since this trend started, the party has never matched its immediate postwar success, when the lines between the DC and Italy's statist parties were sharpest.

CHRISTIAN DEMOCRACY IN BELGIUM

In Italy and France, the Christian Democratic parties abandoned their adherence to Christian Democratic principles in the name of political pragmatism. In both cases, the parties emerged with neither their integrity nor the political success they expected.

Yet the argument is often made that a political party in the twentieth century simply cannot hope to succeed adhering to principles as stringent as those of Catholic social thought. To do so is to buck a seemingly irresistible trend toward greater state involvement in the economy, or at least to cede political success to those willing to adapt themselves to this trend.

The experience of Christian Democrats in Belgium challenges this conclusion. Belgian Christian Democrats have found that political success does not come from abandoning first principles. Rather, the close and principled adherence to Catholic social thought helps to prevent electoral setbacks.

The Catholic Party

Belgian Christian Democracy was born of the anti-Catholic policies of Belgian liberals in the nineteenth century. The Belgian Catholic Party was born in the 1890s as both Belgian Socialists and the Catholic hierarchy became friendlier to the idea of Catholic participation. The Belgian Catholic Party developed from below, following the impetus of priests and lay people determined to take control over education and to protect independent social groups. Its original platform called for independence for labor and professional organizations and for labor representation in government.

The Catholic Party, like the MRP, the PP, and the DC, acquired access to political power almost immediately after its formation. Like the PP, it maintained its commitment to the antistatist principles of Catholic social thought. Under Catholic Party Prime Minister Auguste Beernaert, it abolished female mine labor, instituted workmen's compensation, forbade work on Sunday, and limited the other working days to nine hours. It opposed the growth of government power.[34]

Much of the party's support has come from the Belgian Large Families League, formed in the interwar period to put pressure on businesspeople to pay a family wage and to offer higher salaries to workers with more children. By 1939, the League had grown to 250,000 members, which gave it considerable influence on issues such as taxation, family allowances, and even railway rates.

The Catholic Party supported the goals of the League. The party stressed the importance of the family, called for additional votes for household heads over 30 years of age, and proposed that the government build more single-family homes and require profit sharing from Belgian firms.[35]

The Catholic Party was also strong among workers, the Socialists' natural base. While refraining from criticisms of capitalism itself, labor unions connected to the party demanded accident and sickness insurance, old-age pensions, a graduated income tax, and Sunday rest. The party supported these demands.

After World War I, the Catholic Party entered into a coalition with the Socialists but did not abandon its traditional principles in the process. It made adherence to its program by the Socialists the price of their participation. Working together, the two parties promoted progressive taxation, a government housing policy, old-age pensions, and an eight-hour day. Both supported the right of unions to organize.

Still, the alliance was not without cost. Working with the Socialists cost the Catholic Party some of its hard-core support, and so it lost the absolute majority the party had retained before the war. At the same time, the Socialist Party became more strident in its Marxism. The Catholic Party decided upon a coalition with the liberals, the party's old opponents.

Unlike their French and Italian counterparts, the Belgian Christian Democrats were not haunted by fear of the political right. Since they could not govern alone, they joined the party whose views were more compatible with their own. Commitment to ideology, in other words, outweighed short-term political gain. In the end, the Catholic Party secured this anyway.

Belgium's shifting political alliances made this coalition short lived. Liberals and Socialists were able to coalesce after World War II, putting the Catholic Party in the minority. In 1954, however, with the Catholics out of government altogether, the alliance between the Liberals and the Socialists sought to cut the subsidy given to private schools. This galvanized Belgian Catholics. Since the Catholic Party had not abandoned its position in favor of independent private schools, it could take advantage of Catholic anger and win a large majority in the 1958 election.[36]

Belgium's Christian Democratic Parties Today

In 1968, ideological and regional differences split the Catholic party into the Walloon Social Christian Party (PSC) and the Flemish Christelijke Volksparity (CVP). The two groups work closely together and can be considered two branches of the same party. The CVP is more conservative, perhaps because Flanders is more agricultural and conservative than Wallonia. Its support comes from Catholic workers, the Flemish middle class, and small farmers. Several Christian trade unions are linked with the CVP. The PSC, representing the Latin part of Belgium, is smaller but still germane to this discussion. The CVP-PSC retains much of the support the Catholic Party acquired when it represented what one expert calls "the most conservative Catholic tendencies."[37]

During the 1970s, Belgium's Christian Democratic parties developed two identifiable tendencies. The right was represented by CEPIC, a businesspeople's organization, and the left by the workers. During most of the decade, the left dominated the PSC, resulting in a steady leftward movement reminiscent of French and Italian Christian Democracy. The PSC began to lose votes from traditional supporters, particularly among young people, who like their counterparts in France and Italy soon grew tired of complacent, insider politics.

At the same time, the pressures of an almost constant presence in Belgium's governing coalitions made the Christian Democrats less hesitant about embracing state power. Like their French and Italian counterparts, they sought votes through patronage and clientism, rather than through commitment to ideology. As the 1970s ended in recession and high inflation, their ability to use government largess to persuade voters eroded. This, plus their ideological drift, made the 1981 election the all-time low for the CVP-PSC partnership.

Unlike its French and Italian counterparts, the Belgian CVP-PSC retained a coherent conservative wing ready to take advantage of the weakness of social democracy in the 1980s. This electoral slippage provided an opportunity for the CEPIC wing of the party to reassert itself.

The CEPIC wing pushed the Christian Democrats to champion the viability of the commercial firm, reducing state intervention in the economy and staking out a strong position on defense. During the 1980s, in spite of pressure from its left wing, the Christian Democrats opposed the automatic (and inflationary) indexation of wages, at the same time opposing state intervention in the economy and increased public expenditures.[38]

The CVP-PSC coalition has found that political success follows adherence to roots in Catholic social thought. In 1985, a CVP-PSC-led coalition was reelected. It is rare for Belgians to reelect governing coalitions. Even more surprising was that the Christian Democrats had imposed austerity measures on Belgium during their term. Aligned with the antistatist Liberal Party, the Christian Democrats promised to restrain both wages and public expenditures. The CVP-PSC found that such a forthright stand did not have to mean electoral failure.[39]

CONCLUSION

In France, Italy, and Belgium, Christian Democratic parties have emerged in the twentieth century. With significant differences, all the parties began with a firm commitment to the tenets of Catholic social thought. At some point, Christian Democrats in France, Italy, and Belgium abandoned Catholic social thought in the search for short-term political success. In doing so, they lost votes from their traditional supporters while failing to gain either the votes or the respect of their opponents.

Pragmatism, in short, turned out to be anything but pragmatic. As Luigi Sturzo said about the actions of Italian Catholics during Italy's reunification, "The mistake of many in those days was to consider an attitude of practical expediency as good for all times and places, almost as a theoretical and universal truth."[40]

In France, the Christian Democratic MRP imitated the economic policies of its political rivals and disappeared. In Italy, the DC tried the same thing and almost lost the 1975 elections to the Communists. The DC has yet to regain the electoral strength that it had when it stood for Catholic social thought. Only in Belgium have Christian Democrats halted the trend toward accommodation of statism and imitation of political rivals. There, Christian Democratic parties have recommitted themselves to the political economy of the Catholic Church and have revived.

Latin American Christian Democrats traveled the same rocky path as their Latin European counterparts. Only in the 1990s did they realize the false promise of statist-directed "pragmatism." In Parts 2 and 3, I will examine the economic policies of Christian Democratic parties and movements in Latin America. To a large degree, the experience of Europe has repeated itself. Imitation and pragmatism have failed to bring success. Commitment, on the other hand, has never led to failure.

NOTES

1. For further discussions of the various theories that explain political parties' behavior, see Gabriel A. Almond and G. Bingham Powell, Jr., eds., *Comparative Politics Today* (Glenview, Ill.: Scott, Foresman, 1988), Chapter 6. For a discussion more directly related to parties in multiparty systems, see Arend Lijphart, *Democracy in Plural Societies* (New Haven, Conn.: Yale University Press, 1977).

2. For the purposes of this study, the French, Italian, and Belgian Christian Democratic parties are the most important. Not only did they develop in areas as predominantly Catholic as Latin America, and with a similar political culture, but they also provided the most direct guidance to Latin American Christian Democrats. The experience of the German Christian Democrats, especially their revival under Helmut Kohl, confirms the thesis of this chapter.

3. Michael P. Fogarty, *Christian Democracy in Western Europe, 1820–1953* (Notre Dame, Ind.: University of Notre Dame Press, 1957), p. 155.

4. R. E. M. Irving, *Christian Democracy in France* (London: George Allen & Unwin, 1973), p. 33.

5. Ibid., p. 34.

6. Fogarty, p. 331.

7. Ibid., p. 218.

8. Jacques Maritain, *Man and the State* (Chicago: University of Chicago Press, 1951), p. 195.

9. Latin American Christian Democrats would frequently conclude that their societies were weak and that greater state power was therefore necessary. They made no effort to strengthen society so that state intervention would be short lived.

10. Jacques Maritain, *Freedom in the Modern World* (New York: Charles Scribner's Sons, 1936), p. 197.

11. See Thomas Aquinas, *Summa Theologica*, II-II Art. 57, Q. 3.

12. Maritain, *Freedom*, p. 208.

13. Ibid., p. 209.

14. Ibid., p. 212.

15. Irving, *France*, pp. 53–54.

16. Mario Einaudi and François Goguel, *Christian Democracy in Italy and France* (Notre Dame, Ind.: University of Notre Dame Press, 1952), p. 127.

17. Ibid., p. 143.

18. Irving, *France*, p. 125.

19. Fogarty, p. 276.

20. Ibid., pp. 319–21.

21. Luigi Sturzo, *Italy and the Coming World* (New York: Roy Publishers, 1945), p. 144. (Italics in original.)

22. Luigi Sturzo, *Politics and Morality* translated by Barbara Barclay Cater (London: Burn Oates and Washbourne, 1938), p. 5.

23. Luigi Sturzo, *Church and State* (New York: Longmans, Green and Co., 1939), p. 532.

24. Sturzo, *Politics and Morality*, p. 153.

25. Sturzo, *Coming World*, p. 140.

26. Sturzo, *Politics and Morality*, pp. 15–16.

27. Emil Kirchner, *Liberal Parties in Western Europe* (Cambridge: Cambridge University Press, 1988), p. 35.

28. Einaudi and Goguel, p. 37.

29. Ibid., p. 42.

30. Alan Zuckerman, *The Politics of Faction: Christian Democratic Rule in Italy* (New Haven, Conn.: Yale University Press, 1979), p. 83.

31. Roger Morgan and Stephano Silvestri, *Moderates and Conservatives in Western Europe: Political Parties, the European Community and the Atlantic Alliance* (London: Heinemann, 1982), p. 118.

32. Ibid., p. 19.

33. Geoffrey Pridham, "The Italian Christian Democrats after Moro: Crisis or Compromise?" *West European Politics* 2, 1 (1979): 78.

34. R. E. M. Irving, *The Christian Democratic Parties of Western Europe* (London: George Allen & Unwin, 1979), p. 170.

35. Ibid., p. 173.

36. Ibid., p. 166.

37. John Fitzmaurice, *The Politics of Belgium: Crisis and Compromise in a Plural Society* (New York: St. Martin's Press, 1983), p. 144.

38. Ibid., p. 149.

39. For lengthier discussions of the 1985 and subsequent Belgian elections, see Chris Rudd, "The Aftermath of Heysel: The 1985 Belgian Election," *West European Politics* 9, 2 (April 1986): 282–88; John Fitzmaurice and Guido Van den Berghe, "The Belgian General Election of 1985," *Electoral Studies* 5, 1 (1986): 73–83; and various analyses in *Parliamentary Affairs*.

40. Sturzo, *Coming World*, p. 114.

II

The Political Economy of Latin American Christian Democracy

3

Christian Democracy in Latin America: Compromising with the State

ORIGINS AND EARLY COMMITMENT TO CATHOLIC SOCIAL THOUGHT

The European Christian Democratic movement attracted a great deal of attention among young Latin American intellectuals in the 1930s and 1940s. The Catholic Church supplemented the call to action that its social encyclicals represented with a series of seminars, training sessions, and conferences for young political leaders throughout the world.

Latin America's large Catholic population, and the prevalence of Catholic intellectuals, convinced the Catholic Church that the continent merited a special effort. Conferences in Rome in the 1930s brought together potential Christian Democratic leaders from all over the area, and soon most Latin American states had a Christian Democratic party or movement.

In the early days of the Christian Democratic movement in Latin America, its leaders were outwardly committed to the broad outlines of Catholic social thought. This was particularly true in the case of limiting state power. Living for the most part in countries with strong military governments, Latin America's early Christian Democratic theorists and leaders shared the traditional Catholic suspicion of state power.

If the Latin American movement had retained this commitment, Christian

Democratic parties could have become genuine alternatives to the left-and right-wing statism that has plagued the continent. Such an alternative, based on clear Christian principles, would have had a broad and loyal constituency among Latin Americans left out by statist, insider politics. Christian Democracy could easily have become a major, mass-based political movement.

The movement did not hold to its beliefs, however. I will show in this and subsequent chapters that Latin America's Christian Democrats quickly became even less reluctant to use state power than the Europeans. Once they made this decision, they jettisoned their opportunity to build mass support and became just another elite political movement. After a promising start in Latin America, the Christian Democratic movement foundered. As we shall see in Chapters 7 and 8, some Christian Democratic movements revived as the 1980s ended. These successful Christian Democrats have rediscovered the antistatism of Catholic social thought. They were able to take advantage of the shift toward neoliberal economics in Latin America.

Catholic social thought is difficult to sustain in practice. Critics of Catholic social thought have maintained that it is too vague to be of any use as a policy guide to politicians in the real world. The high levels of ideological consistency demanded by the social encyclicals also persuade some politicians that it is impossible to be faithful to Catholic social thought and succeed politically.

The philosophy is indeed short on specifics. But its first principles indicate certain directions that could not be clearer. One major fundamental idea is a distrust of state power and a determination that it should not be increased, unless there is no other choice. Equally important is a commitment to sustaining independent social groups at the expense of government power.

Christian Democratic parties in Latin America adhere to these general principles until they taste political power for themselves. Then, either because they believe they are better than other political parties or because they have concluded that society is not as strong as the popes thought it was, they embrace state power and seek to use it to fulfill specific social goals while neglecting Catholic social thought's more essential goals.

Because they accept the major premises of their opponents while still presenting themselves as "moderates," Latin Americans perceive Christian Democrats as simply less committed and less consistent shadows of their Social Democratic rivals. This largely accounts for the movement's disappointing history since the glory days of the 1960s.

Latin American Christian democracy did not achieve political power anywhere until Eduardo Frei's 1964 victory in Chile. Thus the Latin Americans did not have the same immediate pragmatic temptations that proved so enticing to the European Christian Democrats. Nevertheless, once they did achieve power, the Latin Americans would prove no more reticent in their embrace of state power than their European precursors.

The continent's Christian Democrats were always more protective of independent social groups than they were of private property. Their enthusiasm for state-directed land reform, nationalization, and business regulation was always fairly strong. But even their determination to protect families, independent schools, and other important social groups failed to last past the earliest formative stages.

Their early days in the political wilderness only serve to highlight how complete the turnaround was. Initial Christian Democratic attitudes and statements reflect a strong suspicion of state power and a strong determination to keep the state within well-defined bounds. At that time, Latin American Christian Democracy sought to protect society, especially independent social entities like families, private schools, professional organizations, and labor unions.

All these, according to Christian Democratic theory, are anterior to the state and have rights that the state cannot suspend or eliminate. In Venezuela, Christian Democrats under a military dictatorship created women's, youth, and workers' organizations to undermine the dictator's power. In Peru, José Luis Bustamente y Rivero, a major Christian Democratic theorist, blasted Marxism for its statism. In Brazil, Christian Democracy started with a movement dedicated to ensure that the "sacredness of the family" would be enshrined in the 1934 constitution through the prohibition of divorce and the protection of parents' rights in education.[2]

In El Salvador, the party warned against the expansion of "centralized, all-powerful, impersonal government." To prevent this expansion, Salvadoran Christian Democrats supported diffusion of power to the local level and promoted the autonomy of independent social groups. The Costa Rican party adjured the state to respect the rights of the family, especially in education. Argentine Christian Democrats promised to protect the independence of the Church, the rights of the family, and the right of parents to oversee their children's education.[3]

In Venezuela, Rafael Caldera began his Christian Democratic career by declaring the importance of the family and warning against state intrusion on its prerogatives. The 1949 Christian Democratic conference in Montevideo stated, "The State ought to recognize the professional organization as a juridical institution with normative, executive, and jurisdictional powers."

Christian Democrats believed that claims of power by the state were prejudicial and egoistic and must give way to the prior claims of the individual or the social group. Independent social groups effectively limit the power of the state by confronting it with institutions more difficult to coerce than isolated individuals. The early Christian Democrats made no assumption that directives from the state were necessarily more just, more moral, or more compelling than directives from any other group of flawed human beings.

Although the Christian Democrats insisted that they desired revolutionary political and economic change for Latin America, they were reluctant to radically increase state power to make revolution occur. Such an increase, they believed, would threaten the moral base for their revolution and would lead to an imposed revolution, rather than the organic revolution, in liberty, that Latin American Christian Democrats originally desired.

Early Christian Democratic theory also opposed centralization of political power. It championed the rights of provinces and municipalities, based on the Catholic principle of subsidiarity. The Bolivian party, for example, said: "Popular government must be decentralized. The concentration of all power, in the communist style, is anti-popular and, consequently, retrogressive."[4]

Other Christian Democrats tried to revitalize the municipal governments of Latin America, with one party promising to revamp the tax system to give localities their own source of revenue. Eduardo Frei of Chile came to the presidency with plans to use tax incentives for businesses to move out of Santiago.

Chile

Latin America's Christian Democratic parties have much in common regarding their origins. Most grew out of the efforts of young, middle-class intellectuals, who were inspired by the social encyclicals and devoted to the immediate application of Catholic social thought. Chilean Christian Democracy started when Chile's Conservative Party sponsored a youth movement in the 1930s. Its leaders included Eduardo Frei Montalva, Radomiro Tomic, Manuel Garretón, and Bernardo Leighton. All these men had taken part in the struggle to remove Carlos Ibáñez from the presidency in 1931.

This introduction to political activity spurred Frei to investigate Catholic social thought. With the other youth movement leaders, he joined the Falange Nacional, which claimed its intellectual heritage from *Rerum Novarum* and *Quadragessimo Anno*. Most Falangist leaders were students under Fernando Vives de Solar and Alberto Hurtado Cruchaga, whom one expert described as "progressive" members of the Society of Jesus.[5]

The strong influence of these priests, and of Jacques Maritain, convinced Frei that Chile needed political and economic changes that the Conservatives opposed. He decided in the 1950s to form a new party, one openly supportive of the social encyclicals and committed to basic social change.

From this platform, Frei became a Chilean senator from Santiago in 1957. His large plurality in that election spurred his national political ambitions, and Frei ran for president in 1958. He finished third behind Jorge Alessandri and Salvador Allende. Almost immediately after the votes were counted, Senator Frei began preparations for 1964.

Frei's 1964 victory was convincing. Winning an outright majority of the votes, he avoided throwing the election to the Chilean National Assembly and claimed a mandate for sweeping changes in Chile's politics and economy. His victory was the first by a Christian Democrat in Latin America and seemed to presage a bright future for the movement. (The victory of Rafael Caldera in Venezuela four years later seemed to confirm this.) Many Latin

Americans, as well as policy makers in Washington, saw the Christian Democrats as a centrist movement that would rescue Latin America from the polarized politics of left and right.

Yet there were disturbing shadows over the victory. Frei's critics on the left pointed to the sudden shift in the 1964 campaign's last days to a hard anti-Communist line. They pointed out that this shift coincided with contributions from West Germany's Christian Democratic party, which many Chileans perceived to be a conduit for money from the North American Central Intelligence Agency (CIA).[6]

Chile's traditional right, represented by Alessandri's National Party, failed to run their own candidate in 1964 and had to back Frei against Salvador Allende. Thus, the president-elect could not depend upon the support of many people who voted for him once he started to govern. It also meant that a large number of his supporters opposed those elements of Catholic social thought that challenged their privileged economic and social position. To offset this opposition, and to undercut the charges of collaboration with the CIA, Frei found it expedient to move leftward during his presidency.

Frei wrote before becoming president that Christian Democracy desires "meaningful economic development." This requires a state that protects individuals and allows them to feel that they have power and are creating wealth.[7] Frei did believe that the state had an economic role. It should, he said in 1955, offer economic development plans, make basic investments in research and development, and "fix inequalities in international trade." He added, however, that "the wide field of economic life within this rationally defined area . . . will not be uselessly invaded by the state."[8]

In the 1964 campaign, Frei warned of the effects of an Allende victory. The Socialists, he said, would expropriate large landholdings and nationalize minerals, mining facilities, utilities, insurance companies, and banks. They would levy heavy redistributive taxes and control the distribution of consumer goods.[9] Frei, for his part, promised to decentralize Chile's economy and politics and avoid "socialist" policies. Writing in 1977, he pointed with pride to the formation of independent social groups like neighborhood associations, peasant co-ops, guilds, and unions that had taken place during his presidency.

Frei was unable to succeed himself in 1970. His party, split between statists and antistatists, was unable to gain reelection. The Christian Democrats came in third, behind Allende's Popular Front and a revived National Party. This set a pattern for the continent's Christian Democratic parties. Not one of them has ever been reelected.

Venezuela

A youth conference in Rome provided the impetus for Venezuela's Christian Democratic party as well. Rafael Caldera, like Frei a leader of anti-Marxist university students, attended the First Conference of Catholic Youth in Rome in 1934, joining Frei and other future Christian Democratic leaders. A featured speaker at this conference was Vatican Secretary of State Eugenio Pacelli, who would later become Pope Pius XII.

The death of dictator Juan Gómez in 1935 provided the political space for student movements to become more overtly political. When Eleazar López Contreras replaced Gómez, he offered the Labor Ministry portfolio to the youthful Caldera. Refusing the top post, Caldera served as deputy director from 1936 until 1938. He is the author of Venezuela's 1936 labor code.

After graduating from university, Caldera created the Acción Nacional in 1942, linking his fledgling Christian Democratic movement with rightist regional groupings. The union was based on a common suspicion of centralized state power. Caldera's future electoral strength came from the Andean states of Tachira, Mérida and Trujillo, where the tradition of anti-Caracas feeling was strong.

Like Frei, Caldera was heavily influenced by a "progressive" Jesuit. Manuel Aguirre Elorriaga introduced Caldera to Luigi Sturzo at the 1934 Rome conference. Aguirre also emphasized to Caldera the importance of political tools like grassroots organizing and public speaking. With Sturzo, he spoke to the young Caldera of the importance of gaining political power to implement the social encyclicals.

Because of his influence on Caldera, the future career of Father Aguirre is worth noting. By the 1960s, Aguirre had concluded that only violent revolution could end the misery of Latin America's lower classes. While retaining the critique of capitalism spelled out in the social encyclicals of Pius XI, Aguirre rejected the pope's suspicion of the state and instead looked to the state to assume an active role in the economy.

Christian Democracy in Venezuela got its biggest boost from the democratic government that appeared in 1945. To compete in elections to be held that year, Caldera founded the Comité de Organización Política Electoral Independiente (Copei) to identify and recruit likely Christian Democratic voters. The leaders of this movement identified themselves most closely with French Christian Democrats like Maritain and with the French Popular Republican Movement.[10]

The 1946 Copei electoral program supported the social encyclicals and promoted the legitimate rights of independent social groups above individual or class rights. At the same time, it stipulated that the state was not the primary repository of these collective rights.

During these formative years, Caldera retained some outward suspicion for the state. As late as 1959, he wrote that Christian Democracy means "a doctrine of renascence, of reformation, sanely revolutionary, which aims at putting an end to the injustices of extreme individualism without falling into the opposite error of social hatred, worship of the state, or anarchy."[11]

Venezuela's democratic forces were determined to make the most of the 1945 opening and so formed a coalition to minimize intrademocratic competition. When Rómulo Betancourt of the Social Democratic Acción Demo-crática (AD) claimed the leadership of this coalition, Caldera became attorney general in the early months of the 1945–1948 Triennio. He quit the coalition in 1947 after AD roughs attacked Copei electoral workers in Tachira.[12]

In 1948, a military coup ended the Venezuelan democratic experiment. Marcos Pérez Jiménez, the new dictator, suspended all political parties and exiled most democratic leaders. Copei, which was technically an electoral commission, and not a political party, was not dissolved. Caldera's collabo-ration with the military regime continued until 1952, when Pérez Jiménez sought to legitimize his rule through fraudulent elections.

In 1957, Pérez Jiménez turned his repressive energies toward the Church and Copei. Clerical opposition to the Pérez Jiménez regime supplemented oppo-sition from other groups and brought the regime close to collapse. Caldera, after taking refuge in the Vatican embassy, left for New York City and a crucial conference with Betancourt. At this meeting, arranged through the good offices of the international Christian Democratic organization, Caldera again acceded to Betancourt's desire to lead a democratic coalition. Despair-ing of becoming president himself, he decided to join with Betancourt.

The practical results of this decision were not long in coming. Following an election in 1958, won by Betancourt's AD, Copei received the Ministries of Agriculture, Development, and Justice. All of these portfolios came with extensive patronage power, but the first two also brought a temptation to extend state economic power. Caldera used this new power to extend Copei's influence outside of its Andean strongholds.

By extending Copei's influence from the top down, through patronage, instead of committing himself to a unique and attractive ideology, Caldera alienated many of his Christian Democratic colleagues. Many were disap-pointed that he did not try for the presidency, pointing to his five years of opposition to the military regime and his extensive grassroots organization inside Venezuela.

This, one former companion argued, would have assured his election if he presented a coherent alternative to Social Democratic statism.[13] Further evidence that Caldera's popularity was more widespread than he believed came from student elections in the early 1960s. Although the Communists won, Copei's 37 percent of the vote was more than triple that of AD. Stu-dents were normally considered part of AD's base. Other Venezuelans also perceived the AD as lukewarm Marxists, and they preferred Copei.[14]

Perhaps a more antistatist platform would have garnered more Copei votes in 1958. No one can say for sure, since Caldera chose not to find out. Instead, Caldera sought AD votes and abandoned not only his principles but also his former colleagues. These he attacked and insulted, taking every opportu-nity to link the conservative wing of his own party with the Pérez Jiménez dictatorship.

Caldera followed a path that became popular with Latin American Christian Democrats by making basic ideological compromises, and embracing Social Democratic programs, because he thought that this would result in greater popularity. By the 1960s, the continent's Christian Democrats saw political power as an end in itself, not just a means to carry out the social encyclicals.

Copei's early platforms emphasized its belief in the family as the fundamental base of Venezuelan society and its support for whatever elevates and dignifies family life. Caldera also defended private property in a 1966 speech to Copei youth. These pronouncements, even if insincere, helped Caldera win the presidency in 1968. In his 1969 inaugural address, he promised to protect the family as the fundamental core of society.[15]

Copei's traditional support came from rural states leery of interference in their affairs by Caracas. Copei served this rural constituency by promising political decentralization. A 1946 Copei document promised a regime that would "harmonize" the decentralized principles of a federal republic with the necessities of the Republic.[16] A similar document in 1948 called for the decentralization of administrative agencies and the strengthening of municipal government.

Like the Chileans, the Venezuelan Christian Democrats lost after their first term in office. Although they returned to the presidency five years later, that administration also lasted only one term. Their electoral fortunes since 1983 have been poor.

El Salvador

Christian Democracy in Central America got off to a later start than it did in South America. In El Salvador, the Christian Democratic party started at the 1954 Pax Romana conference in Rome. Delegates returned to El Salvador determined to make the principles of the social encyclicals a reality. They started with a series of informal study groups, made up of mostly middle-class students. The embryonic movement was led at the time by Abraham Rodríguez and Roberto Lara Velasco.

When El Salvador's military rulers decided to allow an election in 1960, the Christian Democratic Party (PDC) appeared. It began as a purely ideological party whose programs would be based on the principles of social Christianity. This committed, ideological definition coexisted with a strong pragmatic, anti-ideological wing that depended more on machine politics and economic promises to gain votes.

José Napoleón Duarte, elected party secretary-general in 1961, was a leader of the "pragmatic" faction. He immediately took over the office in charge of organizing local party cells. This was not only the least controversial of the posts available at that time but also the one most likely to enhance Duarte's personal power.

The Salvadoran party made reasonable progress, given El Salvador's checkered experience with democratic government. By 1968, Christian Democrats held mayoralties in San Salvador and 80 other cities and towns. In 1972, Duarte won a presidential election, only to have the victory stolen, and by the time El Salvador began another democratic experiment in 1980, the Christian Democrats were the country's largest party.

Carlos Alberto Siri was one of the founders of Salvadoran Christian Democracy, before the movement was taken over by Duarte's pragmatists. Siri believed that the state is inadequate to provide for most human needs and should be content with merely coordinating the initiatives of society.

Duarte himself said early in his career that Christian Democratic philosophy reflects the "fear of the expansion of centralized, all-powerful, impersonal government in [Christian Democracy's] emphasis upon social pluralism and the diffusion of power to local levels through community organizations, religious societies, service groups, labor unions and producers' associations."[17]

As late as the 1972 presidential campaign, the Salvadoran Christian Democrats agreed that private property was beneficial and that the party's "scheme of development [would] reserve a dominant role for private sector investment and [would] contain a call for measures to protect small and medium entrepreneurs and landholders."

In his 1964 campaign for mayor of San Salvador, Duarte demanded increased local autonomy from the central government, particularly in administrative and financial affairs. Such decentralization would make local government more accessible, more responsible, and more accountable.[18] When Duarte became president in 1984, however, he made no moves in this direction. Salvadoran Christian Democrats failed to achieve reelection in 1989. The PDC has revived its interest in decentralization, now that its rightist opponent is in power.[19]

Guatemala

The record of democracy in Guatemala is even more brief than in El Salvador, yet the Christian Democrats have been able to take advantage of the tiny democratic openings that have existed over the years. The party started during the last years of the Arévalo-Arbenz regime, under José García Bauer, a labor lawyer like Frei and Caldera. He started a Catholic study group to examine the social encyclicals. The Guatemalan party started as a right-of-center movement committed to Catholic social thought. Nevertheless, it supported much of Arbenz's economic policy, especially in the areas of labor law and agrarian reform.

After Arbenz was overthrown in 1954, the Christian Democrats survived to become one of the country's three major parties. However, by the mid-1960s most of the original leaders who were dedicated to Catholic social thought were gone and pragmatic elements had taken over. This new leadership found its political horizons terribly narrow. In 1970, they tried to win partly open elections by persuading General Efraín Ríos Montt to carry their banner. They repeated this strategy in 1974 and 1978.

Like the Salvadoran party, the Christian Democrats used their campaign experience and insider maneuverings to become Guatemala's largest single party when a new democratic experiment began in 1984. Guatemalan Christian Democracy (DCG) was the clear winner of the Constituent Assembly elections that year, and their Secretary-General Vinicio Cerezo Arévalo convincingly won the 1985 presidential election. Trying to extend their mandate in 1990, the Christian Democrats barely placed third.

Ecuador

The story of Christian Democracy in Ecuador is the story of Osvaldo Hurtado and León Febres Cordero. Hurtado launched the original Christian Democratic party in the 1960s and tried to crack the extremely closed, personalist Ecuadoran political system. He was elected vice-president in 1979 and became president on the death of Jaime Roldós in 1981. Febres was a member of the small, conservative Social Christian Party (PSC), and he became the presidential candidate of a coalition of conservative parties in 1984.

As Ecuador entered the 1970s, it had a large and growing middle class of government officials and others whose incomes depended on government spending. This statist middle class turned against the military in the late 1970s after the generals denied them sufficient access to state funds. The withdrawal of support from this class was a sore blow to the military government.[20] The statist middle class created the parties that appeared when Ecuador began its democratic transition, including the Democratic Left Party (ID) and the Christian Democratic Party of Hurtado.

Hurtado's own account of the formation of the Christian Democratic Party mentions the merger of several Christian political groups that existed in Ecuador's major cities. In addition, the new party attracted members of Christian labor unions and young members of the PSC who were dissatisfied with the "conservative positions of the parent party." The driving force behind the Christian Democrats was university students, who desired "progressive" policies, including the formation of alliances with Marxist movements. Writing in 1977, Hurtado described the outcome of the party's electoral participation as "negative."[21]

When Ecuador's leadership returned to civilians, they moved to satisfy the demands of its statist middle class for greater government spending. Roldós embraced such spending. Rising oil prices, for a time, provided the wherewithal. By 1982, the public sector had grown to 33 percent of Gross Domestic Product (GDP), up from only 22 percent in 1969.[22]

When Hurtado succeeded to the presidency, he found that such spending could not continue. Soon after his elevation, oil prices started dropping and Hurtado found that he had to cut spending to keep the deficit from growing out of control. Hurtado had been a forceful advocate of fiscal restraint while vice-president. He wanted to see oil money used for diversification of the economy, not for political patronage. Vice-President Hurtado had also opposed a 1979 proposal to double the minimum wage.

Responding to the oil glut, Hurtado raised taxes on some luxury items, halved the government gasoline subsidy, and eliminated the wheat subsidy. He also made concerted efforts to cut government spending. The Ecuadoran Congress, dominated by representatives of the statist middle class, opposed this at every turn. Hurtado had spoken of the need to use benevolent government power to direct the economy before he was elected. Once in power, he tried, even if only in response to circumstances, to reduce government power. León Febres Cordero, Hurtado's long-time personal opponent, did exactly the opposite.

Febres Cordero, for his part, started public life as a businessman; he cared little for the ideological questions that would occupy Hurtado. He had been a severe critic of Hurtado both as a private citizen and later as a congressman. In 1983, his PSC joined other conservative parties, and a number of independent Guayaquil businesspeople, to form the National Renovation Front to contest the coming election.

During the first-round campaign, Febres sounded a decidedly free market note in his rhetoric. He was particularly adamant about reducing the economic power of the state, which, he said, the Hurtado Christian Democrats had allowed to become too paternal and too powerful. This charge was not entirely fair.

Febres said, baldly: "There is a big difference between making the state into the first servant of the people and making people servants of the state. This is the great difference between Democracy that respects private initiative and the populism and communitarian socialism that [Abdala] Bucaram, Roldós and Hurtado are trying to impose."[23]

Febres's 1984 platform included promises to cut regulations, abandon import substitution, end price and exchange controls, and reduce tariffs. His most famous campaign quotation was "I am more Reagan than Mitterand." Febres expected that this program would win him a clear first-round victory.

Having done less well in the first electoral round than he expected, Febres quickly discovered and followed the common Christian Democratic path of imitating his Social Democratic rivals. Promising that the government under a Febres administration would deliver "pan, techo y empleo," he sacrificed any chance he might have had to alter Ecuadoran politics. After holding power himself, Febres said, "The state is a barrel without a bottom."[24]

Febres's experience is unique among Christian Democrats in that he switched from an antistatist to a pro-statist message during a campaign and still won. The victory that he gained in this fashion, however, was an empty one. His confusing statements eviscerated his mandate, making it difficult for him to govern, even before his erratic personality made it impossible. The PSC lost badly in 1988.

Peru

Christian Democracy has never held political power in Peru, nor in the remainder of countries in this section. Nevertheless, the parties are important, either because they contributed something to the movement elsewhere or because their failure to attain political office is itself instructive.

Peruvian Christian Democracy began in the 1950s as a centrist movement committed to the social encyclicals. By the end of the decade, however, Hector Cornejo Chávez, the movement's founder, had moved to a more statist position. This split the party into statist and antistatist factions. The antistatists took the name Popular Christian Party.[25]

Cornejo Chávez found it almost impossible to break the traditional deadlock in Peruvian politics in which the social democratic American Popular Revolutionary Alliance (APRA) of Raúl Haya de la Torre, the conservative Popular Alliance (AP) of Fernando Belaúnde Terry, and the leftist sectors of the military (later the civilian United Left) all command the allegiance of one-third of the electorate. It frequently seemed that Cornejo Chávez was not interested in winning electoral majorities but contented himself with leading the crucial block in any coalition government.

This required a great deal of ideological flexibility, which Cornejo Chávez enforced on the party. Like Caldera's Copei, the PDC did manage to reap some political rewards, in the form of cabinet positions under Belaúnde in 1963. The price of this entry to insider politics was support for Belaúnde's increasingly populist and statist policies.

Supporting populism helped to cause the 1966 split that formed the Popular Christian Party (PPC). Luis Bedoya Reyes led a number of his conservative colleagues out of the PDC to protest this pragmatic policy. The PPC based its ideology on the anti-Marxist and antistatist thought of José Luis Bustamente, who had attended the Christian Democratic conferences in Rome in the 1930s. Bedoya himself became a forceful advocate of free enterprise and an enemy of government restrictions on the activities of domestic firms. Such government interference, he thought, made Peruvian businesses unable to compete with foreigners.

When leftist military officers overthrew Belaúnde in 1968, Cornejo Chávez was supportive of the new regime's "anti-imperialism." Bedoya, for his part, was suspicious of the military's long-term commitment to democracy and its intention to use state power to enforce questionable economic policies.

Bedoya's PPC would eventually support the radical reformist candidacy of Mario Vargas Llosa in 1990.

Argentina

In Argentina, the movement began in the 1950s and immediately confronted the dominance of Juan Perón. Following the lead of the Argentine Catholic Church, the Christian Democratic Junta for National Promotion became openly anti-Perón in the mid-1950s and, along with the Church itself, bore the brunt of Peronist repression. In its first electoral test in 1957, the new party scored a respectable fifth.

Like the Peruvian Christian Democrats, however, the Argentine Christian Democrats found little political room for a new party and quickly decided to collaborate with the Peronists to gain marginal political power. This was a complete repudiation not only of Catholic social thought but also of the party's own origins. The Christian Democrats who later joined the outlawed Peronists were most enthusiastic about Peronist proposals to nationalize oil and seize large landholdings.

Brazil

Brazil's Christian Democratic movement started with the formation of Catholic labor groups between World War I and World War II. In 1937, these workers' clubs formed the National Confederation of Catholic Workers, giving the Brazilian Christian Democrats a stronger labor wing than they had elsewhere.[26]

An intellectual movement, similar to those that preceded Christian Democratic parties in other countries, began in the 1920s and later supplemented the labor wing. Under the guidance of Archbishop Sebastião Léme, study groups of Catholic laymen began appearing in Rio and São Paulo.[27] Léme intended these groups to concentrate on personal morality and to remain apolitical.

Opposing this tendency was Jackson deFigueiredo, who founded the Centro Dom Vital to coordinate Catholic political action in the 1920s. With deFigueiredo's sudden death in 1928, Alceu Amoroso Lima took over the center and continued the development of a Christian Democratic party. Lima, more than deFigueiredo, opposed any connection with the Brazilian Church, which he said was too closely identified with the Brazilian state.[28]

With the suicide of Gertúlio Vargas in 1954 and the return to democratic rule, a full-fledged Christian Democratic party did compete in presidential elections. The movement remained extremely heterogeneous, however, which prevented it from offering a coherent democratic alternative to the Brazilian people. Perhaps the party's sorriest episode was its embrace of the radically nonideological Jânio Quadros in the 1960 election, even though he made it clear that he had no commitment to Catholic social thought.

The 1964 military coup found the Christian Democrats divided over the presidency of João Goulart, who had become president upon Quadros's unexpected resignation in 1961. Opposition to Quadros's successor prompted some Christian Democrats to collaborate with the military regime, a collaboration that would last until the army suspended all political parties in 1965.

Uruguay

The most important Christian Democratic contribution to come from Uruguay affected the international movement far more than the political system in Uruguay itself. In the 1960s the tiny Catholic Civic Union organized and played host to two international conferences. The Uruguayan movement itself was not able to penetrate the country's bipolar political system.

Frustrated by the complete domination of the Blancos and Colorados, the Christian Democrats were a driving force behind a coalition of extreme left parties, called the Frente Amplio, in 1971. Not only did this opportunism fail to attract new party members, it resulted in a split that damaged the already minuscule Christian Democratic political prospects. A recent invitation to join a coalition government notwithstanding, the party failed to take full advantage of Uruguay's political opening in the 1980s.

Nicaragua

Unlike most Latin American Christian Democratic parties, the Nicaraguan Social Christian Party never pretended to be uncomfortable with state power. Its most important founder was Reinaldo Téfel, a sociologist. Writing in 1972 about the plight of Nicaragua's slum dwellers, Téfel deprecated the attempts of private groups to alleviate the suffering.[29]

Family groups, he said, were not strong enough to provide any real assistance. Charitable organizations lacked coordination, were overly paternalistic, and tended to act sporadically, until rich people have salved their consciences. Church groups concentrate too heavily on the next world. Political parties are not really interested in poor people.

Even poor people themselves cannot form their own charitable organizations. Téfel's survey data showed a drop in what he called "social solidarity" once newly arrived migrants to the Managua slums attained the first rung of the economic ladder. Téfel evidently did not consider it significant that many were attaining this first rung without government help.

The Nicaraguan party has also demonstrated the highest level of ideological flexibility and has, at different times, demonstrated a willingness to collaborate with the Conservative Party, the Sandinistas, and the rightist groups supporting the Nicaraguan Resistance. Yet they insisted on running on their own in the 1990 election.

EMBRACING THE STATE:
SOME CHRISTIAN DEMOCRATIC SOCIAL PROGRAMS

The Nicaraguan party may have been more consistent than other Christian Democrats, who embraced state power only once they acquired it themselves, but they have been no more successful electorally. Political success for Christian Democrats in Latin America has been reserved for the committed and the coherent.

In spite of many promises and rhetorical exercises, Latin American Christian Democratic parties, once they have tasted political power for themselves, come to regard it as far less threatening than their early statements indicate. The Christian Democrats are certainly not unique in this regard, since most Latin American political parties have sought to concentrate more power in their own hands.

Other parties, however, did not have to jettison so much of their ideological heritage to justify this. Other parties, moreover, did not claim an intellectual and ideological heritage from the Vicar of Christ. Although analysts may disagree about the wisdom of statist economic policies in Latin America, it is difficult to justify pursuing such policies while insisting that one is committed to a philosophy that censures state economic power.

Christian Democrats defend their apostasy by saying that increases in state power were necessary and proper to carry out Christian Democratic social reforms. Thus, where early Christian Democrats might defend the autonomy of private schools, Christian Democrats in power would insist on subsidizing such schools, which tied them more closely to the state.

According to some observers, the religious lineage of the Christian Democrats induced them to see the state as a supermissionary, one that could order the mobilization of a country's resources, not for its own sake, but to achieve Christian Democratic ideals. In the economic sphere, Christian Democrats account for their embrace of state power by saying that the problems of Latin America are more complex than they could have imagined before coming to power and require a strong state to "solve" them. Frei, for example, insisted that the emergence of private "power centers" that sought to compete with the state, or even to control it, made a strong state indispensable.

At the base of this change in attitude toward the state is an even more basic change of attitude toward the civil society they had defended so strongly. Once they came to power, Christian Democrats lost faith in the ability of civil society, and of the independent social groups that compose it, to solve problems or to make progress on their own. Following Maritain, they came to believe that some private groups need the help of a wise and benevolent government. The Christian Democrats would even view some independent social groups themselves with suspicion.

Family Protection and Education

As we have seen, protecting the family from state power was paramount to Catholic social thought and in the formative pronouncements of Latin America's Christian Democratic parties. The 1946 Copei Electoral Platform stated emphatically that the state should defend the family and that family property should be inviolate.[30] The family, according to Copei, must also be the primary educator, even before the state.

Venezuela's Christian Democrats chose a decidedly un-Catholic manner of "protecting" the family, however. Point 5 of the 1946 Copei platform embraced the family wage, but in the form of subsidies from the state. This departure from Catholic social thought appeared elsewhere. In Uruguay, one of the few legislative proposals for which the Christian Democrats were responsible was a law providing for family allotments from the state. The Brazilian party managed to get a similar law enacted there in 1963. In Costa Rica, Christian Democratic President Rafael Calderón created the Institute for the Family in his first 100 days. This state agency was charged with promoting the family to attain a higher standard of living.

Protecting the family and subsidizing the family are two different things. The first recognizes the primacy of the family, acknowledges its importance to society, and seeks to promote the family by doing it no harm. It is a negative view of state power, based on the notion that the state is capable of more harm than good.

A subsidy, on the other hand, turns the family into just another interest group, seeking the most favorable spot at the public trough. Once subsidies are instituted, families must go to government agencies to persuade public officials they should receive them.

There is a sharp contrast between providing subsidies and simply allowing families to keep more of their own money by increasing tax deductions. Later Christian Democratic policy seemed to base itself in the idea that the state could spend the money of families better than the families could themselves. This belief completely reverses traditional Catholic social thought. Yet by promoting family subsidies, the Christian Democrats could pose as the family's friend.

Eduardo Frei showed the logical conclusion of an ideology that places greater wisdom in the state than in private citizens. At one point in his presidency, Frei decreed a "compact day" for Chileans, telling them to work from nine to five, without the siesta. To ensure that workers spent their evening hours at home, Frei also ordered Chile's bars closed from four to seven P.M. This well-meaning but intrusive scheme was soon abandoned.

Christian Democratic education policy followed the same pattern as its family policy. Early Christian Democratic statements uphold the rights of parents to be primarily responsible for their children's education. Before coming to power, Christian Democrats supported educational pluralism to provide parents with the widest choice of schools possible. Copei stated that state intervention in education should amount to nothing more than ensuring a patriotic and moral teaching profession. This was particularly important to rural Venezuelans, who for the most part attended Catholic schools.

Copei retained its commitment to educational pluralism even during its stint in the Triennio government. The party fought to keep Betancourt's AD from taking control of private schools, and it almost left the coalition government over the issue. The bitterness of this fight, however, convinced Caldera that it was a divisive issue and could threaten future collaboration with other democratic parties. It also forced him into what was for him a distasteful collaboration with conservative Venezuelans.

When it later joined the Betancourt cabinet in 1958, therefore, Copei dropped its insistence on genuinely private schools and accepted the AD notion that the state, not the parents, was Venezuela's primary educator.[31] Lorenzo Fernández, the party's 1973 presidential candidate, defined human development as the use of state money to promote education, housing, youth, sports, and family life. By 1976, Copei's leaders were promising to outdo their AD opponents in providing money to promote education.[32] In 1978, Luis Herrera Campins promised to be the "president of education" and to put more government money into Venezuelan schools.

Venezuelans were not alone among Christian Democrats who embraced state subsidies to schools. The Argentine party sought subsidies to private and confessional schools to ensure educational pluralism. Innocently, they also insisted that state control be kept to an absolute minimum. In Chile, Frei's party promised to increase educational spending along with similar promises in other social areas.

The Christian Democrats departed from Catholic social thought by supporting school subsidies. The reason the popes insisted on private schools was to protect children from an overbearing state. Schools must be independent from state control. Increasing educational subsidies for nominally private schools, though seemingly supportive of Catholic social thought, really makes these schools wards of the state. Interference from that state is inevitable.

Independent Social Groups and "Communitarianism"

Before coming to power, Christian Democratic parties and movements in Latin America organized many independent social groups. The purpose of such groups, in many cases, was to establish centers of opposition to military governments. During the Pérez Jiménez dictatorship, Copei, for example, organized women's and youth groups, as well as labor unions, especially in Tachira. The ideology behind the formation of such intermediate social organizations was to make the work of government coercion more difficult.

What allows intermediate social groups to perform this function is their independence from government. A comment by Duarte, however, shows that his definition of such groups is slippery and that the line between independent social groups and groups dependent upon the government for their existence is not always clear to him. He said, "A democracy cannot function without the intermediary structures such as a free press, political parties and a fair judicial system."[33]

What Duarte describes here, except for the press, are either government agencies or agencies close to government. After coming to power, Christian Democrats abandoned the spirit of Catholic social thought on societal independence. Communities, according to the papal documents, must evolve naturally, and then perhaps receive recognition from the state. Christian Democrats in power seemed to want to create communities and social groups themselves, and to tie these groups either to government or to a Christian Democratic party. Far from reducing the power of the state, this increases it.

Truly independent social groups will have a difficult time surviving under any government that seeks to be more dynamic and more active than any private group. Such governments will desire to centralize and consolidate power. They also tend to be suspicious of potential sources of opposition.

Christian Democrats, perhaps because of a messianic belief in their own fitness to rule, have created such governments wherever they have come to power in Latin America. In El Salvador, for example, far from defending the existence of independent social groups, the Christian Democrats threatened to leave the civilian-military junta in 1980 if the government officially recognized the existence of professional or labor organizations.

In Chile, Frei came into office highly suspicious of existing professional and private organizations and sought to create new "popular" organizations to counteract their claims. This *"Promoción Popular"* involved the development of basic community organizations designed "to bring the individual to some meaningful sense of himself."[34] Once the government instituted these community organizations, they became part of the Christian Democratic political machine. They were never truly independent.

In Venezuela, Caldera came into office deploring the "lack of organization" in Venezuelan society and sought to repair it by government action. Herrera Campins carried his plans even further, naming his program *comunitaria*. Herrera inherited a state from AD President Carlos Andrés Pérez that, in his mind, had grown too large and powerful. To balance the power of the state, the Copei administration created mass organizations to increase the "people's power." Herrera promised a "promoter state" to stimulate the activity of persons and associations.[35]

Still, the initiative remained with the government. Copei created the societal groups they wanted, gave or withdrew government support as they wished, and used their own social groups to undercut the existing private groups that performed the same functions. The long-term effect was to disable private groups who lacked access to government money and power, leaving the promoted government groups in their place. Independent groups, as a potential source of protection from state power, had no place in this structure. Even the "functional organizations" created by Copei complained that they were mere appendages of the party.

Copei youth groups advocated such top-down societal organization in advance of their elders, and they were less reticent about its logical conclusion. All three Copei youth factions insisted to Herrera that socialism was necessary to enforce the goals of communitarianism. Basic to this insistence was the assumption that people cannot create and sustain social groups on their own. Christian Democrats expect that governments can create social groups better than ordinary people, just as they suppose that governments better promote the welfare of families and schools.

Writing in 1977, Frei defended what he described as the efforts of his administration to make Chileans more organized. The "independent" groups that his government created were meant to help people, and, he added, "all of [my] measures were embodied in a systematic government program." State initiative, he insisted, is the only way to make reforms. If this is communism, he fumed, "only the Tsar was anti-Communist."[36]

Christian Democratic Housing Policies

Latin American Christian Democracy's commitment to adequate housing is part of their commitment to the family. In the words of Eduardo Frei, "No home is possible without a house." Frei's 1964 campaign platform promised more public housing.

Housing policy, however, is another area in which the Christian Democrats have allowed a specific social goal to supersede their general policy of avoiding the growth of state power. The 1960 Lima Christian Democratic conference stated that the primary support for any housing program in Latin America must come from the private sectors of the economy. Public money, the delegates believed, should be complementary, providing services, institutions, incentives, and, perhaps, indirect subsidies.[37]

Frei's original housing promise was consistent with this conference statement. He proposed that the Chilean government provide the land and materials for a house, with the occupant supplying the labor and construction skills or costs. More importantly, such a contribution would allow the citizen to own a home, not just occupy a government facility.

Still, Frei operated from the assumption that if houses were to be built, it would have to be the government that initiated the construction. Frei's proposals did not include tax incentives that would spur private home building and thus remove the visible government presence in the project altogether. There is, of course, no political return in such a tax plan; new homeowners do not realize that they owe their house to the Christian Democrats and cannot be persuaded to vote for Christian Democrats on that basis.

In Venezuela, Copei's concern about public housing became an obsession. Before coming to power, Caldera spoke of the importance of housing and promised to provide incentives for more home construction. By the 1963 election, however, Copei found itself in an escalating bidding war with AD over how many houses the government could build during a five-year period.

Copei promised voters in 1963 that they would build 100,000 houses per year. Caldera repeated this pledge in the 1968 campaign. In 1978, after AD repeated the same pledge, with the same number, Copei candidate Herrera Campins bested it by promising 600,000 new houses in five years.

In Ecuador, after failing to win the first round of the 1984 election, Febres Cordero promised more housing as a major priority in the second-round campaign. His first order of business on becoming president, he said, would be to acquire World Bank funds to allow his administration to provide concessionary loans for the construction of 200,000 new homes.[38] Febres later attempted to overcome political problems by authorizing more housing projects.

This is the type of bidding war that Christian Democratic parties get into when they abandon their original principles. A leftist Social Democratic party such as AD, with an unabashed belief in the worth of state power, can always promise to spend more government money than a moderate, centrist party like Copei, especially if Copei is still using the rhetoric of Catholic social thought to gain votes.

Consciously besting one unkeepable promise with another keeps the Christian Democrats from performing the one function for which they are best suited: providing an alternative to the statist and populist politics of so many Latin American political parties. As enthusiasm for state-directed economic projects has decreased around the world, and in Latin America, the Christian Democrats have found that although they have acted in the same way as their political rivals, they have ideological roots that better position them to offer some genuinely new solutions.

There is some indication that Latin America's Christian Democrats are coming to realize this. Copei's defeated 1988 presidential candidate Eduardo Fernández, for example, advised the AD government to offer mortgage protection for 200,000 homeowners rather than building 200,000 houses per year, as Copei might have suggested under other circumstances. This is not a drastic change, but it is a start.

The new Christian Democratic president of Costa Rica has moved further in this direction. President-elect Rafael Calderón promised to attend to the plight of Costa Rica's 120,000 citizens who lack adequate housing. His inaugural address recalled that his father, Costa Rica's first Christian Democratic president, had initiated low-cost housing programs under government supervision.

These statements suggest that he might follow a Copei-like statist housing policy. The younger Calderón added, however, "I view private enterprise as the motor of development. I believe in free enterprise with social responsibility." It remains to be seen whether Calderón enacts these sentiments any more successfully than other Christian Democrats, who made similar pronouncements before they exercised political power themselves.

CONCLUSION

Latin America's Christian Democrats made their strongest antistatist declarations when talking about the family, education, the Church, and other independent social groups. They began their political life determined to protect these entities from state power. Once in power themselves, however, their fear of state interference with independent social groups disappeared.

The continent's Christian Democrats were never so forthright in defending private property or the rights of domestic or foreign businesspeople. Since they embraced the state in the areas where they were most determined to limit it, it is not surprising that they have rushed headlong into statist policies in other areas. The following chapters will trace this development in Christian Democratic policies on land reform, nationalization, and regulation.

In many cases, Christian Democrats have embraced the state because they truly believed this would serve their country best. Their methods of increasing state power, however, indicate that they also thought about improving their electoral fortunes. Christian Democratic parties have been most successful, however, when they have made promises that most closely adhere to Catholic social thought. I have noted that each Christian Democratic party that has come to power in Latin America has had to leave after only one term.

Whether or not closer adherence to Catholic social thought would have gotten them reelected is a question I will address. It is clear that abandoning Catholic social thought has not brought electoral success. "Pragmatic" compromises, as noted, have proven to be anything but pragmatic. Perhaps this is why, as early as 1961, delegates to the International Union of Christian Democrats Annual Congress recommended "purification of aims and recovery of first principles."[39]

NOTES

1. The following discussion is not intended to be a comprehensive survey of each Christian Democratic party in Latin America. Rather, I attempt here to highlight the important steps to establishing Christian Democratic parties in order of their national importance. I also emphasize the early, antistatist philosophies of these parties. See Edward Williams, *Latin American Christian Democratic Parties* (Knoxville: University of Tennessee Press, 1967).

2. Emanuel deKadt, *Catholic Radicals in Brazil* (London: Oxford University Press, 1970), p. 57.

3. *Ave Maria*, 20 August 1955, p. 6.

4. Williams, p. 99.

5. Robert Alexander, *Latin American Political Parties* (New York: Praeger Publishers, 1973), p. 318.

6. Leonard Gross, *The Last, Best Hope: Eduardo Frei and Chilean Democracy* (New York: Random House, 1967), p. 110.

7. Miguel Jorrín and John Martz, *Latin American Political Thought and Ideology* (Chapel Hill: University of North Carolina Press, 1970), p. 413.

8. Williams, p. 125.

9. Gross, p. 98.

10. Alexander, p. 340.

11. *Christian Democratic Review*, no. 56 (November 1959): 5.

12. Gehard Cartáy Ramírez, *Política y partidos modernos en Venezuela* (Caracas: Ediciones Centauro, 1983), p. 99.

13. Germán Borregales, *Copei Hoy: Una Negación* (Caracas: Ediciones Garrido, 1968), pp. 28–29.

14. *America*, 17 October 1964, p. 433.

15. Alexander, pp. 348–49.

16. "Platforma Electoral de Copei," in Paciano Padrón, ed., *Copei: Documentos fundamentales, 1946* (Caracas: Ediciones Centauro, 1981), p. 87.

17. Stephen Webre, *José Napoleón Duarte and the Christian Democratic Party in Salvadoran Politics, 1960–1972* (Baton Rouge: University of Louisiana Press, 1979), p. 65.

18. Ibid., p. 78.

19. San Salvador, Canal Doce, 16 February 1990 (Foreign Broadcast Information Service, Latin America *Daily Report*, hereinafter FBIS, 26 February 1990, p. 4).

20. For more details, see Catherine M. Conaghan, "Party Politics and Democratization in Ecuador," in James M. Malloy and Mitchell A. Seligson, eds., *Authoritarians and Democrats: Regime Transition in Latin America* (Pittsburgh: University of Pittsburgh Press, 1987), pp. 146–47.

21. Osvaldo Hurtado, *Political Power in Ecuador*, translated by Nick D. Mills, Jr. (Albuquerque: University of New Mexico Press, 1980).

22. David Schodt, *Ecuador: An Andean Enigma* (Boulder, Colo.: Westview Press, 1987), p. 147. This did not include public enterprises or public financial institutions.

23. Ramiro Rivera, *El pensamiento de León Febres Cordero* (Quito: Ediciones Culturales, 1986), p. 72.

24. Ibid., p. 49.

25. Alexander, p. 357.

26. Philippe Schmitter, *Interest Conflict and Political Change in Brazil* (Stanford, Calif.: Stanford University Press, 1971), p. 192.

27. deKadt, p. 56.

28. Jorrín and Martz, p. 411.

29. Reinaldo Antonio Téfel, *El infierno de los pobres: Diagnóstico sociológico de los barrios marginales de Managua* (Managua: Ediciones el Pez y el Serpiente, 1972).

30. "Platforma Electoral," p. 94.

31. Donald Herman, *Christian Democracy in Venezuela* (Chapel Hill: University of North Carolina Press, 1980), p. 57.

32. Enrique Baloyra and John Martz, *Electoral Mobilization and Public Opinion* (Chapel Hill: University of North Carolina Press, 1976), p. 136.

33. Quoted in Max G. Manwaring and Court Prisk, eds., *El Salvador at War: An Oral History of Conflict from the 1979 Insurrection to the Present* (Washington, D.C.: National Defense University Press, 1988), p. 19.

34. Gross, pp. 158–59.

35. Donald L. Herman, "The Christian Democratic Party," in Howard R. Penniman, ed., *Venezuela at the Polls: The National Elections of 1978* (Washington, D.C.: American Enterprise Institute, 1980), p. 146.

36. Eduardo Frei, *The Mandate of History and Chile's Future* (Athens, Ohio: Center for International Studies, Papers in International Studies, Latin America Series, no. 1, 1977), pp. 21–23.

37. Williams, p. 97.

38. *New York Times*, 9 May 1984, p. A10.

39. *Tablet*, 4 November 1961, p. 1055.

4

Christian Democratic Land Reform

There are several different ways to assess Christian Democratic land reform efforts. First, an analyst can test their programs against a general theory of land reform. Second, one can examine how closely Christian Democrats adhere to Catholic social thought, which they claim as antecedent. Third, one can compare Christian Democratic land reform programs with the statements on land reform that Christian Democratic politicians have made in initiating those programs.

In this chapter, I will show that land reform programs that Latin American Christian Democratic parties have initiated have been seriously flawed from all three standpoints. Christian Democrats have overseen major land reform programs in Chile, El Salvador, and Venezuela. In Chile and El Salvador, the programs failed to live up to the expectations, and they failed to conform to the Christian Democrats' own statements about land reform. Only in Venezuela did land reform bear any resemblance to the principles of Catholic social thought. It was here that the Christian Democrats had the least influence over the strategy of the reform.

THE CRITERIA OF JUDGMENT

Robert Alexander writes that land reform has social, economic, and political results. Breaking up large tracts of land and distributing this land to the people who could not own land previously makes a society more just. Access to a minimum standard of dignified living comes from a successful land reform program. Land reform also eases the social burden on the cities by removing one of the strongest motivations that peasants have for leaving the countryside.

Economically, a successful land reform program will increase agricultural productivity by eliminating the unproductive and unjust land use practices of large landowners. This will, in turn, increase the purchasing power of the peasants and thus spur development in other areas of the economy as well. By creating more rural landowners, and freeing peasants from tenant-labor obligations, land reform also raises the cost of labor, spurs mechanization, and thus increases production.

Politically, land reform blunts, or even destroys, the attraction of radical political philosophies, including communism. By making peasants into small landowners, land reform also makes them politically conservative. In addition, land reform often acts as a recruitment instrument for the party that carries it out.

For a land reform program to perform all these desirable functions, however, it must have certain characteristics. Among these are expropriation from large landholders and distribution to smaller farmers. "Distribution," if it has any meaning at all, must mean that peasants own their new land outright They must not simply trade domination by the hacendados for domination by state bureaucrats. If this occurs, peasants simply will not act like owners, and the desired social, economic, and political results will not appear.

This is not to say that government should simply hand out deeds and disappear. Successful land reform requires that government perform the same minimal functions in the countryside that it does in cities. It should provide a predictable legal system and basic law enforcement. The absence of either one will discourage private investment or improvements.

In addition, government can provide roads, ports, docks, and other infrastructure to allow more efficient marketing. This does not mean that government must take over the actual marketing of crops, unless the peasants in a reformed area demonstrate a persistent lack of ability to do this themselves. No such incapacity has appeared in Latin America.

Since unjust landholding patterns have resulted from oligarchs using government power to create and to protect their haciendas, it may require government action of a different sort to level the playing field again. This done, governments should allow peasants to do what the oligarchies had always prevented them from doing, namely, to freely use their talents and property to earn a living.

These are the characteristics needed for successful land reform. Therefore I will use these characteristics as a criteria to judge the efforts of Latin America's Christian Democrats. These characteristics correspond to Catholic social thought. As we saw in Chapter 1, the social thought of the Church is specific on the subject of private property. Although the popes laid down significant restrictions on the use of private property, their social goal is to replace the capitalist system of "few proprietors" and the socialist system of "no proprietors" with a Christian system of "all proprietors."

Thus, a land reform program consistent with Catholic social thought will be one that creates new owners, rather than one that creates new state employees. Even though Catholic social thought restricts what owners can do with their land, there is nothing in the political theory of the Church that encourages, or even allows, the state to enforce these and other restrictions so tightly that the meaning of "private ownership" is lost.

Catholic social thought commits the state to helping the new owners succeed on their own. The popes' support the building of infrastructure and the creation of temporary government agencies to market agricultural produce. However, simultaneous with such government efforts should be efforts to turn these functions over to organized groups of peasants.

Land reform therefore requires the presence of independent social groups. Such organizations can negotiate the best price for seed and machinery, organize communal use of property or equipment, market produce, and most importantly of all, protect the newly won independence of the peasants against either disgruntled former oligarchs or encroaching state officials.

Christian Democratic land reform proposals and programs fail to conform to the strictures of Catholic social thought. Latin America's Christian Democrats also failed to live up to their own statements and promises on land reform. They consistently preferred rural cooperatives with substantial government intervention to private ownership. Far from encouraging the growth of independent rural organizations, they tried either to turn such organizations into organs of the party or to destroy them altogether.

BOLIVIA: SHOWING THE WAY

Bolivia serves well as a control case.[1] Its land reform program took place in the early 1950s, before any Christian Democratic party had come to power in Latin America. Thus, all Christian Democrats were aware of Bolivia's land reform before attempting reform themselves. In addition, Bolivia's land reform achieved the results that most theorists look for in a successful land reform program. Finally, the Bolivian reform conforms closely to Catholic social thought on land reform.

Bolivia before Land Reform

In 1950, Bolivia had the most polarized landholding structure in Latin America. Peasants in Bolivia lived in a subsistence, almost barter, economy. Their purchasing power was almost nil, and they were prevented from improving their lot by a traditional land tenure system that was outmoded, inefficient, and irrational. Many landowners spent little or no time on their farms, employing managers who had no interest in improving productivity or modernizing methods. Bolivia had, in short, a double helping of all the rural social and economic problems that plagued the rest of the continent. If a land reform program could work here, it could work elsewhere too.

The 1953 Land Reform Process

A decree from Victor Paz Estenssoro's Nationalist Revolutionary Movement (MNR) in 1953 expropriated Bolivia's latifundia immediately, totally, and without compensation if the landlords were absentee, if farming methods were archaic or if workers on the latifundia were abused or exploited.[2]

Size itself was not an unpardonable sin in Bolivia. Large farms that had a landlord on site, that used modern methods, and that recognized certain workers' rights could be exempted from expropriation. Medium and small farms were left alone unless they exceeded a regional maximum. Modernized estates were allowed to keep from 80 to 800 hectares, depending on the land's quality, as a "reserve."

Once the government expropriated offending latifundia, it gave parcels of the confiscated land directly to the *colonos* who had formerly been employees. Whatever the tenants had been farming under the old landlord they retained, pending the distribution of the remaining land to provide what the decree called a "vital minimum size."

Rural chaos followed the announcement of this ambitious program. The government had little information on the quality of reformable land, on how it was used, or even how to get to it, owing to a lack of good maps or survey data. Many peasants, impatient for the government to act, began invading large estates themselves, often at the behest of local peasant syndicate leaders. The peasants benefited from the efforts of José Rojas, who organized independent peasant unions in the Cochabamba Valley in the 1940s.[3] Many resident landlords, fearing the worst, left their farms or even left Bolivia.[4]

Other landlords quickly enacted more modern methods, hoping to present their farms as exemptible when government survey teams arrived. Still others sought, and found, ways to evade expropriation through political favoritism. Such insider deals were of no use when peasants used violent means to occupy land.

The most widespread reform took place in areas where peasant organizations were strongest. In the Altiplano, for example, "land reform" consisted largely of peasants simply refusing to perform the traditional labor obligations that went with their land. In the Yungas, by contrast, unions were weak and land reform took place from the top down. It was also here that the MNR would make its most heavy-handed political demands of peasant beneficiaries, making a vote for the party the "price" of land reform.

Catholic social thought emphasizes that land reform should increase rural productivity. Some popes have specifically suggested "colonization" of unused land to accomplish this. Such colonization was an important part of the

Bolivian land reform. In Bolivia, there was unoccupied land in the eastern lowlands. The 1953 decree awarded every highland peasant the right to 60 hectares of eastern frontier land, over and above what he got in his home community.[5] The Bolivian government also built a highway to the Oriente. Thousands of peasants, accepting the role of colonist, now commute seasonally between highland and lowland, while others have moved permanently to the frontier.

By 1965, the land reform had given some 4 million hectares of arable land, and another 2 million hectares of grazing land, to 173,557 peasants.[6] The Bolivian reform was much more extensive than anything the Christian Democrats have accomplished since.

As important, Bolivia's land reform made owners of the peasants. According to the land reform decree, at least 10 percent of the expropriated land was to be reserved for cooperative farming, a method La Paz bureaucrats thought was favored by traditional Indian communities. From the beginning, the peasants were hostile to cooperatives. For many peasants, government co-ops and syndicates merely introduced new masters, who, like the old masters, would make them work for nothing.

In spite of substantial inducements to form co-ops, the peasants invariably divided the expropriated land into individual holdings. In many cases, strong rural unions defended this type of rural privatization against the wishes of the MNR government that had encouraged and legalized the unions' existence. Their actions confirm the importance of independent rural unions, such as those the popes envisioned.

Since the Bolivian government never controlled the unions, farmers were free to organize their own marketing schemes, their own purchasing agents, and their own credit. They could also choose their own technologies without government intervention. As we shall see, it was the overabundance of well-meaning government intervention that caused Christian Democratic land reform projects to fail. Repeating an error they make in many areas, the Christian Democrats assumed that government officials knew more about farming than farmers.

The Results

In the short term, agricultural productivity fell dramatically. By 1955, Bolivia was producing only 70 percent of what it had produced in 1952. Production did not recover until 1960, and even then, much of the increase came from colonized land in the Oriente. One author is careful to point out, however, that the mid-1950s were drought years in Bolivia.[7]

Again, a crucial variable is the strength of peasant unions. Where these were strong, they could ensure that markets and fairs opened nearby, providing an incentive to produce more. The produce of the Compí hacienda in the Altiplano, for example, filled two trucks before the reform. Afterward, eight trucks were required.[8] In the irrigated lower Cochabamba Valley, the value of agricultural land has increased tenfold as a result of postreform changes in land use.

Left largely on their own, with their land divided into individual parcels, Bolivian peasants formed their own marketing and credit institutions or expanded existing ones. They dealt with the persistent rural problem of extortionist moneylenders by using their peasant unions to encourage more people to lend money, thus increasing competition, and to negotiate for the best rates. This sort of spontaneous, voluntary cooperation, against a ruthless profiteer, is exactly what Catholic social thought encourages.

After the land reform, the Bolivian countryside was dotted with farmhouses, roadside hamlets and new market towns. Security of tenure encouraged house building and other improvements. The creation of new towns encouraged independent social groups, especially churches, to provide basic social services and schools.

Bolivian peasants have learned to rely either on themselves, or on private organizations like their unions. Self-reliance has softened the impact of the political chaos common to Bolivia. The complete failure of Communist guerrillas under Che Guevarra to incite the Bolivian peasants to revolution, and the relatively low level of spillover from the ferocious Shining Path movement in Peru, also attest to the land reform's long-term benefits.

CHILE: DEVIATING FROM THE CATHOLIC MODEL

Eduardo Frei repeated the Catholic social principle that a society of "all proprietors" should replace the capitalist few proprietors and the socialist no proprietors. Following the popes, he added that private property is a human right but must be directed to the common good. It is not, according to Frei, an inalienable right.[9]

Nevertheless, Frei promised land reform in the presidential campaign, including expropriation with limited compensation and taxation based on what the land might have produced.[10] He never explicitly promised rural landownership, concentrating instead on the sins of the large landowners. Frei also supported independent social groups, saying that rural communities must be viable and form real communities. The Christian Democrats also promoted the formation of Christian Democratic rural unions and promised to ease unionization of rural workers if elected.[11]

With regard to peasant organizations, the Chilean Christian Democrats inherited the results of efforts by Catholic priests to organize rural workers. In the 1950s, Father Rafael Larraín created the Institute for Rural Education to train Christians to take over the rural institutions that other priests were forming.

When President Frei unveiled his land reform proposal in November 1965, he said its "main aim is to create new agricultural entrepreneurs, new legitimate landowners. It ensures the opportunity for those who have worked hard in the fields of becoming landowners."[12] The thrust of the Christian Democratic rhetoric on land reform, therefore, was consistent with both the Catholic and the Bolivian model. Frei's program, however, deviated from these models, and from his own statements, in almost all particulars.

Chile before Land Reform

In the 1940s, Father Alberto Hurtado Cruchaga, S.J., was actively forming rural labor unions and teaching the leaders of these unions the importance of staying independent of government control. The Catholic Church also started land colonization schemes prior to 1964. These Church colonies featured both private and communal holdings. They found that the private plots were far more productive and that most of the peasants preferred private ownership.[13]

In spite of these efforts, land tenure in Chile was badly polarized in 1964. Before land reform, 3,250 large rural estates, or 2.2 percent of the total number of farm units, each over 2,000 acres, accounted for 68.8 percent of Chile's total agricultural land.[14] Farm workers were, for the most part, unable to press for higher wages because of severe restrictions on their right to form unions.

The Christian Democratic Land Reform Program

The victorious Christian Democrats found that their diversity hampered their ability to develop and implement coherent programs on complex issues. On land reform, the party leadership was flanked by Christian Socialists on the left and the Society of Christian Entrepreneurs on the right.[15]

Rafael Moreno, the vice-president of the Corporation for Agrarian Reform (CORA), and Jacques Chonchol from the Ministry of Agriculture drafted the Land Reform Law. Both of these men came from the left wing, or *rebeldes*, of the Christian Democratic party. Chonchol would later become minister of agriculture under Salvador Allende.

The *rebeldes* were against private ownership of land and wanted to create rural cooperatives instead. They desired that the law have few provisions for compensation and almost no provision for landowners to retain a "reserve" from their expropriated property. Frei's backers in the party managed to soften some *rebelde* language before the bill became law in 1967.

Frei's land reform efforts had their best effects before the law was even passed. While the law was debated in Congress, Chile was governed under a mild land reform law passed during the Alessandri administration. This law allowed landowners to volunteer to sell their land to the government under much better terms than Frei seemed to promise. From 1964 until 1967, CORA had purchased a million hectares from willing sellers. Judicious use of this land would have allowed Frei to keep his campaign promise of ten hectares to 100,000 new owners, before the Land Reform Act even went into effect.

The law that finally passed, after a two-year debate, provided for the expropriation of irrigated holdings over 80 hectares. For the purposes of the law, and to take into account the varying quality of Chilean land, the legislature created a new unit of measure, the Basic Irrigated Hectare (BIH), and allotted no more than 80 of these to any single owner.

Grounds for expropriation under the new law included large size, deficient use, abandonment, unauthorized subdivision, corporate ownership, lack of compliance with labor laws, or, bizarrely, small size. The law provided for compensation in a mixture of cash and government bonds with long maturities and low interest rates.

The Christian Democrats also nationalized water rights and gave the government the right to reallocate them, in spite of the fact that Frei himself later insisted that irrigation should come first from "enterprising individuals." Only if they are not present, he said, should the government get involved.[16] Nationalization precludes individuals, enterprising or not, from any involvement. It also increases the potential for corruption and political favoritism.

The 1967 law also provided the terms for compensation. Payment to the dispossessed landlords was to be prompt and in full for any equipment, buildings, or animals on their property. Compensation for the land itself was much less certain. Frei's government used the assessed value of the land, done for tax purposes, to determine the amount of compensation owed. Where the government confiscated land due to excess size, or where the owners transferred their land voluntarily, they were paid 10 percent of the assessed value in cash, with the remainder in 25-year bonds with variable interest rates.[17]

Other grounds for confiscation meant even less compensation. If the land were confiscated from absentee landlords, or from those who had exploited their land inadequately, only 1 percent to 5 percent was payable in cash, with the rest in 30-year bonds at fixed, concessionary rates. Even getting this small amount of cash could be difficult. The land reform agency was at odds with the Chilean exchequer over when to deposit the cash that would allow the government to take possession. Chile's worsening inflation made these cash payments cheaper the longer they could be delayed.

Frei also set up special courts to hear cases involving the land reform process, especially disputes over compensation. Made up of jurists and agronomists appointed by the Frei government, these courts provided what one author called a "rapid, simple and technical process of review." Landlords had only limited access to regular courts, and only special appeals courts could review cases from the special land reform courts. The dispossessed did retain some rights to contest the amount of assessment in civil courts.

Decrees that followed on the original law allowed the government to take possession of the contested land even before it had made the initial cash payments. In some cases, the government took possession even before it and the owner had agreed on the amount of eventual compensation.

The question of compensation brings up an essential contradiction in the Chilean land reform process. If the former owners held the land illegally, immorally, or incompetently, why pay them for the privilege of using the land? If their possession was legal, moral, or beneficial, why take the land at all? If the government is genuinely committed to compensation, why play games with bonds and interest rates? Frei presented his land reform as revolutionary, but like many Christian Democrats, he was also committed to important elements of the status quo. Frei only served to make Allende's genuinely revolutionary platform seem more coherent and more attractive.

More important than the Frei government's treatment of the former landlords was its treatment of the peasants, purportedly the 1967 law's beneficiaries. Country people who had spent their lives working someone else's land wanted their own land and expected the Christian Democrats to give it to them. Even the Mapuche Indians of the south, who had farmed collectively before Europeans dispossessed them in the colonial period, reacted to getting their land back under the 1967 law by immediately agitating for private ownership.[18]

Frei opted against distribution of the land immediately because he feared a disruption in the food supply to the cities (and to the voters who lived there). The government mandated the formation of cooperatives to maintain the economy of scale that had prevailed on the haciendas. The Christian Democrats had previously said that the haciendas' monopoly of land prevented them from using it efficiently.[19]

The Christian Democrats turned the seized haciendas into co-ops for three to five years, after which the peasants could vote on whether to continue the cooperative arrangement or divide the land into individual parcels. This intermediate stage was called the *asentamiento*. Ownership during this period remained with CORA.

Since the peasants lacked the landowners' accumulated wealth, they required an income until harvest time, an income CORA provided in the form of "advances" or cheap loans. These had the effect of making cooperative members dependent on the work of all their fellows. Persuading peasants to work hard for the common good when they could see that their neighbors were not working hard, yet would receive the same share at harvest they themselves did, was nearly impossible. It was not, as some authors believe, a problem of getting peasants to act like independent landowners.[20] It was a more difficult problem of convincing peasants they were landowners when they could see they were really CORA employees.

Even if a peasant lasted the three-to-five-year waiting period and opted for individual ownership of land, he had to pay CORA for his received share, making payments over a 30-year period, during which his ownership rights were subject to restraints on alienation and inheritance. This requirement was one of many ways in which the Frei government encouraged peasants to choose the cooperative path. The waiting period was a prolonged propaganda opportunity for CORA managers.

The Results

One sympathetic biographer of Frei says that 20,000 families received confiscated lands from formerly unproductive latifundia during the Frei presidency.[21] This estimate is probably correct. The great majority of these settlers, however, had no definitive title to their land. Frei had promised in 1964 that by the end of his term there would be 100,000 new Chilean landowners. In fact, there were only 5,688 individual titles distributed by 1970, all of them still conditional.

On the collective farms, CORA completely dominated credit, purchasing, leasing equipment, marketing, and improvements. In effect, peasants had to go through CORA for any contact outside the farm gate. It was as though the hacendados had never left.

Frei's abstract interest in land reform was tempered by a competing desire for a program that promised political rewards for the Christian Democratic Party. Frei never hesitated to connect improvements in the peasants' lives, such as they were, with his land reform efforts. His government gathered peasants onto cooperatives that became recruiting grounds for the Christian Democratic Party. By retaining so much control over the peasants' lives, and by effectively replacing and making obsolete the independent peasant organizations that had preceded the Frei government, the Christian Democrats sought to perpetuate their rural electoral base.

If Frei were not the leader of a party nominally committed to something other than short-term political gain, no one could blame him for using land reform to help his party. He did so, however, at the expense of the most important relevant tenets of Catholic social thought. Not incidentally, he also enacted a program that failed to fulfill the peasants' expectations, and failed to help them much. Like most Christian Democratic efforts at political pragmatism, it failed. Frei's politicization of land reform did not prevent the Christian Democrats from running a poor third in the 1970 election. It did not prevent rural voters from backing Salvador Allende.

EL SALVADOR: PUNITIVE LAND REFORM

In the 1972 presidential campaign, the Salvadoran Christian Democrats agreed that private property was a human right. Their plan for development "reserved a dominant role for private sector investment and it contained a call for measures to protect small and medium entrepreneurs and landholders."[22] Earlier the party had called for increased crop yields by intensifying production, but without exhausting the soil.

The Salvadoran Christian Democrats also recognized, even before they came to power, the importance of independent rural unions. They were the first to try to organize the peasants, creating the Christian Federation of Salvadoran Peasants (FECCAS) in 1965. The federation was built on the work of San Salvador archbishop Monsignor Chávez y González, who had organized the Cooperative Support Foundation for small peasant producers in 1963.[23]

When the 1979 coup took place, the progressive military officers asked the Christian Democrats to take part in government. The latter stipulated that serious land reform be part of the junta's program of government. The prospect of government power resulted, as it usually does, in changes in Christian Democratic policy. The Christian Democrats insisted that the private sector not be allowed in the junta at all. The original Land Reform Law promised "the right to private property in a communal framework."

El Salvador before Land Reform

In the nineteenth century, the term *land reform* meant the theft of communal maize land from native populations for coffee plantations. Although this is often described as a liberal or free market policy,[24] the coffee growers used their government connections not only to prevent the Indians from regaining their lands but also to limit the number of coffee growers. From the very beginning in El Salvador, coffee was a statist enterprise, even if the profits were privatized.

The pre-reform landowners did not use the land rationally or productively. Since they were protected from any significant competition by their government connections, there was little incentive to risk savings in schemes that could maximize production. Since rural labor was cheap, owing to the paucity of rural unions, there was also little incentive to mechanize or modernize. Land use seemed dictated by whim or by the availability of desperate peasants.

Land often remained idle. In the words of one author, "The situation seemed to cry out for an idle lands law to stimulate large, well-run farms to produce more and threaten those holdings that were decapitalizing and/or failing to produce with expropriation."[25]

A government that was friendly to landowners established the Institute for Agrarian Transformation (ISTA) in 1975. This body began a modest land reform program in the eastern provinces of San Miguel and Usulatan. Using U.S. Agency for International Development (USAID) funds, the government gave landowners a deadline by which they had to sell their land to the government for redistribution. By using their government connections, cotton farmers managed to get their farms exempted, and only 150,000 acres were affected.

Landholding patterns were badly polarized by 1979. Although specific estimates vary, it is clear that a tiny minority of Salvadorans held most of the desirable land and that a large majority desired that land forthwith. The civilian-military junta realized that the threat of land reform would cause many landowners either to find ways around the threat of confiscation or to fail to produce. In 1980, therefore, the junta decreed two important prereform measures. The first prohibited transfer of holdings over 100 hectares, while the second forced owners to continue their 1979–1980 crop-year tenancy arrangements into the 1980–1981 season.[26]

Meanwhile, important changes were taking place outside the government. FECCAS, which had begun as a self-help organization, became more militant in the 1970s. At the same time, it came under the control of radical priests who were hostile to the Christian Democrats. This was fatal to FECCAS.

The Salvadoran Christian Democrats, like their counterparts elsewhere, have little tolerance for independent social groups they do not control. While negotiating with the military in 1979, the Christian Democrats entered into a side agreement with the Salvadoran Communal Union (UCS), a long-time rival of FECCAS. Under the agreement, the Christian Democrats agreed to aggressively pursue land reform, while the UCS agreed to enter the government and take control of ISTA. Thus FECCAS, the peasant union most committed to independence, was excluded from power and the UCS was effectively co-opted.[27]

Unlike the Bolivian and Catholic models, land reform in El Salvador came from the top down and was vigorously supported by both Democratic and Republican administrations in the United States. United States involvement limited the influence of independent peasant forces like FECCAS and all but ensured that land reform would increase government power.

The Salvadoran Reform

Land reform began in March 1980 with the promulgation of Decrees 153 and 154. The minister of agriculture at the time was Enrique Alvarez, who had held the same position in the Sánchez Hernández cabinet ten years earlier. The major author of the land reform decrees was Antonio Morales Ehrlich. True to their promise, the Christian Democrats named Rodolfo Viera, secretary-general of the UCS, to head ISTA.

Phase 1 of the reform authorized the government to seize properties of more than 500 hectares. It was massive, drastic, and rapid. No large landowners escaped. Seizures occurred suddenly and sometimes violently, with trucks of soldiers turning up at dawn and ordering families off the land with little more than the clothes on their backs.

According to observers skeptical of land reform,

. . . the Salvadoran land reform in its first few months had distributed far more land (in percentage of total agricultural land available) than any other land reform in Latin

America, including Mexico, Cuba under Castro, and Allende's Chile and probably more than any 20th century land reform in the world, including the People's Republic of China.[28]

By June 1980, all farms larger than 500 hectares, numbering 376 and covering about 224,000 hectares, were seized and turned into peasant co-ops.

The government determined compensation by looking at tax records from several years earlier, when productivity was lower. Compensation was often late or absent. Owners frequently waited a year for the first interest payment on their single-digit interest rate bonds.

Phase 2 of the land reform authorized the seizure of farms of 250–500 hectares, but this did not take place in 1980. Nevertheless, many Phase 2–sized properties were affected, with at least 60 being seized in the belief that they were larger than 500 hectares (and thus Phase 1 property). Many medium-sized owners sold to the government voluntarily, hoping either for a better price or to be spared the indignity of being escorted off their land by soldiers.[29]

As in Chile, the government denied the peasants ownership of the confiscated land. As the soldiers arrived on the larger farms, ISTA employees gathered the peasants, announced that they now "owned" the land, and proceeded to hold an election, on the spot, for cooperative officials. Gaining individual title to land was all but impossible.

The cooperatives were beset with problems from the start. According to a U.S. government survey, undertaken by the inspector general's office, ISTA structured the co-ops "without fully considering the basic ingredients necessary for profit-making productive enterprises."[30] In addition, the co-ops were saddled with the compensation bill, even if the landowner had not yet received any compensation.

Proceeds from the co-ops went directly to the Banco de Fomento Agropecuario, which held the debts. Anything left over after debts were paid went into escrow. Only ISTA could release funds to the peasants. Not surprisingly, the peasants came to regard these advances as wages, confirming their suspicion that they had merely changed masters. Accordingly, if a bank advance came late, co-op members preferred to sit idle rather than work anyway to protect what one author calls their "future profits." Again, peasants completely understood the difference between being an owner and an employee.

Since a rural union was running ISTA, and since the Christian Democrats regarded the co-ops as prime recruiting sites, it is not surprising that the government placed far more members on the co-ops than had worked the same lands earlier. In most cases, the newcomers were more than the co-op could support. Consistent problems in getting credit in time for planting also put many co-ops in great trouble. Perhaps worst of all, the land reform decrees did not create any process for "graduation" to self-management.

The ISTA managers wielded great power. They were comanager with the elected leader, with veto power over all major decisions and control over the co-op checkbook. A USAID official remarked that the co-ops needed "significant support to handle the burden of paperwork." Since the ISTA managers were salaried officials, their presence was yet another financial burden that was for some co-ops the final factor leading to bankruptcy.

Managing positions in ISTA often went to Christian Democratic faithful, regardless of their qualifications for farming. It often seemed that the less they knew about farming, the more determined they were to make decisions about it. For example, many ISTA staffers believed the co-ops should raise subsistence crops, rather than the cash crops the old owners had raised. The result was an immediate glut of basic grains in 1980–1981, with the resultant low prices. The U.S. Inspector General (USIG) survey also reported a high level of corruption among ISTA officials.

The heavy bureaucratic burden, the difficulty of transfer, and above all the enormous uncertainty that land reform brought induced many peasants to sell their land privately and illegally. This exodus has been the source of the heralded return of the hacendados to the countryside. There have also been reports of soldiers extorting new crops in return for protection from former landowners and for other services.

Phase 2 was to affect farms between 250 hectares and 500 hectares. This included large percentages of El Salvador's coffee, sugar, and cotton land, and its transformation into subsistence growing would have destroyed the country's ability to earn foreign exchange.

Conservative elements in the Salvadoran Constituent Assembly, however, managed to delay this part of the reform. In the Constituent Assembly's final product, the 1983 constitution, the maximum permissible amount of privately owned land was raised to 245 hectares. The same document also prohibited expropriation for two years, giving owners plenty of time to subdivide their land to avoid expropriation altogether.

Phase 3 of the reform was the "land-to-the-tiller" provision. Decree 207 of April 28, 1980, promised up to seven hectares of land to tenant farmers free of charge. The only requirement was that the proposed beneficiary be a former lessee. While the Christian Democrats may have intended this provision to help peasants who worked for large landowners, many of the farms confiscated under Phase 3 turned out to be owned by other campesinos just as poor as the tenants. Phase 3 titles were easier to attain, however, and new owners gained incentive to improve their parcels through soil conservation, permanent crops, or irrigation. Many are doing so.[31]

Even here, though, the problem of reforming land while maintaining production appeared. Provisional president Alvaro Magaña had the Constituent Assembly exempt cotton, sugar, grain, and cattle land from Phase 3. These exemptions, plus the delays of Phase 2 and the generally belligerent attitude of the rightist National Republican Alliance (ARENA) majority, convinced many peasants that the land reform was over.

Former landowners, employing thugs and taking advantage of the poor communications in the countryside, began expelling the co-op members and taking the land back. It was here that the failure of Christian Democratic rural organizing was most evident. By 1982, FECCAS and the UCS were either gone or part of the government. When the government changed hands in 1982, new ISTA officials appeared, no longer even nominally friendly to the peasants. Genuinely independent rural unions would have had a much better chance of defending peasants' rights.

The new government also made the granting of Phase 3 titles a nightmare. Again, the Christian Democrats seemed to believe that government power was necessarily benign or that it could never fall into reactionary hands. Had they been truly committed to granting permanent titles, the ARENA coalition would have found land reform virtually irreversible in 1982.

The Results

Supporters of the Salvadoran land reform, such as Roy Prosterman, insist that productivity on the co-ops increased when compared with the 1975–1979 average. They are equally insistent that 1981 yields should not be compared with 1979 yields, which were much higher, since 1979 was El Salvador's best crop year ever. What they do not explain, or even address, is why 1979 was such a good year.

There is, however, little doubt that productivity did go up on many of the co-ops. In most cases, co-ops produced more than the national average. Since these were, for the most part, underused lands to begin with, the reform here was more in the nature of a colonization program. Like the Bolivian Oriente colonization program, this supported overall production figures when they were falling on other co-ops.

For individual peasants, the results have been almost invisible. Those on the co-ops work for the government rather than for landowners. The promise of independent ownership is still just a promise. The poorest of the rural poor, those who had no access to land before 1980, still have no access, since the land reform decrees did not affect them. At least 18,000 such landless Salvadorans still work as day laborers.

Some of what little change has occurred has been reversed. With no independent rural unions, land reform follows the shifting sands of Salvadoran politics, placing the burden of uncertainty on those least able to bear it. By 1986, only 127 Phase 1 recipients had definitive titles to their land, and only 16,992 Phase 3 recipients.[32]

Despite this failure, land reform remained in the 1989 Christian Democratic platform. Proving that the Salvadorans have learned nothing from their experience or that of Chile, Christian Democratic presidential candidate Fidel Chávez Mena promised to carry out Phase 2 and to create 160,000 rural jobs.[33]

LAND REFORM IN VENEZUELA

In most of Latin America's early history, landed elites have desired a weak central government that would leave them alone. Virtually self-sufficient, haciendas needed little from government. Moneyed elites, on the other hand, have always required a strong and stable government to ensure the value of their paper holdings. Venezuela was no exception to this rule. Before the discovery of oil, Venezuela had one of the most rudimentary and inactive governments in Latin America. The landed elites were secure in their relative isolation, and there were no moneyed elites to speak of. With the advent of oil wealth, however, things changed. The relative value of farmland decreased, rural labor became more expensive as peasants went to the cities to work for oil companies, and political power shifted irrevocably from the countryside to the capital.

Venezuela's modern political parties were born of this social division. The strength of the Christian Democratic Copei originally came from the rural Andean states of Tachira, Mérida, and Trujillo. Landowners depended upon Copei to protect them from Social Democratic policies of Acción Democrática, which was centered in the cities.

Copei did promise land reform in its early platforms. The group also promised, however, that this reform would be effective and "without hatred." In these early days, Copei evidently hoped that educating the rich in the principles of Catholic social thought would induce them to parcel out land among their peasant tenants themselves, perhaps in the hope of increasing productivity.

The 1946 Copei Manifesto states the party's position on land reform. Point 4 of this manifesto says that private property is guaranteed, that private initiative will be respected, and that insofar as the government should redistribute wealth at all, it should do so through the tax policy. They did add, following Catholic social thought, that individual interests must bow to the social function of property.[34]

Point 6 states that land should be owned by those who work it, and that a just and "scientific" land reform will reward individual initiative. This point also upholds the right of the state to seize properties, with fair compensation. As late as 1960, Rafael Caldera told the delegates to the Fifth International Christian Democratic Congress that while the state must play a decisive role in agrarian reform, it must do so "without prejudice to private enterprise."[35] Later that same year, speaking in Quito, he expressed the hope that between 120,000 and 150,000 families would be settled *on their own land* by 1963.[36]

Germán Borregales, an anti-land reform Copei leader, wrote in 1968 that land reform does not have to be heavy handed, arbitrary, or confiscatory. Such a land reform only gives peasants a false sense of proprietorship, since it destroys the entire meaning of private ownership in the first place. A true nationalist, he continued, would devote his energies to making the country-side productive and thus reducing the country's foreign dependence.[37]

Luis Herrera Campins, Caldera's successor as Copei party leader, said in 1978 that Copei does not seek to prohibit private property, but, he added, the public, through the state, does have the right to proscribe harmful uses of private property, especially in areas of economic importance.[38] Herrera spoke often of a new sort of ownership called *comunitaria*. This is a form of private property overseen by social groups. It is, he insists, entirely consistent with the "all proprietors" mandate of Catholic social thought. If the groups he mentioned had indeed been private, not created and maintained by the state, Herrera would have been correct.

Venezuela before Land Reform

Unlike that in Chile and El Salvador, Venezuela's land reform problem was not concentration of ownership but the existence of large unsettled areas that could be cultivated more intensively but that were for the most part isolated. They required social services like roads, schools, markets, irrigation, and medical services. Venezuela needed, not confiscation, but colonization.

Existing farmland was highly concentrated before 1958, however. Holdings of less than ten hectares accounted for 67 percent of all farms, but for only 2 percent of the land then under cultivation. By contrast, the largest 1.7 percent of all farms had 75 percent of the cultivated land. While the military governments promoted European immigration to settle southern Venezuela, and while large landowners used their government connections to best advantage, the small Venezuelan farmer lived at a subsistence level.[39]

When AD came to power in 1945, beginning the Triennio, it passed an agrarian reform law based on three precepts: first, that land reform should be measured and legislated, not illegal and confiscatory; second, that reform should not affect large holdings where efficient and modern means of production are employed; and third, that expropriated landowners should receive just prices. These precepts are entirely consistent with Catholic social thought, and perhaps even more generous to large landholders than Catholic social thought. Acción Democrática had no chance to enact them before the Triennio ended.

Like Chile and El Salvador, Venezuela had a strong rural labor movement before land reform got started. The Venezuelan Peasants' Federation (FCV) was stronger than any of the rural unions examined thus far. This union was instrumental in carrying out the Venezuelan reform.[40]

The FCV had close ties to AD, but it was not under the party's control. Its members seized land well in advance of AD directions, especially in 1957–1958 as the Pérez Jiménez dictatorship was collapsing. Their actions ensured that AD would retain its commitment to land reform through the transition period. Thus it performed exactly the function that independent social groups are supposed to perform: It defended the interests of its members without regard to the wishes of the government.

When the democratic regime came to power in 1958, Rómulo Betancourt recognized that getting a land reform law passed might take more time than the unions were willing to wait. He also discovered that Pérez Jiménez and his friends had turned much of their private land into state land to endow it with tax money. When the dictator left the country, AD confiscated this land. Starting with these extensive tracts of public land, Betancourt began distributing it to appease the FCV. He also established a procedure for the FCV, not individuals, to petition the government to confiscate land.

At the same time, oil wealth began flowing into Venezuela. Many land-owners invited peasants to "invade" their land, so that the government would buy it at a satisfactory price. The former owners were then free to invest this money in oil. For its part, the Betancourt administration discouraged free-lance land invasions and announced in 1961 that it would not grant land to peasants who had taken the law into their own hands.

The Venezuelan Land Reform Program

In the 1958 election, AD received the votes of many peasants connected with the FCV. The federation successfully showed its political potency. Since 1960, most members of the National Agrarian Institute (IAN), which managed the reform, have come from the FCV. In spite of their strength, however, the countryside in 1958 was still largely a Copei preserve. This rural strength earned the Agriculture Ministry for Copei. Víctor Giménez Landínez held this position throughout the Betancourt administration. He authored the 1960 land reform law, and Copei has taken credit for Venezuelan land reform since 1960.

The 1960 law sought the "transformation of the agriculture of the country and the incorporation of the rural population into the economic, social and political development of the country, through the substitution of the latifundia system for one of a just system of property, tenure and exploitation of the land."[41] It began with public land, which included about a million hectares, although most of this was poor. It also promised to distribute the better land taken from the former dictators. In addition, the law provided for the confiscation of private land. To be liable to seizure, such land had to be uncultivated, badly farmed, or used extensively for cattle grazing.

It made no promises about future individual ownership, although one of its stated purposes was to "create a new class of small family farmowners." Instead, the law said that it guaranteed the right of every individual or population group to agricultural or livestock work.

In practice, the government limited expropriations to the states of Miranda, Aragua, and Carabobo, all known for their polarized landholding patterns. In much of the rest of the country, the distribution of public land was enough to satisfy the demands of the landless. The power of the FCV was reflected in the requirement that for land to be expropriated, it must be in the vicinity of groups of peasants who have asked for land.

The government was not burdened with compensation costs because relatively little land was confiscated and also because oil money enriched the public treasury. The IAN paid 10 percent in cash and the rest in nontransferable agrarian reform bonds. The bonds came in three classes, all with single-digit annual interest rates. Unlike their counterparts in Chile and El Salvador, Venezuelan landowners had access to regular courts for land reform disputes. These were rare, indicating that most owners were satisfied with the settlement.

Venezuela's land reform law was almost unique in Latin America in its emphasis on production. The drafters of the law recognized that parceling land would not by itself make Venezuela productive; vigilant credit and technical assistance, along with adequate infrastructure, especially to colonized areas, was also important. The law created *asentamientos*, as in Chile, and the government concentrated government services on these settlements.

For the most part, the *asentamientos* were given to individual owners, although the government retained substantial control over how they used the land. Using credit as leverage, the Central Bank steered most peasants into crop production, contrary to a national trend toward livestock. Credit also served to induce farmers to remain part of the *asentamientos*.

The committees that ran these co-ops were often politically divided, especially where the FCV was weak. This sometimes resulted in paralysis, which encouraged farmers to move toward de facto private ownership. As they did, the IAN had a more difficult time persuading farmers that they were better off as part of the collective.[42] In Venezuela, as elsewhere, peasants knew the difference between being an owner and an employee.

Loose government supervision meant greater control for farmers, but it also meant the lack of a reliable legal system to provide the certainty required for investment. Peasants could, however, buy restricted amounts of land adjoining the co-ops. They could sell this land to other eligible peasants, and there were far fewer limitations on inheritance than in Chile or El Salvador. Still, under certain conditions, the government retained the right to deny land to a recipient.

Providing sufficient infrastructure was a recurring problem. Sustaining a level of skilled bureaucrats and properly supported public minimal services was difficult. The government made every effort to build neighborhood roads, to make some start toward public housing, sewage and water facilities, schools, and medical dispensaries. The state also began some sizable irrigation projects. The state did not create its own marketing co-ops, but it did encourage the formation of private markets.

The reform created numerous opportunities for corruption. Loans from the official Central Bank, for example, usually went uncollected. They were, in fact, a subsidy for peasants well connected enough to receive them. The privilege of borrowing became a corruption-potent plum. The government also set minimum prices, but the "loan" subsidies allowed some peasants to undercut this price, so that the minimum became a maximum for independent, incorrupt peasants. By 1961, the bank directorate ordered that no more loans be advanced to any individual or group in arrears in payment.

Copei's Limited Involvement in the Venezuelan Land Reform

The Venezuelan land reform, both by design and by accident, resembles the Catholic and Bolivian models far more closely than the Chilean or Salvadoran reforms. This does not mean, however, that Venezuela's Christian Democrats deserve all the credit for this. There is good reason to believe they had limited control over the details of the reform, in spite of controlling the Ministry of Agriculture, and in spite of Giménez Landínez's authorship of the land reform bill.

President Betancourt effectively replaced the Copei-dominated Agrarian Reform Coordinating Council, chaired by the minister of agriculture, with the Coordinating and Planning Board, whose members the president appointed. When the 1960 law established the IAN, its four directors, nominally responsible to the minister, were all named by the president.

Copei acknowledged their lack of control by complaining about AD favoritism in the distribution of land reform benefits. Most of these went to areas of AD control. Eventually, Copei took issue with the whole idea of AD land reform, calling the government's program "socialistic" and expressing a preference for more local, and less national, control.[43]

Control over the FCV became a joint goal of AD and Copei. Formerly dominated by the Communists, the FCV remained determinedly independent of the coalition government and a target of Betancourt's increasingly strident anti-Communism. As Betancourt removed the FCV leaders he did not like, Copei got control of FCV units in Mérida and Tachira, two of Copei's traditional strongholds. It did not vie for control of all the FCV units. More importantly, it did not fight to keep the unions independent, as a party committed to Catholic social thought would have.

Acción Democrática eventually purged the FCV of Communist elements and gained a large majority in the union's national leadership. So overwhelming was the AD majority that it felt it could share some offices with Copei.

The Christian Democrats, typically, took what they were given and tried to form their own peasant union in 1964. The effort was ten years too late.

The Results in Venezuela

The most critical observer of the Venezuelan land reform is Copei renegade Germán Borregales, who wrote that the land reform decreased production, made food more expensive, and hurt the poor, who, he said, used to eat better for less money.[44] Robert Alexander disputes this, saying that output increased significantly while redistribution was going forward. In his final message to Congress, Betancourt claimed a 10 percent decrease in agricultural imports since 1958, coupled with a 15 percent rise in exports.[45]

Figures on grain production provide an incomplete, but still informative, picture of the program's success. The IAN itself reported that in 1959, 280,000 hectares of maize land had yielded 336,000 metric tons, while in 1960, an additional 120,000 hectares increased the total yield to 440,000 metric tons. Rice production climbed from 38,500 metric tons on 28,500 hectares in 1959 to 72,000 metric tons on 42,000 hectares in 1960.[46]

There were problems in getting the peasants final title to their land. Partly, this was due to a lack of sufficient personnel to write out proper deeds. By December 1961, 36,295 families had received land, of the 84,676 that had requested it in the first 21 months of the law's existence. By the end of 1962, however, most peasants who had titles had individual titles, which were not dependent on *asentamiento* membership.

CONCLUSION

This chapter has traced the development of four Latin American land reform programs. In Bolivia and Venezuela, the social, economic, and political results that their creators desired actually appeared. In the same two programs, the land reform reflected the precepts of Catholic social thought. Peasants became owners, independent social groups became stronger, the growth in state power was limited, and eventually production rose. The Bolivian and Venezuelan programs were very different from those in Chile and El Salvador.

It was in Chile and El Salvador, however, that the Christian Democrats had the most complete control over the land reform program. In Venezuela, while the Christian Democrats stayed reasonably close to Catholic social thought, they were constantly nudged in that direction by political forces they did not control. In Bolivia, there was no Christian Democratic participation at all.

Besides the programs examined here, Christian Democrats contributed to land reform proposals in Peru, Nicaragua, and Ecuador. In these cases, they imitated their fellows in Chile and El Salvador, who had the chance to implement reforms themselves. In every case, the Christian Democrats ignored the most basic precepts of Catholic social thought.

Had they been interested in consistency with their stated ideological roots, the Christian Democrats would have implemented policies that would increase the number of rural landholders. They would have encouraged the formation of truly independent social groups. They would have allowed a variety of service providers, from marketers to lenders, to compete to serve the farming communities.

With the qualified exception of Venezuela, Latin America's Christian Democrats replaced the "few proprietors" of the unjust pre-reform systems with the equally unjust "no proprietors" of socialized agriculture. For the most part, only the government owned land. In Chile, this allowed the Allende regime to make the countryside even more tightly controlled. In El Salvador, it allowed the rightist opposition government to stop land reform altogether. Only the Venezuelan land reform withstood future government challenges, largely because of the strong independent social groups the Christian Democrats did not control.

It is difficult to persuade rural people that they are owners when they can see they are still employees, even for a different master, or even for a more benevolent master. Yet in one program after another, Christian Democrats expected peasants to act as if they owned land they occupied only at government pleasure.

Agricultural labor is difficult and often unrewarding. It is unrealistic to expect people to work hard if they have no personal stake in the outcome of their efforts. The Christian Democrats failed, in other words, to instantly overcome the importance of self-interest to an economic system.

To be sure, Catholic social thought condemns excessive self-interest. Its developers, however, did not expect to eliminate selfishness altogether. In their statements on private property, the popes recognized the importance of self-interest. Their suggestions for overcoming it, however, involved establishing independent social groups that would help peasants to spontaneously place the needs of others above their own needs. Such independent social groups ideally function to protect peasants from the state, as they did in Venezuela, or from rapacious moneylenders, as they did in Bolivia.

Land reform based on Catholic social thought, therefore, seeks to make peasants as independent as possible from both government control and capitalist exploitation. It does so without permanently increasing the state's role in agriculture. For Latin America's Christian Democrats, however, the chances to gain politically from land reform were too attractive to ignore.

By tying programs in Chile and El Salvador so closely to the state, Christian Democrats hoped to turn the land reform program into a partisan windfall. Extending their own power became the priority, while the welfare of the peasants, and the principles of Catholic social thought, were far less important.

NOTES

1. Although the Bolivian program did not occur under a Christian Democratic regime, it demonstrates that land reform that is consistent with Catholic social thought can, in fact, take place. I include no similar control case in Chapter 5 (nationalization) because none exists in Latin America.

2. Russell King, *Land Reform: A World Survey* (Boulder, Colo.: Westview Press, 1977), p. 117.

3. John Powelson and Richard Stock, *The Peasant Betrayed: Agriculture and Land Reform in the Third World* (Boston: Oelgeschlager, Gunn and Hain, 1987), p. 99.

4. Ibid., p. 119.

5. Ibid., p. 118.

6. Doreen Warriner, *Land Reform in Principle and in Practice* (Oxford: Oxford University Press, 1969), p. 244.

7. King, p. 120.

8. Powelson and Stock, p. 102.

9. Edward Williams, *Latin American Christian Democratic Parties* (Knoxville: University of Tennessee Press, 1967), pp. 113–14.

10. Leonard Gross, *The Last, Best Hope: Eduardo Frei and Chilean Christian Democracy* (New York: Random House, 1967), p. 104.

11. Williams, p. 106.

12. Warriner, p. 342.

13. Ibid., p. 333.

14. Joseph R. Thome, "Law, Conflict and Change: Frei's Law and Allende's Agrarian Reform," in William C. Thiesenhusen, ed., *Searching for Land Reform in Latin America* (Boston: Unwin Hyman, 1989), p. 191.

15. Warriner, p. 335.

16. Eduardo Frei, *The Mandate of History and Chile's Future* (Athens, Ohio: Center for International Studies, Papers in International Studies, Latin America Series, no. 1, 1977), p. 61.

17. Thome, p. 197.

18. Ajit Kumar Ghose, *Agrarian Reform in Contemporary Developing Countries* (London: Croon Helm, 1983), p. 253.

19. Ibid., p. 250.

20. Warriner, p. 339.

21. Mark Falcoff, "Eduardo Frei Montalva, 1911–1982," *Review of Politics* 44, 3 (1982): 324.

22. Stephen Webre, *José Napoleón Duarte and the Christian Democratic Party in Salvadoran Politics, 1960–1972* (Baton Rouge: University of Louisiana Press, 1979), p. 157.

23. Robert Armstrong and Janet Shenk, *El Salvador: The Face of Revolution* (Boston: South End Press, 1982), p. 148.

24. Martin Diskin, "El Salvador: Reform Prevents Change," in Thiesenhusen, p. 431.

25. Ibid., p. 435.

26. Roy Prosterman and Jeffrey Riedinger, *Land Reform and Democratic Development* (Baltimore: Johns Hopkins University Press, 1987), p. 147.

27. Ibid., p. 148.

28. Powelson and Stock, p. 237.

29. Diskin, p. 414.

30. Quoted in Powelson and Stock, p. 231.

31. Diskin, p. 422.

32. Ibid., p. 440.

33. San Salvador, Canal Doce, 3 March 1989 (Foreign Broadcast Information Service, Latin America *Daily Report*, 7 March 1989, p. 23).

34. "Platforma electoral de Copei," in Paciano Padrón, ed., *Copei: Documentos fundamentales, 1946* (Caracas: Ediciones Centauro, 1983), p. 89.

35. *Christian Democratic Review*, no. 60 (March 1960): 15–16.

36. Robert J. Alexander, *The Venezuelan Democratic Revolution: A Profile of the Regime of Rómulo Betancourt* (New Brunswick, N.J.: Rutgers University Press, 1964), p. 181. (My italics.)

37. Germán Borregales, *Copei hoy: Una negación* (Caracas: Ediciones Garrido, 1968), pp. 214–15.

38. Alfredo Peña, *Conversaciones con Luis Herrera Campins* (Caracas: Editorial Ateneo de Caracas, 1978), p. 91.

39. Raymond J. Penn and Jorge Schuster, "Venezuela," in Oscar Delgado, ed., *Reformas agrarias en la América Latina* (Mexico City: Fondo de Cultura Economica, 1965), p. 550.

40. Warriner, p. 351.

41. Penn and Schuster, p. 551.

42. Ibid., p. 557.

43. John Duncan Powell, *Political Mobilization of the Venezuelan Peasant* (Cambridge, Mass.: Harvard University Press, 1971), pp. 185–86.

44. Borregales, p. 216.

45. Alexander, p. 184.

46. Ibid., p. 183.

5

Control of Natural Resources: Christian Democratic Nationalization Policy

Christian Democrats in Venezuela, Chile, and El Salvador have been most active in pursuing the nationalization of basic industries. While nationalization per se is not necessarily inconsistent with Catholic social thought, the actual processes of nationalization the Latin American Christian Democrats have pursued have violated the spirit of Catholic social thought in a number of areas.

Catholic social thought is not strong in its defense of private property rights when important natural resources are involved. Christian Democrats believe that an individual's responsibility to promote society's common good is most important. The temptation to abuse that responsibility is strongest when important natural resources are involved. Venezuelan, Chilean, and Salvadoran Christian Democrats, among others, follow policies ostensibly designed to prevent narrow, selfish individual interests from gaining excessive control of resources on which the entire country depends.

The Roman Catholic popes, as well as early Catholic social thinkers and Christian Democrats, have emphasized that the economic power of the state should not be increased except under very specific circumstances. These thinkers have also stated that it is acceptable for a nation to acquire control of its nonrenewable mineral resources to prevent foreign domination.

Thus, a nationalization policy that did not increase the economic power of the state would be, at least theoretically, consistent with the strictures of Catholic social thought. It is difficult to imagine a nationalization policy that did not immediately increase state power. This power need not be permanently increased, however. Catholic social thought warns against such an outcome. The popes did not believe that natural resources left in a state monopoly would necessarily be better managed on behalf of the entire nation. If a private monopoly is bad, a public one can be even worse.

Latin America's Christian Democrats have stated that increased state power over basic natural resources is necessary. If this is the case, however, they should also insist that the state enterprise perform as nearly as possible the same functions as a moral private enterprise. They should insist that the state enterprise be efficient, productive, and professional. The Christian Democrats do not insist on these characteristics, however. Instead, to varying degrees they have used state intervention as a partisan political tool. They have been no less selfish and short sighted than the most exploitative foreign capitalist might have been.

Catholic social thought acknowledges the temptation to misuse great power, and it teaches that a nationalization policy should protect the natural patrimony from destructive self-interest, but without permanently placing that patrimony in state hands. Such a policy might include government regulations on ownership, or at least on majority ownership. A nationalization policy consistent with Catholic social thought might use tax money to purchase shares of stock from foreigners and then expeditiously make this stock available to local entrepreneurs. It might also support diversification of the national economy to reduce dependence on a single commodity. Christian Democrats, however, have consistently pursued nationalization policies that increase state power at the expense of private enterprise. This includes their native private enterprise, not just MNCs.

CHRISTIAN DEMOCRATIC STATEMENTS ON NATIONALIZATION

Latin America's Christian Democratic parties started as movements of intellectuals. They were heavily influenced by the thought of European Christian Democrats in the late 1950s and early 1960s. At that time, the Europeans were enthusiastic about the ability, and the duty, of the state to ensure economic development. Thus, when the exiled leadership of Venezuela's Christian Democrats attended the International Christian Democratic Congress in 1955, they endorsed the nationalization of industry, focusing especially on industries under the control of American MNCs.

An early conference of Latin American Christian Democrats, while avoiding the use of the word "nationalization," did maintain that the State should make national economic plans. Private capital, the communique went on, should be allowed so long as it did not become "a danger to the commonweal." The conference neglected to say who would make that determination.[1] Key industries (again, undefined) and underutilized properties should be subject to immediate government takeover.

Even in their early theoretical pronouncements in Latin America, the Christian Democrats were not reticent about the need to increase the state's control over foreign economic activities, especially enterprises involving basic resources. At this early point in their history, Christian Democrats were also promising to protect civil society from overbearing state power. That they thought they could do both simultaneously indicates that Christian Democrats believed the power of the state could grow in some areas and not spill over into other areas.

Venezuela's Copei

Among the most enthusiastic in their belief in a stronger state was Venezuela's Christian Democratic Copei. This was true in spite of the fact that Copei represented Venezuela's landed elite, which had traditionally preferred a weak central government and opposed the moneyed elite of Caracas, which needed a strong government.

The discovery of oil in the 1920s, and its rapid rise to national economic importance, made the moneyed elite Venezuela's dominant class. Realizing this, Copei sought to make its peace with this class, even while using the rhetoric of weak government to maintain landed support. Part of Copei's rapprochement with the state was the embrace of nationalization of oil.

Christian Democrats were aware that oil had been, from the very start in Venezuela, an enterprise with a good deal of government involvement. Multinational corporations desiring drilling rights or territorial concessions received them from the government. In the early days, this normally involved bribery. Thus oil immediately became a source of government revenue. During the Gómez dictatorship, this revenue was illicit, irregular, and privatized. This partnership between a corrupt dictator and foreign oil companies might have colored Copei's view of private oil enterprise.

Under the direction of Rafael Caldera, the National Student Union, which was a precursor of Copei, was highly critical of the role of the U.S. petroleum companies in Venezuela and suggested they exerted control over the economy. Later, Caldera included a commitment to the idea of a national oil organization in the statement announcing the 1958 Pact of Punto Fijo. Copei, according to one author, "did not find it difficult to agree that the state should assume a major role for national development."[2] Looking ahead, Copei also tried to make inroads into the petroleum workers' union at this time.

Caldera himself tried to strike a balance in his speeches between his concern for free enterprise and his evidently equally strong determination to limit free enterprise. I have alluded to a number of such confusing pronouncements in earlier chapters. What Caldera stated unequivocally, however, was that proper respect for private enterprise did not preclude nationalization of basic resources or creation by the state of basic industries.[3]

Early Copei documents reflect this determination. Latin America's urgent need for economic modernization, an early Copei treatise said, means the state must follow a series of new public policies, among them land reform, political modernization, and "participation" in the oil industry. The party promised to protect the natural resources of Venezuela and to limit private initiative "by law, by morality and by the national interest."[4]

Copei statements on the oil industry seem almost ingenuous, for they are so contradictory. Claiming to be the party that would protect private initiative, Copei also promised that foreign oil companies could continue their operations in Venezuela. This welcome would last, however, only as long as these operations were consistent with the security of the state, the conservation of the oil riches, and the participation of the nation in the exploitation. Copei gave itself three open-ended excuses to intervene in the oil industry.

Copei might have achieved its goals by encouraging more Venezuelan companies to start exploration and drilling on their own. A party truly committed to Catholic social thought would consider such activities "national participation" in the industry. It would also increase the number of oil companies and induce competition, consistent with Catholic social thought. For Copei, as we shall see, the nation became synonymous with the state. Venezuelan participation, therefore, meant state participation. The Venezuelan state became a competitor with private Venezuelan economic concerns.

Once in power, Copei prepared the country for the nationalization of oil. Caldera received much of his support for this policy from the Frente de Trabajadores Copeyanos (FTC), Copei's labor group. This organization supported the immediate nationalization of natural gas, the suspension of concessions to oil companies, and the replacement of such concessions with "service contracts" that would limit the foreigners' participation.

Luis Herrera Campins, Copei president from 1979 until 1984, was defensive about the fact that Copei did not take the final steps toward nationalization, instead unwillingly leaving that decision to the administration of Acción Democrática's Carlos Andrés Pérez. In a 1978 campaign book, Herrera insisted that it was Copei that declared Venezuela's oil independence from the United States and took the necessary steps toward nationalization. If Copei had won in 1973, he added, it would have nationalized the oil more quickly than AD.[5]

Christian Democratic Nationalization Theory in Chile

Like his Venezuelan counterparts, Eduardo Frei insisted that more complex economic problems required a larger state. Even more important to Frei than modern complexity was what he called "the emergence of power centers that seek to control [the state]."[6] He must have been thinking of fairly large private economic interests. Frei believed that because Latin America entered the modernization phase without accumulated capital for development, a luxury the North had, detailed state planning, and the "unavoidable" nationalization of basic resources, was necessary.[7]

Again like his brother Christian Democrats in Venezuela, Frei tried to retain

some rhetorical commitment to Catholic social thought. He condemned collectivism and statism because these "absorb and subjugate man," but he almost simultaneously proclaimed a "new form of nationalism . . . which is not only concerned with recapturing control over natural resources but also with achieving independence in industry, agricultural and commercial development."[8] The instrument of this recapture was the state.

Thus Frei condemned and supported state power at the same time. It is possible that he believed state power could be fenced into discreet sectors. In this case, he could increase its power over copper without endangering other economic concerns he thought should remain free. Catholic social thought has no illusions about the possibility of confining an expanding state economic apparatus.

In the 1964 campaign, Frei gave more examples of his inconsistency. He insisted that the government had to engage itself in more and more economic decisions, and that reliance on private business was insufficient. "Our businessmen," a Christian Democratic official complained, "do not go out and create markets."[9] At the same time, Frei warned that an Allende victory in 1964 would mean, among other evils, the nationalization of minerals and mining facilities; nationalization of utilities, insurance, and banking; and government control over distribution of consumer goods.

The only way to resolve this inconsistency is to assume that Frei thought government intervention in the economy was bad only if undertaken by a non-Christian Democratic government. There is no other basis on which he could conclude that Allende's nationalizing of mines was bad but Eduardo Frei's doing the same thing was economic nationalism. Frei repeated a common failing of Christian Democrats: They do not analyze or judge economic policies apart from the government that is enacting them.

Frei completely neglected the possibility of neutralizing foreign domination of the copper industry by encouraging more private Chilean participation. Had he encouraged such participation, even through temporary government action, he would have left behind a weaker state, more independent social groups, and, not incidentally, an economy less dominated by foreigners. All these goals reflect the Catholic social thought with which Christian Democrats profess agreement.

NATIONALIZATION IN PRACTICE: VENEZUELA'S OIL

The Caldera Administration

Copei has ignored important tenets of Catholic social thought related to the issue of nationalization in Venezuela and merely followed the lead of Rómulo Betancourt's AD. Even though the actual nationalization in Venezuela occurred during an AD administration, Copei prepared the way. Copei's preparation bears no stamp of a particularly Christian Democratic perspective.

Juan Pablo Pérez Antonio, as Betancourt's minister of mines and hydro-carbons, was the architect of AD policy. After 1958, Copei broadly shared the objectives of this policy and agreed with its strategies. Pérez Antonio did not want to nationalize the oil immediately, since Venezuela in 1958 lacked the capital and technical expertise to run the wells at a profit. Instead, AD put the foreign oil companies under an increasingly specific regulatory regime and demanded an increasingly large percentage of the profits.

First, AD replaced the traditional concessions of territory with service contracts, which strictly limited what the companies could do and how much profit they could secure. At the same time, AD deepened the tax bite by basing taxes not on oil's market price, which fluctuated, but on a steadily increasing government-set price. By 1968, these taxes amounted to 68 percent of the companies' profits.

Although AD's policy was gentle compared to what the companies expected in 1958, it caused enough concern to induce Venezuela's two largest pro-ducers, Creole and Shell subsidiaries, to contribute heavily to Caldera's 1968 campaign. Perhaps the oil companies hoped that Copei would adhere to Catholic social thought and not radically increase the state's economic power. They were to be disappointed.

In his first days, Caldera established the National Committee for the Defense of Oil, a government agency charged with taking over part of the companies' marketing responsibility. Its task was to press for a larger share of the U.S. market.[10] Copei also sought to get control of local government in oil areas. In the department of Zulia, which produces most of the coun-try's oil, Copei and AD agreed in 1969 to name officials of the Legislative Assembly and municipal councils. It is difficult to find a motive for this other than the desire to prevent government control from being diluted by indepen-dent local officials. It was exactly this sort of manipulation that the Catholic social principle of subsidiarity was designed to prevent.

Caldera's original finance minister, Pedro Tinoco, opposed an oil tax in-crease in 1970 — a year of falling oil prices — and his position seemed to pre-sage some relief for the foreign companies. Caldera originally supported Tinoco, then changed his mind when public opinion polls demanded higher taxes. Caldera also raised the benchmark price and pushed the Organization of Petroleum Exporting Countries (OPEC) to agree to set higher prices. Among those calling for higher taxes were Venezuelan businesspeople who thought that their own taxes would fall as foreigners paid more.

While waiting for the opportunity to take over the oil industry, Caldera introduced a bill to nationalize natural gas, which required far less technical expertise to market and was not so closely connected to powerful MNCs. The bill passed in late 1971. Somewhat incongruously, Copei said that al-though the gas belonged to the nation, they were willing to compensate the displaced gas companies.[11]

Also in 1971, Tinoco tried a second time to protect Venezuela's productive

industries. As part of a tax reform bill that would increase sales and income taxes, he sought to exempt foreign petroleum companies from any tax changes. The early 1970s, it must be remembered, was a time of falling oil prices, and Tinoco was justifiably concerned about the future of Venezuela's oil industry. A policy of no tax changes would increase the security of the foreign companies and perhaps induce more investment.

Caldera rejected his advice. In December 1971, Copei assessed an additional $.32-per-barrel tax on oil and imposed a fine for changing output more than 2 percent from the 1970 level.[12] Any quarterly decline in a company's output below the level in the corresponding quarter of 1970 meant a higher benchmark price for the 1971 oil sales, and thus a higher tax, on the whole output of that quarter. This regulation applied only to marginal drops in output, however. It was no less profitable for a company to decrease production by 30 percent than by 10 percent.

The burden fell most heavily on small companies, the ones most likely to decrease production marginally and least able to absorb new taxes. The 1971 law, therefore, kept newcomers out of the market and actually protected the market share of the largest foreign subsidiaries. At the same time, it removed the incentive for these companies to explore or to develop new areas. The MNCs' failure to explore became a major justification for nationalization five years later.

One of the most important steps in the nationalization process was the Hydrocarbons Reversion Law of 1971. The law stipulated that all foreign-owned properties would "revert" to the government when the concessions expired in 1983. Unexplored concessionary areas were liable for immediate reversion. Companies had to put up a bond worth 10 percent of all assets to "insure good working order." Finally, plans for exploration and drilling had to be submitted to government authorities, in advance and in writing.

Proponents of nationalization believe that a developing nation is better off with its natural resources in government hands. Venezuelan governments, however, have demonstrated a consistent inability to anticipate the future of the oil market. After demanding that prices go up in Venezuela while they were dropping everywhere else in the early 1970s, Caldera allowed prices to rise slowly in 1973, when the world price was quadrupling. In June 1973, Caldera sponsored the Internal Market Law, which nationalized the storing, transportation, distribution, and dispensing of hydrocarbons for the domestic market. Thus Caldera insisted on taking over more of the industry while demonstrating his inability to make the most of the oil resource.

Pérez and the Nationalization

Although AD takes credit for the oil nationalization, Caldera as a lame duck worked closely with incoming AD President Carlos Andrés Pérez to pass a law preparing for the nationalization of oil. Copei had already taken most of the preliminary steps. These preliminary steps all increased costs and severely limited the number of companies that could afford to drill in Venezuela. They also prevented almost all Venezuelan entrepreneurs from getting involved in the oil business. Herrera Campins of Copei was an especially enthusiastic supporter of these measures in the Chamber of Deputies.

During the first two years of the Pérez administration, taxes on oil company profits kept rising, reaching 97 percent by 1976. When nationalization finally took place that year, the government found itself the new owner of over 20,000 wells producing over 3 million barrels per day and the new employer of 22,000 employees. Gross income from oil was $10.8 billion.[13]

The MNCs did not walk away from Venezuela empty handed, however. Pérez paid more than $1 billion to them in the wake of the expropriation.[14] He also signed service contracts with the former owners for drilling, marketing, and exploration. Pérez was more willing than Caldera to admit that the Venezuelan government knew little of the oil industry. The Venezuelan left was outraged at Pérez's concessions. As one labor leader put it, the oil MNCs now have "no strikes, no laborers, no assets, no fires, no sabotage. All they have is the oil."[15]

The Herrera Administration

Copei sought to exploit this leftist dissatisfaction by attacking Pérez for the oil nationalization. Herrera insisted that Copei not only would have nationalized more quickly but would have refused compensation. He pointed out that Caldera had nationalized more businesses than Pérez. His administration changed the nature of the service contracts by demanding a "bonus" be paid to the Venezuelan state oil company before and after any contracted exploration.

Herrera also tried to get Exxon, Lummus, Texaco, and Bechtel subsidiaries to develop the heavy oil in the Orinoco river belt, which is more difficult and expensive to extract. Herrera's foreign minister José Alberto Zambrano, however, insisted that any Orinoco oil they found be sold to the government oil company at bargain prices.[16] Given the high cost of drilling and refining Orinoco oil, this demand removed all incentive to explore. After removing the incentive, the Herrera government then insisted that government control was necessary because private companies would not act as the government wanted.

Results of Nationalization

A central tenet of those who favor nationalization of basic industry is that private companies, and especially foreign companies, are self-centered and completely fixated on profits at the expense of national development, conservation, or even decent wages for workers. State officials, on the other hand, are impartial, oriented toward the benefit of the country as a whole, and committed to judicious and fair use of the nonrenewable mineral resources.

Venezuela's experience, however, shows the wisdom of Catholic social thought's insistence that the economic power of the state be limited. It also shows the pervasiveness of human imperfection, even among humans who work for governments. There is nothing to indicate that the Venezuelan government was more able or more willing than private companies to make the best use of Venezuelan oil.

Herrera's minister of energy and mines, Humberto Calderón Berti, insisted that the central reason why Venezuela was still poor, in spite of its oil wealth, was "the tremendous politicization, administrative corruption and general lack of efficiency" in the state oil company. His sentiments were echoed by a North American expert who agreed that "a considerable share of Venezuela's petroleum revenue has been squandered because of government mismanagement and corruption."[17]

The image of North American oil companies as single-mindedly searching for greater profits through greater exploitation of Venezuela also requires some modification. It is true that the first reaction of U.S. oil companies to Betancourt's inauguration was to move some of their funds to Canada, Mexico, and North Africa. They made no systematic attempt to remove assets from Venezuela, however.

When the Hydrocarbons Reversion Law was passed, foreign oil companies decreased their long-range planning and began thinking day to day. This was exactly what the bill provoked. The bill was a breach of earlier contracts and agreements between the government and oil companies, which only made the latter more wary of the government's intentions.

At the same time, Creole Company, Exxon's subsidiary, was putting money into Venezuelan businesses. Their primary motive was to make a profit, and the company established a rigorous screening process for investment requests. In addition, Creole desired to increase the confidence of Venezuelan investors in their company and in the companies they supported. They also hoped to improve the overall Venezuelan economy, create consumers, and perhaps even soften leftist rhetoric directed against them.[18]

None of these motives are particularly altruistic. Creole was looking after its own interests but aiding Venezuela at the same time. Individuals who desired backing for some capital project could present a proposal to Creole. Hundreds of Venezuelan entrepreneurs received Creole money. Far from creating colonies within the Venezuelan economy, Creole provided seed money and then withdrew from the projects. Venezuelan investment replaced that of the foreigners.

Creole's actions were helpful in realizing the Catholic social goals of diversifying the economy, providing as many different employers as possible, creating jobs, and creating balanced economic growth, all without resorting to increased state power. As such, they should have had the support of Copei. Instead, the party sought to force the companies to pay a higher percentage of their profits to the state. There was then less money available to support Venezuelan businesses. As a result, Venezuelan companies lost an independent source of backing.

Creole was also the moving force behind the "Dividend for the Community" program, under which Creole and other large companies would donate 2 percent to 5 percent of their profits to schools, hospitals, and other community projects.[19] For the Christian Democrats, however, this support meant removing these institutions from government control. Copei opposed the program.

Besides the assumption that private companies are always harmfully selfish, which the activities of Creole belie, the Christian Democrats also held the equally questionable belief that state agencies will always be professional and selflessly concerned with the common good. Nationalization provides no evidence for this belief, and a good deal of evidence for the opposite belief.

Betancourt created the Venezuelan Petroleum Company (CVP) to provide a vehicle for Venezuelans to learn the inner workings of the oil industry. A secondary purpose was to enable the government to tax oil companies more efficiently. Through the 1960s, the CVP slowly forced oil companies to accept service contracts under its control and for its profit. The state agency proved early on that it was no less committed to profit than the foreign companies.

The CVP realized that for the changeover to total state control to work, they would have to rely heavily upon the assistance of "Venezuelans now working for the foreign oil companies, many of whom have a highly critical attitude toward the state."[20] That the CVP desired to keep these experienced employees on the job, doing the same thing they had been doing before, raises serious questions about why the nationalization was necessary in the first place.

When the nationalization took place, the CVP was renamed Petróleos de Venezuela, called PDVSA or Petroven. Its first president, the AD-appointed General Alfonso Ravard, ran Petroven "with a no-nonsense realism and an insistence that the agency be kept as immune as possible from the normal rigors of Venezuelan political administration."[21] The state duplicated the efforts of private companies.

For Ravard, the whole idea of Petroven was "to keep as much as possible of the present structure of the industry, with as many people doing their present jobs, doing what they are familiar with according to established principles." Acción Democrática also allowed Petroven to set up ventures with private companies, hoping to get some international help with the development of the Orinoco heavy oil belt. Herrera Campins and Copei were against all these provisions.[22]

Under Copei's 1979–1984 administration, however, the political independence of Petroven eroded as Herrera attacked its independence and self-sufficiency. What had been an oasis of efficiency in Venezuela's state economic structure began to disappear. Plans for further development, which involved joint ventures with foreigners, were delayed or abandoned as the foreign partners lost confidence in Venezuela.[23]

Selection of Petroven officials became increasingly partisan under Herrera. In September 1983, General Ravard was forced out and replaced by Herrera's energy and mines minister, Calderón Berti. Petroven became virtually a branch of the Christian Democratic party. Many of these political officials were arrested in the early 1980s for selling industrial secrets, a practice thought to be reserved for self-serving businesspeople.[24]

Under the Christian Democrats, Petroven postponed plans to explore the Orinoco fields, preferring to make quicker profits from squeezing more oil from older fields.[25] Again, political officials' actions were hardly an improvement on the perceived faulty behavior of the private investors.

It was not long before the Herrera administration cast avaricious eyes at Petroven profits and sought to absorb them into the general budget. Under AD, they were supposed to be earmarked for specific domestic uses. In 1982, Herrera approved the transfer of $4.51 billion from Petroven to the Central Bank for use in servicing the foreign debt.[26] A frequent complaint about private oil companies was that they sent Venezuela's oil profits abroad. Under the Christian Democrats, however, Petroven's profits went abroad faster and in larger amounts. The Christian Democrats invested what was left in government bonds that paid interest below the inflation rate.

Herrera might have found some justification for increasing state control over oil. There is no justification, however, for using that power for the exclusive benefit of one political party. In effect, Venezuela's oil remained in private hands, since the public officials in charge of its exploitation treated the oil like a private preserve. It is exactly this sort of misuse that the authors of Catholic social thought had in mind when they warned about permanently increasing state power.

It would be left to the returning Pérez in 1988 to reverse some of the decisions of his first administration. During the 1988 campaign, Pérez promised to invite foreign oil companies back to develop refining facilities. He reversed his earlier policy of using state funds to buy into foreign refinery operations.[27] Pérez has pursued a number of other policies that tacitly admit to the damage caused by Venezuelan statism.

NATIONALIZATION IN PRACTICE: CHILE'S COPPER

In Chile, copper was the single largest source of wealth to foreign MNCs, and the Christian Democrats devoted most of their efforts to this commodity. Contrary to Christian Democratic claims, Chilean state intervention in minerals did not start with the Frei administration. Anaconda, a large foreign copper company, had been subject to a heavy tax since 1962, and nitrate had been a state monopoly for years before Frei became president.

Frei promised a new style of nationalization during his 1964 campaign. He proposed to buy 51 percent of the foreigners' stock, slowly and with minimum disruption. He called the new policy "Chileanization." He contrasted this with what he called the socialistic or Marxist policy of outright nationalization, which, he maintained, would result in Chile's international isolation and the loss of valuable technical expertise.

Frei at first seemed to be reasonably friendly to the copper companies, lowering their taxes in 1964 to 44 percent, from 86 percent in 1963.[28] Frei hoped to spur current production as well as encourage new production before negotiating the purchase of stock. He also followed an early policy of import substitution, which put more pressure on U.S. copper companies to do more refining in Chile. In addition, Frei promoted tax and tariff incentives to spur manufacturing in Chile.[29]

In December 1964 Frei announced a pact with Kennecott, the largest U.S. copper company operating in Chile. Under the terms of the agreement, the U.S. company would increase investment in Chile and triple production. Frei also announced his government's intention to acquire 51 percent of the stock in Braden, the Chilean branch of Kennecott. In return, the company's management would remain North American and company profits would be taxed at a lower rate.[30]

Chileanization itself started in October 1966 with the publication of Decree 2167. This decree was, in the words of one observer, an attempt by government to involve itself in exploiting Chilean resources to a degree never before accomplished.[31]

During the negotiations with Braden, the Christian Democrats stipulated that the 51 percent payment (about $80 million) would be paid over 20 years at low interest.[32] Kennecott, the parent company, had to agree to lend back the $80 million and acquire another $100 million for Chile from the Export-Import Bank for use in Chilean social projects.[33]

Anaconda, the second largest U.S. copper company operating in Chile, got essentially the same conditions in their deal, arranging Chile's purchase of 25 percent of its stock. Anaconda agreed to invest some $216 million in Chile, and it did manage to persuade the Christian Democrats to lift tariffs on machinery inputs. In 1966, Anaconda agreed to keep no more than $.42 per pound and to pay whatever profit remained, in addition to their regular taxes, for six months.

The company was simply buying time. The agreement had no legal basis and was in fact a breach of contract. But concerned about the advent of a leftist regime, Anaconda determined that its interest lay in keeping Frei in power. The Americans evidently believed that if Frei successfully claimed that he had nationalized copper, then the appeal of Allende's promises of immediate nationalization would shrink. Frei used their fear of Allende unabashedly.

At the same time, Frei's administration demanded that the new joint copper companies increase production 66 percent by 1972, hoping to greatly increase Chile's income from copper. In early 1967, however, copper prices fell by 20 percent to $.45 per pound. The Frei government was first disappointed, then vaguely suspicious of these results. Betraying little knowledge of the most basic laws of supply and demand, the government assumed that falling prices must be the result of a North American plot.

As the 1970 election approached, the international copper picture was better due to upheavals in Zaire. The rise in price made Christian Democrats, and especially 1970 presidential candidate Radomiro Tomic, even more determined to pursue Chileanization, and on terms even less favorable to the copper companies.

Anaconda had hitherto been a secondary target of the Frei administration, which spent most of its efforts on Kennecott. As the election approached and fears of an Allende government grew stronger, Frei demanded 51 percent of Anaconda's two largest mines, El Salvador and Chuquicamata.[34] Tomic, for his part, promised to attack Anaconda immediately after his election. The Christian Democrats' copper policy started to look less like a way of increasing Chile's participation in the industry and more like the use of economic power for political gain.

Chileanization involves some basic logical problems. If the U.S. copper companies were so harmful to the Chilean economy, or so exploitative of their workers or of Chilean resources, then there was no justification for buying them out, as opposed to simply ordering them out, as Allende later did. On the other hand, if they were not doing harm, there was no reason to replace them at all.

A second problem is the source of the copper companies' alleged shortcomings. If they were due to foreign control, then the answer would have been to allow Chileans to purchase stock, either directly from the companies or perhaps from the government after a forced sale. Frei did not do this. If these shortcomings were due to the presence of capitalists, why leave the capitalists with 49 percent of the stock?

A third inconsistency of Chileanization involved the way the Christian Democrats implemented the details of the policy. When copper prices were down, Frei was friendlier to the copper companies, hoping to get them to continue producing. When they went up, even slightly and temporarily, Frei and then Tomic promised tougher terms for Chileanization. If a major complaint about the foreign MNCs was that they were selfish and shortsighted, why base the details of nationalization policy on short-term trends in the copper price?

Fourth, the Christian Democrats never explained why having only two major foreign owners was dangerous, but having a single state owner was not. They seemingly never considered methods to increase the number of owners. In addition, Chileanization did not produce a copper agency free from politics. The Chilean copper company suffered from the same problems of politicization as nationalized oil in Venezuela.

Chileanization was an attempt to steer a middle course between what Frei saw as the subservient policies of past Chilean administrations and the demands of the left for immediate nationalization. If Frei really expected to appease the left with Chileanization, he was disappointed. According to one of Frei's leftist opponents, he paid $175 million (the author inflated the actual price and seemed to include the interest also) for 51 percent of Anaconda, when the value of the company's Chilean holdings was only $181 million. It was the Allende government, this Chilean insisted, that was the real nationalizer of copper.

Left-of-center observers in the United States were also dissatisfied with Chileanization. According to one such commentator, copper companies were "running scared" in 1965, and Frei could have gotten a much better deal. During purchase negotiations, Frei did not challenge Kennecott's value estimate. One observer also contended that by allowing the foreigners to retain management posts, Frei failed to acquire real control over the industry. He merely made it less risky for the MNCs. Like Venezuelan leftists, critics of Chileanization insist that Kennecott's and Anaconda's agreements with the government gave them all the advantages they had had earlier, with none of the problems.[35]

In Chile, the state copper company became a haven for political friends of the government, both under Frei and Allende. In 1971, the president of the Andina mine was a Communist pharmacist.[36] One U.S. copper manager resigned rather than replace all his executives with Allende's political appointees. Frei's Christian Democrats are somewhat less culpable than their counterparts in Venezuela, since the party did not make the same concerted effort to use the copper company for partisan political gain. But the Christian Democrats can take little comfort from the fact that these particular excesses took place under the Popular Front government, for their policies had provided the opening for this sort of political manipulation. This points up the danger, once again, in suspending distrust of the state merely because a friendly party happens to be in power.

What Allende did with the issue of compensation also points up a failing of Christian Democratic nationalization policy. The principles behind nationalization, such as the demand that Chileans control Chilean resources, do not lend themselves to the sort of moderation the Christian Democrats want to project. If the copper belongs to the nation, then settling for partial control makes one a timid and reluctant nationalist.

Less concerned about moderate language than Frei, Allende was neither timid nor reluctant about taking over the copper industry. He argued that copper companies deserved no compensation and instituted a series of "back excess profits" taxes to charge against what Frei had promised the companies.

Far from paying compensation, Allende presented Anaconda and Kennecott with huge tax bills.[37] When Allende fell in 1973, Kennecott was still waiting for interest on its loan-back of $80 million.

It did not have to happen this way. Frei could have maintained that a genuine nationalist desired not only greater Chilean participation in the copper industry but also increased production. Frei could have sought additional foreign investors for Chilean copper to reduce the power of the two giant U.S. MNCs. He could have purchased 51 percent of the stock and then sold it to Chilean entrepreneurs, perhaps favoring these entrepreneurs with tax breaks. He could have sought more markets for Chilean copper.

All these efforts would have had the effects that the Christian Democrats profess to desire. More Chileans would have had a hand in the copper industry, its production would have gone up, and the dominance of two MNCs would have eroded. Allende would have faced a new class of Chilean capitalists instead of a population accustomed to state economic intervention.

NATIONALIZATION IN PRACTICE: EL SALVADOR'S COFFEE

Although discussions of nationalization usually involve mineral resources or industrial organizations, the actions of the Christian Democratic party in El Salvador toward that country's coffee growers can appropriately be considered in the same context. Since so much of El Salvador's wealth comes from coffee, the same motivation to nationalize exists. In addition, Christian Democrats themselves have drawn a connection between their actions toward coffee marketing and Venezuela's oil nationalization.

José Napoleón Duarte stated the basic theory behind nationalization in 1986 when he said on national television, "Coffee does not belong only to those who grow it, but to the entire nation."[38] During his stint as leader of the civilian-military junta, and later during his presidential administration, coffee growers were increasingly burdened by taxes and regulations. Production suffered in direct proportion.

Prior to the 1979 coup in El Salvador, coffee was the major source of El Salvador's prosperity, and coffee growers used their close government protection to insulate themselves from any domestic competition. Because the government could not regulate the international market, however, coffee growers did have to compete either with each other or with foreigners.

But coffee was a source of national income and national economic diversification long before it became nationalized. Its profits financed more coffee planting and paid for the development of cotton and sugar as export crops. In the late 1960s, coffee growers provided the investment to spur light industry. Private coffee growers were, in other words, accomplishing exactly what Catholic social thought recommends.

Such an enormous source of wealth did not escape the notice of El Salvador's new leaders in 1979, however. Decree 75, passed soon after the October coup, created the Instituto Nacional del Café, or Incafe. Duarte would later point to this event as the "nationalization" of El Salvador's coffee, which he compared to Venezuela's oil nationalization.

Incafe became the only legal marketing institution for coffee in El Salvador. Growers were required to sell their crop to Incafe for a government-set price below the market price. In theory, the difference is a tax on growers that the state can use to finance projects in economic development and diversification. Again in theory, this is no different from an income tax, except that collection is more efficient.

The tax soon became quite high, however. Incafe offered prices that were not only below the world market price but also below costs. Duarte announced in 1986 that farmers would receive $80 per quintal for their current crop, at a time when coffee was quoted on the New York exchange for $250 per quintal. In addition, Incafe was often months late in making payments.

The low prices Incafe offered forced many growers into short-term debt. Since the 1979 revolutionary government had also nationalized the banks, growers had to borrow from the state monopoly at 15 percent interest. At the same time, Incafe received payment for coffee in dollars and then paid farmers in local currency at an artificially low rate of exchange.

Not surprisingly, many coffee growers stopped production in the face of these multiple penalties. During the 1980–1981 season, Incafe's first, El Salvador's coffee yield fell 21.4 percent from the 1978–1979 base year. During the next three years, production fell from this base by 31.2 percent, 30.5 percent, and 35.3 percent, respectively.

Even Incafe did not attribute this drop to El Salvador's guerrilla war. Speaking in London in 1985, an Incafe representative said, "It is not guerrilla war but production costs above sales prices that depress Salvadoran coffee productivity."[39] This drop in productivity prevented El Salvador from taking advantage of problems in the Brazilian coffee crop in 1985–1986. Even with the higher prices, there was little incentive to get coffee to market.

Nationalization did nothing to solve the alleged problems of private ownership. Where government officials acted differently from private owners, it was to the detriment of El Salvador's economy. Incafe also represented a serious increase in government economic power, coupled with a multipronged attack on private entrepreneurs.

To argue that the nationalization was necessary to wrest the coffee crop from the few families that controlled it begs the question. If few families with concentrated ownership is bad, one government with monopoly ownership is no better, unless one assumes a particular wisdom or goodness from government officials.

As elsewhere, there is no evidence of any such moral superiority. In fact, there is little evidence one way or the other about Incafe's operations. There is no audited statement for four of the agency's first five years. What is known is that by 1988, Incafe was $100 million in debt. The industry that even in the hands of self-serving oligarchs had at least turned a profit became a serious drag on the economy once the government took it over. It also became a source of corruption.

Duarte's successor, ARENA president Alfredo Cristiani, has sought to reverse Christian Democratic policy. Having abolished Incafe immediately after coming into office, Cristiani reestablished a free internal market in coffee and is moving slowly toward freeing sales to the international market as well.

CONCLUSION

The above is by no means a comprehensive list of the capitalistic enterprises that Christian Democrats coveted while in power. Christian Democrats were also enthusiastic in their attempts to control banks. Copei, for example, nationalized foreign brokerage houses in 1972 and required that foreign banks sell 80 percent of their stock to Venezuelans. At the same time, Venezuelans were discouraged from opening savings accounts in foreign banks.[40]

After his party lost the 1973 election, Caldera recommended that the Venezuelan government should use its decree powers to nationalize electric companies, television stations, radio stations, and milk companies, in addition to the oil industry.[41] Copei also established the Corporación Venezolana de Guyana (CVG), a government holding company that controlled iron, steel, and hydroelectric power. The CVG is known for its grandiose plans based on overestimates of future Venezuelan demand for steel.[42]

The reach of the Venezuelan state into the economy has grown since the oil nationalization. The country's Internal Market Law, for example, required all 1,800 petrol outlets in the country to buy from the national oil agency. About 90 percent of the owners of these outlets were middle-class Venezuelans.

Copei also attacked the provisions of the 1976 nationalization laws that allowed for mixed corporations, making no distinction between foreign owners and Venezuelan owners. Herrera insisted that domestic investors also be excluded from the oil industry, saying, "The oil industry must be commanded, basically, by the state."[43]

Chilean Christian Democrats also desired to nationalize more than copper. They created or expanded government participation in Chile's steel, auto assembly, nitrates, and pulp paper industries.[44] The Salvadoran government wholly or partially controls the sugar, cement, and textile industries, while controlling marketing of basic foods produced or imported, including rice, beans, and powdered milk. This control has become a scandalous source of waste and corruption, with the government destroying 1.6 million pounds of food in 1988 that had rotted in government warehouses.

This disaster gives an indication of the Christian Democratic attitude toward commercial capitalism even in nonessential industries. It is difficult to examine the record of Christian Democratic nationalization policy without concluding that the real reason for undertaking such policies had little to do with foreign owners and a lot more to do with a basic preference for state economic activity and an equally basic distrust of private, uncontrolled economic activity.

Catholic social thought is no great friend of capitalism, but the popes did seek a way to retain capitalism's positive aspects, such as its productivity and its rewards for initiative and imagination. To limit capitalism's negatives, including radical individualism, materialism, and the resulting exploitation, the popes preferred to use persuasion to make capitalists less immoral. They also wished to use moral and economic persuasion to make capitalists more concerned with the long-term effects of their actions. Nationalization, for its part, has encouraged the bureaucratic managers that it creates to be more shortsighted than the capitalists.

In addition, Catholic social thought seeks to blunt the hard edges of capitalism by multiplying the number of capitalists. This sets some capitalists against others, forcing them to compete on prices and wages. Small capitalists are also more likely to form independent social groups and far less likely to have the dominant economic position that allows large capitalists to induce the state to protect its interests.

It is possible to outline the elements of a nationalization policy that would achieve all the stated goals of the Christian Democrats, as well as the goals of Catholic social thought. It is possible to find ways to increase national participation in an industry without permanently increasing state power. The Christian Democrats in Chile, Venezuela, and El Salvador did not even make a perfunctory attempt to develop or to enact such a nationalization project. Rather, their actions indicate a single-minded attempt to empower the state and then, to varying degrees, to use that power for private purposes.

The Christian Democrats' attitude toward foreign as well as domestic participation in basic industries mirrors their entire perspective toward business and commercial capitalism. As we shall see in Chapter 6, the attitudes of Christian Democrats in this regard have become decidedly unfriendly.

NOTES

1. Edward Williams, *Latin American Christian Democratic Parties* (Knoxville: University of Tennessee Press, 1967), p. 124.

2. Donald Herman, *Christian Democracy in Venezuela* (Chapel Hill: University of North Carolina Press, 1980), p. 51.

3. Miguel Jorrín and John Martz, *Latin American Political Thought and Ideology* (Chapel Hill: University of North Carolina Press, 1970), p. 422.

4. Gerhard Cartáy Ramírez, *Política y partidos modernos en Venezuela* (Caracas: Ediciones Centauro, 1983), p. 95.

5. Alfredo Peña, *Conversaciones con Luis Herrera Campins* (Caracas: Editorial Ateneo de Caracas, 1978), pp. 58–59.

6. Eduardo Frei, *Latin America: The Hopeful Option* (Maryknoll, N.Y.: Orbis Books, 1978), p. 205.

7. Eduardo Frei, "The Second Latin American Revolution," *Foreign Affairs* 50, 1 (1971): 89–90.

8. Ibid., pp. 93–94.

9. Williams, p. 141.

10. *Time*, 2 May 1969, p. 30.

11. Williams, p. 159.

12. *Business Week*, 11 March 1972, p. 50.

13. *Business Week*, 13 October 1975, pp. 59–60.

14. *New York Times*, 30 November 1978, p. 11.

15. Ross Miloy, "The Venezuela Story," *Progressive*, February 1981, p. 40.

16. *U.S. News and World Report*, 6 July 1981, pp. 33–34.

17. Donald E. Blank, "Oil and Democracy in Venezuela," *Current History* no. 78 (February 1980): 71.

18. *Business Week*, 27 October 1962, p. 50.

19. *Time*, 22 May 1964, p. 96.

20. *Intellect*, January 1976, p. 279.

21. Blank, p. 73.

22. *Business Week*, 13 October 1975, p. 60.

23. John D. Martz, "The Crisis of Venezuelan Democracy," *Current History* 83, 490 (February 1984): 74.

24. *Business Week*, 12 September 1983, p. 42.

25. *Business Week*, 5 December 1983, p. 101.

26. *Business Week*, 18 October 1982, p. 51.

27. Latin America Regional Reports, *Andean Report*, 7 September 1988, p. 3.

28. *U.S. News and World Report*, 4 January 1965, p. 69.

29. *U.S. News and World Report*, 21 September 1964, p. 76.

30. *America*, 9 January 1965, p. 38.

31. Williams, p. 151.

32. *Time*, 1 January 1965, p. 31.

33. *Business Week*, 10 October 1966, p. 81.

34. *Time*, 27 June 1969, p. 75.

35. *Commonweal*, 29 December 1967, p. 407.

36. *Business Week*, 21 August 1971, p. 38.

37. *Newsweek*, 11 October 1971, p. 77.

38. *Wall Street Journal*, 31 January 1986, p. 21.

39. *Wall Street Journal*, 8 March 1985, p. 31.

40. *Business Week*, 11 March 1972, p. 52.

41. Herman, p. 201.

42. *Forbes*, 26 September 1983, p. 85.

43. Quoted in Peña, p. 59.

44. Robert Alexander, *Latin American Political Parties* (New York: Praeger Publishers, 1973), p. 330.

6

Christian Democratic Attitudes toward Commercial Capitalism

Much of the skepticism and distrust that Christian Democrats have traditionally shown toward private capital accumulation was examined in the chapters on land reform and nationalization. The Christian Democrats' anti-business policies in these areas affect only one or two sectors of the economy. They do not form an adequate basis for drawing conclusions about how Christian Democrats act toward other, less economically crucial commercial activities.

This chapter will show that in their policies toward foreign investment, domestic investment, taxes, and foreign exchange regulation, Latin America's Christian Democrats pursue policies designed to limit severely the scope of independent economic activity. Christian Democrats are seemingly motivated by extreme misgivings about the wisdom and virtue of private businesspeople. The parties have consistently acted to increase the economic power of the state at the expense of private citizens.

In doing so, they have abandoned a central tenet of Catholic social thought. As we saw in Chapter 1, the Catholic popes have criticized capitalism's excesses. They have maintained, however, that building up the power of the state to combat it is dangerous. State economic power, because it is more unified and subject to fewer checks, should be increased only with extreme caution. What Latin America's Christian Democrats have done, instead, is to create a new economic oligarchy.

GENERAL CONSIDERATIONS ABOUT BUSINESS

The Christian Democratic attitude toward business is neatly summed up by Leonard Gross in his book on the Chilean Christian Democratic experiment. Chilean Christian Democrats believed that left alone, the Chilean capitalist would not change. "He would have to be taught, perhaps compelled, even coerced."[1] Gross means that capitalists would not voluntarily continue accumulating wealth and producing goods once the government made it clear they would not be able to keep the fruits of their labor. The Christian Democratic insistence that capitalists pretend that they still have incentives, when these have been removed, is the source of their impatience with the business class.

Even León Febres Cordero, the Christian Democratic president of Ecuador, himself a former businessman and candidate of the Guayaquil business class, became impatient with his former comrades once he became president. He directed his ire at businesspeople unwilling to compete: "Those bad businessmen," he said, "who think about the ease of surviving without fighting, without effort, have begun to put themselves at the service of inimical political currents."[2]

In their theoretical statements, Christian Democrats, following Catholic social thought, show impatience with the ethics of business and with the structure of individualism and incentive that makes capitalism work. Christian Democrats in almost all Latin American countries have repeated the belief that capitalism cannot work in the Third World. Without ever clearly examining how free enterprise created wealth in the First World, or how former Third World nations like Japan or South Korea managed to leave poverty behind, and without making the case that genuine capitalism had ever been tried in Latin America, Christian Democrats insist with religious fervor that capitalism has failed and will fail.

Increased governmental "energy," they believe, is needed to make important decisions and to "rectify the economic problems of the country." For Chile's Eduardo Frei, the state must, among other things, plan the country's economic development, correct the international trade inequality, make basic investments, do basic research and development, and defend against monopolies. "The wide field of economic life within this rationally defined area," Frei insisted, "will be open [to private business] and will not be uselessly invaded by the state."

Frei believed that the state should take on the major part of industrial development partly because fledgling industrial economies require protection from competition. In addition, only the state can rapidly accumulate capital. Finally, the state must control prices to protect the lower classes. As the government takes on each of these appointed tasks, Frei's "wide field of economic life" shrinks.

Rafael Ángel Calderón, of the Social Christian Unity Party (PUSC), was elected president of Costa Rica in 1990 and became the continent's newest Christian Democratic president. The long-stifled productive sector of Costa Rica noted hopefully that some of Calderón's advisors were businesspeople, and his Central Bank president an advocate of liberalization. At the beginning of his term, he promised to create thousands of small businesses, many of them related to tourism.

Any hopes for a less intrusive government, however, soon vanished. Calderón's inaugural address revealed his thoughts about the proper role of the state: "We believe in a state that guides, regulates and promotes development, not in a state that smothers, replaces and hampers private initiative." The signal to business was clear: Act under our direction or we will replace and smother you.

Calderón echoed other sentiments of his Social Democratic predecessors in his inaugural address: "We cannot build a future clinging to a liberalism of the last century that promotes the single-minded doctrine of laissez-faire." Christian Democrats are vague in their definitions of capitalism, and even more so when asked to list recent examples of pure capitalism in practice. They are, however, quite clear in their desire to limit independent economic activity and in their perception that any unregulated accumulation of wealth is dangerous.

Catholic social thought suggests limiting the power of large capitalists by forcing them to compete with many smaller capitalists. Thus, Catholic social thought is not allied with laissez-faire capitalism. A complete absence of government regulation of business could result in consolidation of commercial activity under a small number of large capitalists. Government activity may have to be substantial, but it should be directed at preventing serious abuses of labor, avoiding violent swings in the employment or inflation rate, outlawing unfair price gouging, and providing basic services like law and order.

All these goals except the last can be met by ensuring market access for newcomers to the economic system. More businesses mean more competition for labor, steadier employment, more choice for consumers, and more downward pressure on prices. A policy toward business based on Catholic social thought favors small business. Christian Democrats, however, have consistently pursued policies that have, under the guise of limiting capitalism, driven small capitalists out of business while allowing large capitalists to survive and prosper.

ATTITUDES TOWARD FOREIGN INVESTMENT

The attitude of Chilean and Venezuelan Christian Democrats toward foreign investment was described in the chapter on nationalization. Recall that the Chilean and Venezuelan Christian Democrats feared foreign investment and wished their major industries to be under political control. Christian

Democrats believe that productive enterprises can make decisions based on economic criteria, and continue to be productive, under political control.

Even where they have not moved toward outright nationalization, Christian Democrats continue to place significant barriers in the way of foreign direct investment. The confiscation of the most productive and profitable industries in a country is often enough to scare off investment capital. Smaller investors are faced with an unattractive dilemma. If their enterprises grow and prosper, they may attract the attention of the same government that nationalized other growing and prosperous industries. If they fail to prosper, their investment is lost.

In an interview with a North American news magazine just after his election, Frei promised to "try to stimulate private investment, both foreign and domestic." Such foreign capital, he insisted, "had and will continue to have ample guarantees in Chile." These guarantees, however, would be available only to foreign investors who signed a contract with the Chilean government.[3]

Ecuador's Febres Cordero appeared to be friendly to foreign investment. In the first round of the 1984 campaign, he promised to seek foreign investors and criticized what he called the shortsightedness of the Osvaldo Hurtado regime. He even promised that foreign capital would be welcome in areas of high priority to government.[4] Near the end of his term, in one of a number of speeches he made boasting of his success, Febres declared that his administration had lifted the ban on foreign investment in oil exploration, allowing such exploration for the first time in 13 years.[5]

Among Febres's early moves in this direction were the contracts he signed with Exxon and Occidental Petroleum to commence exploratory drilling in the oil-rich Amazon region. Febres promised the U.S. MNCs full capital recovery before they would have to pay taxes.[6] Ecuador withdrew from the Andean Pact regulatory system to make this deal.

For all of this stated confidence in foreign capital, however, Febres offered investors nothing. Once the oil was discovered, it went immediately into government hands. The people he describes as foreign investors, therefore, are really foreign contractors, with little interest in the outcome of their labors. Moreover, their invitation to Ecuador depended on their acquaintance with government officials.

Had Febres been interested in a foreign investment policy consistent with the principles of Catholic social thought, he would have allowed foreigners to explore, drill, and sell oil. Ecuador could have levied a tax on the companies' profits and used tax incentives to encourage Ecuadorans to enter the oil business also. He might have begun a government program to purchase stock in foreign oil companies and sell it to Ecuadoran entrepreneurs. The result would have been diversity of participation in the oil market, not just state control.

Rafael Caldera, the founder of Venezuela's Christian Democratic Copei, is critical of foreign investment in his country. The National Union of Students (UNE), a precursor to Copei, while critical of both the United States and the Soviet Union, was always more critical of the United States and in particular of foreign petroleum companies.[7]

Caldera himself, writing in 1962, spoke of the need to retain the services of foreign capital, but he also disparaged "robber barons" from abroad, who, he insisted, would resist "truly constructive enterprise."[8] Copei initiated the "Venezuelan oil for Venezuela" movement and wished to hurry the nationalization of foreign holdings. Venezuela's oil riches have since enabled it to make its own foreign investments and to provide foreign aid. Even here, Christian Democrats have discouraged independent economic activity.

Venezuela's Copei has imitated the foreign economic policy of Acción Democrática, its rival party. The determination of the AD administration of Carlos Andrés Pérez, which held office during the first oil boom, to keep the tidal wave of petrodollars out of Venezuela's economy prompted the move to foreign investment.[9] Using the money in this way, instead of diversifying the Venezuelan economy or building up the domestic private sector, reveals a statist bias.

Such a bias is also evident in how the petrodollars were used. Venezuela contributed 3 percent of its GNP to its Caribbean neighbors.[10] Most of this was in the form of contributions to multilateral lending institutions, including the World Bank, the Interamerican Development Bank, the International Monetary Fund, the Andean Development Corporation, and the Caribbean Development Bank.[11]

These institutions lend money to governments, and by increasing their liquidity, Venezuela's apparent beneficence served to dramatically increase the debt burden of the Caribbean microstates. At the same time, the central governments of these states were the only entities legally able to borrow from the international lending institutions. Their private sectors were left out completely.

Although Venezuela also sold oil to Caribbean states at cut rates, these transactions tended to be government to government.[12] The governments of these small states became the only entities with access to lending. Venezuelan oil sales also allowed them to nationalize oil distribution with a more or less certain source to use as leverage. In short, Venezuelan statism was exported.

Through the Venezuelan Investment Fund (FIV), Venezuela has directed intensive efforts toward its Caribbean neighbors. Technical cooperation agreements, social welfare programs, health care grants, and infrastructure funding were all part of the Pérez government's efforts. All these were government to government, and all were directed at building up state power in the "beneficiary" state while tying that newly bolstered government more closely to Venezuelan largess.[13]

The election of Luis Herrera Campins in 1978 brought a continuation of the policy of increased Caribbean influence through oil money, albeit with a slightly different slant. Herrera sought to spread Venezuelan influence through the funding of Christian Democratic parties throughout Latin America, and especially in the Caribbean.[14] His wholehearted support for the embattled regime of José Napoleón Duarte in El Salvador was part of this policy and was consistent with Herrera's preference for statist parties.

Christian Democratic regimes have been less hostile to foreign investment than many other Latin American governments, but they certainly have not been friendly. By making the conditions for foreign investment so stringent, they have helped to ensure that only large and powerful MNCs would be interested. The prospects are simply too daunting for smaller firms.

ATTITUDES TOWARD DOMESTIC INVESTMENT

With Christian Democratic governments in Latin American consolidating their control over agriculture through land reform, and over their countries' most important industries through nationalization, there was a shrinking economic sector available to private investors. Even as this sector shrank, however, Christian Democratic governments sought greater control over it. With notable differences in methods, all Christian Democrats were motivated by a basic distrust of business and determined to limit its independent activities.

Chile

Christian Democratic theory does allow private initiative. In fact, Christian Democrats argue that industrial corporations should emerge primarily from private initiative.[15] However, even though Christian Democrats look to the capitalist system to provide such initiative, they insist on managing it. Capitalism based on individualism, Frei wrote, is inimical to the creation of an economic system in which rights can be protected in "a regime based on freedom."[16]

Two of the most crucial factors in encouraging investment are economic and political stability. Christian Democrats have been consistently unable to provide this. In some ways, the Christian Democrats' effects on business were indirect and unintentional. Nevertheless, they were undeniable. In Chile, Frei's economic policies led to uncontrolled inflation near the end of his term. Only the hyperinflation of the Allende years caused many Chileans to forget just how bad conditions were in late 1969 and 1970.

Inflation grew so bad that at one point, a major Santiago construction firm had to announce that its estimates would remain valid for only eight days, instead of a month.[17] Add to this the difficulties in planning even a quarter ahead and the general decline in consumer confidence, and the formula for a general economic slowdown is laid.

Domestic small- and medium-sized businesses bore the brunt of such policies. Chile's copper industry had rising global demand to pull it through. Farmers could at least grow their own food. Large businesses could more easily respond to changing conditions or pay lobbyists to procure exceptions to government regulations. Businesses too small to confront government directly and too small to be an economic subject, rather than an object, suffered the most.

If small businesses cannot survive, then the only remaining capitalists will be huge and threatening, or foreign and uncontrollable. If productive private businesses are denied the chance to earn or to keep income and forced to compete with protected counterparts or even with nationalized businesses having the strength of the national tax base at their disposal, they must eventually fail. The Christian Democrats' contention that investment must come from the state became a self-fulfilling prophecy.

Venezuela

Venezuela's 1961 constitution, on which Copei collaborated, mandates state control of the national economy. Article 97 of this document contains the state's determination to place heavy industry under its control by limiting private participation. Article 98 continues in the same vein. While enjoining the state to protect private initiative, it forbids the latter to interfere in the "state's facilities to plan, rationalize and stimulate production and regulate circulation, distribution and consumption of the national wealth, in order to encourage the economic development of the country."[18]

Caldera himself, writing in 1962, indicates the direction of his thought more clearly when he rejects "conservative [economic] patterns" and speaks of the need to modernize "worn out systems of production." Caldera gives the impression that Venezuela's economy was capitalistic prior to 1958. Internationally, Caldera expresses admiration for the Alliance for Progress, which was marked by high levels of government-to-government transfers.[19]

Venezuelan state control over domestic investment has benefited the large and well-connected in business disproportionately. The experience of the Andean Pact is instructive. Acción Democrática President Raúl Leoni was a strong proponent of the idea of a customs union among Andean states to fight "imperialism," but his apparent enthusiasm for the project was not sufficient to make his countrymen actually agree to join. It would be left to the Caldera regime to work out the details.

Among these details were over 450 exemptions for Venezuelan products from the customs system of the Andean Pact.[20] Once again, the foreign policy goal of economic integration did not outweigh the determination to use the Andean Pact to enhance government ability to create privileged sectors in the Venezuelan economy. By deciding which enterprises would receive the coveted exemptions, the Caldera administration was able to continue government protection for select client industries and to bind the private sector even more closely to government.

Herrera harbored even greater distrust of domestic investment than did

Caldera. For Herrera, this distrust extended to any autonomous property holding. Copei, he insisted, does not prohibit private property. The public, however, has the right to proscribe harmful uses of private property, especially in fundamental areas of economic importance. The agent for enforcing this right is the state.[21]

The Herrera administration took over Venezuela's growing external debt to increase state control over domestic businesses. Much of this debt had been acquired by Venezuela's private businesses. Herrera's government responded to their plight by refusing private businesses permission to raise prices to earn the money necessary to repay their debts. The government first froze prices, then allowed them to rise only with government permission.[22]

At the same time, businesses in the private sector were forced to register their foreign debt in Caracas, providing relevant documents, and to do so during a three-month period in 1983. Copei created a government commission to examine the debt and to take over the payments directly to the creditors. The ability of Venezuela's private businesses to acquire more credit became dependent on the goodwill of the government. Herrera's policy made foreign creditors, even those willing to invest in Venezuela's private sector, regard the country's businesspeople as not fully competent agents. The Copei president helped ensure that creditors would make investment decisions based on a businessperson's government connections, not on the value of his investment project.

Almost overnight, according to one scholar, Venezuela's private-sector interest group, FEDECAMERAS, went from being a major player in Venezuelan politics to a supplicant, dependent upon government largess. Businesses too small to influence FEDECAMERAS, or to pressure the government directly, suffered even more. With all their suspicion of capitalism, Catholic social thought insists on the rights of professional organizations and businesspeople's associations to exist and to function. Herrera's debt policy destroyed the independence of FEDECAMERAS.[23]

Copei also discouraged Venezuelan domestic investment in the oil industry. New laws passed during Caldera's administration discouraged the operation of small oil companies. Increasingly strict regulations on entry into the oil business kept newcomers, including Venezuelan newcomers, out of the oil market.

The principle effects of statism were increases in waste, corruption, and inefficiency. At the same time, the fortunes of Venezuela's economy became inseparable from the fortunes of state enterprises. High oil prices disguised the private sector's withering for a time, but when oil prices dropped in 1986, the shrinkage of the private sector was manifest.[24]

By 1988, small business had largely gone underground in Venezuela. Only nontraditional exports, which had hitherto escaped government notice, and gold, which was mined largely without control by small and secretive prospectors, showed any signs of fueling the Venezuelan economic engine.[25]

El Salvador

The Salvadoran statist economic policies on agriculture were matched by policies equally unfriendly to other business enterprises. From 1979 to 1984, an estimated $1 billion in domestic private investment was lost to other countries. The single most important factor in inducing investors to remove their money was the 1979 nationalization of the banking industry.

Nationalized banks have no flexibility to make lending decisions on economic grounds, nor can they alter their interest rates to take into account greater risk. Rather, their criteria for lending are political, with friends of the ruling party getting loans first. Disgruntled customers cannot go to competing banks in El Salvador, so they place their capital elsewhere.

This situation provided an additional incentive for those who were already considering moving their capital because of El Salvador's civil war. Because of the war, the Salvadoran Christian Democrats had to work harder than any other Christian Democrats to increase domestic investment. Instead of doing so, they provided no incentives and much discouragement.

Ecuador

Christian Democratic president Osvaldo Hurtado's brief administration saw an increase in the size of the country's bureaucracy and a growing burden on private economic transactions.[26] It was this statism that Febres Cordero had vowed to fight, using strong language to separate himself from the Christian Democrats of Hurtado's stripe.

Febres said in 1986, "Chambers of Commerce are instruments to defend businessmen from the continuous attacks of the State." Later he added, "We are either a country with a free economy, or we are communitarian socialists, but we cannot be both."[27] After taking office, Febres recalled, "[In 1984] we had to offer confidence to investors, create productive jobs, diversify production, rescue the farming sector."[28]

Febres had promised to free the economy from the burden of regulation and bureaucracy that was choking it. According to one analyst, traditional exporters stood to gain the most from his economic plans.[29] Febres began his term by freeing interest rates to increase national savings and by freeing controlled prices to encourage producers. He eliminated most price controls, including controls and subsidies on basic foods.

In the early years of Febres's term, these policies seemed to be working. Inflation went from 31 percent in 1984 to 23 percent in 1986. Real GDP grew by almost 4 percent per year, and it grew 2.9 percent in 1986, even with falling oil prices. Ecuador even showed a budget surplus in 1986.[30] In addition, the policy was consistent with Catholic social thought. Far from traditional exports leading the way, nontraditional exports, those attracting Ecuador's more daring entrepreneurs, increased by an annual rate of 10 percent.

Nontraditional exports rose by 10 percent per year during Febres's first three years in office. Shrimp exports, for example, rose from $179.3 million in 1983 to $419.3 million in 1987, nearly double that year's banana earnings. Flowers, in spite of protectionism in the United States, rose from $220,000 in 1985 to $6 million in 1986. Fruit exports rose 407 percent during the same one-year period. The Ecuadoran Export Federation also promoted grains, vegetables, and poultry for export.[31]

For the authors of Catholic social thought, this is exactly what is supposed to happen. More businesses, and more types of businesses, mean more competition, more opportunities, and less chance that businesspeople will work together against workers or consumers. It can, of course, also bring more destructive selfishness. Since government action cannot remove this in any case, expanding and fragmenting the capitalists at least mitigates its effects.

When a series of economic reverses hit Ecuador in 1986–1987, combined with a series of debilitating political problems, Febres reversed his free market course and increased government spending on public works, wages, and subsidies. Drops in the price of oil quickly eliminated the budget surplus, and the deficit swelled to 10 percent of GDP.

At the same time, the declining fortunes of the country made Febres all the more politically vulnerable. He tried to co-opt part of the business class by selectively controlling the exchange rate for import and export transactions. Far from removing government from the operations of business, allowing it to proceed freely as he had promised, Febres, like so many other Christian Democrats, decided to use state economic power for private political purposes.

Guatemala

Vinicio Cerezo's victory in the 1984 election in Guatemala seemed to portend a friendlier relationship between a Christian Democratic government and business. Among other positive signals, Cerezo appointed as finance minister Rodolfo Paz Andrade, scion of a successful business family. Indeed, the country's private sector was willing to help Cerezo establish democracy in Guatemala, and the beginning of his term saw an injection of the investment capital that a skeptical business community had withheld for years.

Cerezo made some attempts to reduce state intervention in the economy. For example, he dropped many price controls and replaced them with free market fluctuations. He did not, however, provide other incentives necessary to spur production. In the short term, uncontrolled prices, after years of being kept at unrealistically low levels, went up rapidly.

Cerezo expressed shock and indignation at this outcome in a 1987 speech, the same speech in which he took credit for releasing prices in the first place. Near the end of the speech he said: "We must control [prices]. However, since some people will not understand the need for such control, we will implement measures to reduce the cost of 240 basic products."[32]

Later in 1987, Cerezo expressed similar dissatisfaction with the private sector for raising prices to meet increases on energy tariffs that went into effect that year. This tariff increase, the president insisted, did not justify any increase in prices. He promised to "talk to the economic minister to create mechanisms to verify that any price increase will be exactly proportional to the energy tariff increase."[33]

Once again, a Christian Democratic president is casting the private sector in the role of omnipotent villain. Cerezo leaves the impression that businesses in Guatemala set prices by administrative fiat, much the way the government does. If this is indeed the case, then it is a symptom of too little competition. Such collusion becomes more difficult with more producers. Multiplying the number of businesses helps to prevent many of capitalism's abuses. Christian Democrats have consistently discouraged the formation of small businesses and their policies have left only large and foreign businesses in operation. The result has brought demands for even more state economic power.

TAX POLICIES UNDER CHRISTIAN DEMOCRACY

U.S. Chief Justice John Marshall once declared, "The power to tax involves the power to destroy." Christian Democratic politicians have realized the potential of using tax policy to destroy private enterprise, or at least to alter the relationship it has with government.

Frei promised Chileans a moderate tax policy when he was elected, although he also promised that land taxes and income taxes would rise. Frei's higher income tax failed to perform as hoped, however. Based on a simple understanding of economics, Frei evidently hoped that increases in income tax rates would bring in more revenue.

What he overlooked was the tendency of such rates, at the margin, to discourage greater productivity. One young Chilean executive lamented in 1967, "I am up in the 40 percent bracket. Where will it end?"[34] Such a person has little incentive to produce. Chile's top tax rate under Frei was 60 percent. Frei once understood the link between incentive and production. In an article published before his election, he said that Chile had a middle class with "an extraordinary human reserve, responsive to the slightest stimulus or the weakest incentive."[35]

At the beginning of Frei's term, the conservative Chilean Senate rejected a government proposal to raise real estate taxes 150 percent. Although land tax rates remained low, reassessment made actual payments soar. Under Frei, the assessed value of urban property rose nearly 600 percent, with rural property assessments rising 145 percent. With help from the U.S. Internal Revenue Service, Frei also increased greatly the number of tax officials in the field. Better enforcement plus higher income taxes allowed revenues to rise from 14 percent of GNP in 1964 to 20 percent in 1967.

How much of this revenue increase was due to more government income or to a shrinking Chilean GNP is not clear. Even more difficult is to measure how much the GNP might have grown had taxes not removed the incentives to invest. Yet under the circumstances, it is very clear why Frei thought that businesses were always large and powerful. His policies had killed the smaller ones.

Frei also planned to use tax incentives to get Chilean businesses to move to less-crowded parts of the country.[36] Like many other Christian Democratic policies designed to get a certain response from business, this policy was undertaken in a vacuum. Chilean businesses might have considered moving from Santiago had Frei combined tax incentives with other measures. The desire to move cannot be created out of thin air. Businesses saw that the best roads and infrastructure were around the capital and, more importantly, that the most important economic decisions were made by politicians. Had Frei more effectively practiced the Catholic social principle of subsidiarity, his efforts to disperse Chilean business would have succeeded.

Febres Cordero did little to lighten the tax burden or even to rationalize Ecuador's bewildering array of tax laws. He made an effort to reduce the burden on consumers of imported goods by lifting import quotas on 600 difference items and reducing tariffs.[37] In a speech on the economy in 1987, Febres said that he had "eliminate[d] once and for all the clever mechanism of bans on foreign trade that create[d] serious distortions and promote[d] contraband."[38]

The effort to reduce tariffs went slowly, however, and advanced only after long negotiations with businesspeople opposed to foreign competition. By the end of his term, tariffs could still raise the cost of manufactured imports 335 percent and the cost of all imports an average of 36.8 percent. Febres's stated intention to provide income tax relief also went unfulfilled. In 1988, there were still 78 separate taxes, with a 60 percent top income tax rate.

Taxes at this level prevent significant rises in national savings. Even Febres's interest rate deregulation could not spark savings. Taxes of such complexity require new businesses to hire teams of tax lawyers, who contribute nothing to productivity. Here again, a Christian Democrat provided no real incentive for citizens to create wealth and then complained when they failed to do so.

Cerezo also maintained high taxes in Guatemala. In 1987, this supposed friend of business imposed a sweeping "tax reform" that threatened his presidency. The plan called for higher rates, a steeper progression, extension of the value-added tax to more goods, a stamp tax on security bonds (necessary to conduct business), and a customs service tax for imports and exports (in addition to the regular tariffs). Along with these new levies went the promise of no new taxes for the remainder of the Cerezo administration.[39]

Guatemalans were not impressed with the promise and were enraged by the higher taxes. In September and October 1987, the business community staged two successful general strikes, with street vendors (small capitalists) prominent among the protestors. Cerezo retained the new taxes, however, sacrificing his early support from the productive community. In 1990 Cerezo claimed that his administration had eliminated many obstacles and taxes.

The new taxes gave the government a one-year increase in revenue. By 1989, however, the tax reform lacked significant effects insofar as tax collections were concerned. Taxes have the invisible effect of stifling productive economic activity that might have taken place, thus reducing the GNP available for taxation.

Again, such policies hurt small businesses most and induce larger businesses to pull back, to go elsewhere, and generally to act like Christian Democrats think they are going to act anyway. Policies that crush the private sector end up confirming the government officials' belief that only government action can bring about economic development.

The Christian Democratic regime in Costa Rica seems determined to pursue the same tax policies as its neighbors in Guatemala and El Salvador. President Calderón's economic policy included a promise to "improve tax and fee collection" while discontinuing tax exemptions on staples and raising the consumption tax from 10 percent to 13 percent. Professionals and businesspeople, as well as workers and retirees, saw their taxes go up 30 percent to 65 percent, depending on their income.[40]

Some might argue that since the tax rates in these Latin American countries are in some cases substantially lower than U.S. income tax rates in the 1970s, these rates are not really oppressive or counterproductive. On the contrary, Latin America's chronic economic stagnation requires even more incentives to save, invest, and produce than were needed in the United States. Not incidentally, the United States eventually found that to encourage investment, its tax rates had to go down also.

CHRISTIAN DEMOCRATIC EXCHANGE RATE POLICY

One of the most effective ways that states without a convertible currency have found to raise revenue is to take advantage of the business community's need for internationally accepted hard currency. In most of Latin America, a private citizen who wishes to negotiate a purchase from a foreigner will have to promise payment in an internationally convertible currency, usually U.S. dollars.

The private citizen must make application to a government bureaucracy for this currency; he is not allowed to purchase it himself. Moreover, in most countries he is required to pay a higher price for the dollars than the current market exchange. In addition, there is frequently a fee for this unwanted service. Thus, the government can gain revenue both from what is called the "exchange spread," the difference between the official rate and the market rate, and from the fee. The result makes buying imports, sometimes already heavily taxed, even more expensive.

Punitive exchange rate policies fall more heavily on smaller businesses, which operate closer to the margin. They are less able to manipulate exchange rates than large businesses, which start with more available capital. In some cases, the government retains the right to reject a private citizen's foreign exchange application altogether. The opportunities for corruption, and for favoring one business over another, are rife. This illustrates why Catholic social thought seeks to limit state economic power.

Herrera partly responded to falling oil prices during his term by taking complete control of Venezuela's foreign exchange purchases. In September 1984, Herrera established a three-tiered exchange plan that would double the foreign debt burden of the private sector, by making their foreign exchange more expensive, while providing the state with cheap money.[41]

Government decrees stated which "categories of debt" were entitled to foreign exchange at the preferential rate.[42] The best rate was reserved for state companies; private importers faced a wider exchange spread. Worst off were businesses without the government connections to have their operations declared eligible for better rates.

It was left to AD to promise to end exchange rate manipulation. Jaime Lusinchi, the AD winner of the 1983 election, loosened exchange rate rules somewhat while in office, but he did not change the fundamental structure. The issue reappeared in the 1988 presidential campaign, when Carlos Andrés Pérez of AD faced Eduardo Fernández of Copei.

During the campaign, both candidates sought the support of FEDECAMERAS, Venezuela's business interest group. (This in itself shows the evolution of the two parties since the 1950s, when business assumed that Copei was a friend and AD an enemy.) The business group itself desired an immediate move to a freely floating exchange rate. Pérez promised a policy much friendlier to private business than his Copei opponent. Speaking before FEDECAMERAS in July, he promised not only a single exchange rate but also substantial privatization of state industry and more liberal rules on foreign investment.[43]

In a speech before the business group in November, Fernández promised a single foreign exchange rate "eventually." In the short term, what his government deemed "essential" or "strategic" sectors of the economy would continue to receive preferential treatment. In the end, FEDECAMERAS decided that its economic plans were more broadly in line with AD's than with Copei's.[44]

In El Salvador, the Christian Democrats nationalized banking and exchange transactions upon entering the military-civilian junta in 1980. Anyone wishing dollars to pay for imports had to seek Central Bank approval. The Salvadoran Christian Democrats established different exchange rates for different sorts of transactions, inviting inefficiency and corruption.

The chances for corruption increase because government agencies retain access to the lower, preferred rate for their transactions. Any private Salvadoran who even indirectly competes with a government agency is thus at two immediate disadvantages. First, a foreign exchange application from such a business is likely to be turned down by Central Bank officials. Second, even if the exchange application receives approval, the private citizen must spend more local currency for the same number of dollars.

Christian Democrats in Ecuador and Guatemala have made some effort to close exchange rate gaps in their two countries. Febres Cordero had promised exchange rate relief in his 1984 campaign. He made no serious moves in this direction until August 1986. Febres had started on the road toward exchange rate reform in March 1985, when banks were allowed to offer savings accounts with floating interest rates. Whereas these accounts marginally increased the national savings, they did nothing to correct the gap between the sucre's official exchange rate and the market rate.

Two years after his inauguration, Febres ended the sucre subsidy and allowed the rate to float against hard currencies. This policy had the effect not of lowering rates, however, but of raising them. Febres's problem was different from that of Venezuela's and El Salvador's. Preceding administrations had used oil money to subsidize the rate, making imports artificially cheap. Within days of the subsidy's end, the sucre went from 110 to the dollar to 150. By the end of Febres's term, it required 500 sucres to buy one dollar.

Regardless of its economic effects, Febres was moving in a direction consistent with Catholic social thought by getting the state out of the exchange rate business. But Febres's temptation to raise revenue through exchange regulation proved too strong for the floating rate to survive. Nineteen months after he established it, Febres abandoned the floating exchange system and replaced it with a tiered system, ostensibly to allow "vital" imports to enter the country by purchasing them on the international market with subsidized dollars.

This policy again made businesses dependent on the state. Successful exporters, that is, those with surplus dollars, had to direct their extra dollars to the controlled market, where they would receive far fewer sucres than in a free market. It also allowed the state to favor some purchasers over others and forced all businesses to register their transactions with the government in an effort to receive the preferential rate. Not incidentally, the tiered system also presented opportunities for corruption.

Guatemala's Vinicio Cerezo campaigned on promises of rigid price controls and strict government control of the exchange rate. While suggesting that the gap between the official and the market rate would shrink somewhat during his presidency, he maintained the belief that government intervention was necessary in this area.

In 1988, Cerezo finally took steps to adopt a uniform exchange rate, though not a freely floating one. In part, he wanted to end the frequent devaluations that made business in Guatemala so uncertain. He coupled the exchange rate reform with increased social spending, however, driving up the government deficit, along with inflation, and assuring that numerous future devaluations would be necessary. He added no significant incentives for production, which could have mitigated the price rises caused by the uniform exchange rate, and indeed presented the exchange reform as a temporary measure.

He then proceeded to blame inflation on "exchange rate speculators," having made such speculation attractive by floating the rate and fueling inflation at the same time. His brief rhetorical support for productivity ended abruptly, and Cerezo, like most of his Christian Democratic counterparts, left an economic mess for his successor.

Unfortunately, Costa Rica's Christian Democratic President Rafael Ángel Calderón seems to have learned little from the experiences of his Christian Democratic counterparts. His New Economic Policy, announced in May 1990, includes a doubling of the controlled exchange rate gap, as well as other attacks on Costa Rica's productive sector.

The best that can be said of these policies is that they have failed to provide the economic relief they were supposed to provide. Their political effects, however, are of more interest. Christian Democratic policies on foreign investment, domestic investment, taxes, and foreign exchange vastly increased state economic power. They did so at the expense of independent economic activity. In country after country, the Latin American Christian Democrats consolidated state power while simultaneously emasculating small business, a potential obstacle to further consolidation. This is a thorough rejection of Catholic social thought.

CHRISTIAN DEMOCRATIC LABOR POLICY

The disparity between Catholic social thought and Christian Democratic policy is equally clear in the parties' policies toward labor. Catholic social thought teaches that the most efficient way to provide a living wage, and the way least likely to increase government power, is through profit sharing. The Catholic popes and most Latin American Christian Democratic theorists sought to promote worker ownership of stock as a first step toward eliminating the wage system altogether. Co-ownership would mean worker participation and worker self-determination.

Worker representation on company boards of directors, representation earned by the ownership of stock, is a second step toward greater worker control over the workplace. Finally, Catholic social thought envisions the blurring of the lines between capitalists, managers, and workers. Like agricultural laborers targeted by Christian Democratic land reform theory, workers would eventually all become proprietors.

In the meantime, Catholic social thought encourages the development of strong, independent unions. In their theoretical statements, Christian Democrats support free labor unions and oppose government interference in labor-management relations. Once in power themselves, the Christian Democrats imitate other Latin American political parties by seeking to gain political control of the labor movement.

According to Catholic social thought, workers, like families, have rights that are anterior to the state and which the state cannot repress. The first of these is the right to a just wage, defined as one that would allow one bread-winner to support a family. The second is the right to organize independent labor unions. In their early days, Christian Democratic parties and movements strongly defended these rights.

They have gone beyond rhetorical support and acted to make labor rights a reality by starting some unions, infiltrating others, uniting others, and working to unionize rural workers, whom the Socialist and Communist labor organizers had largely ignored. The Christian Democrats built on actions by Catholic priests who were strongly committed to the strong, independent unions that Catholic social thought envisioned.

Early Christian Democratic efforts in the labor field emphasized the independence of unions while also contrasting the "responsibility" of Christian unions with their Socialist and Communist counterparts. The Chilean Falange was involved in labor organizing in the 1930s. During the 1950s, the Christian Democratic party demanded that rural workers be allowed to organize their own independent unions. Legalizing such unions was one of President Frei's first acts.

It was not long, however, before Christian Democratic leaders realized the usefulness of a strong, party-oriented labor wing. Frei saw labor as a needed counterweight to the upper class as he became more and more anti-capitalist.[45] One way of acquiring such support was to tie labor, and labor unions, closer to the Christian Democratic party in power.

Frei failed to gain significant union support because he did not reform Chile's labor code to allow shop stewards and other union officials to hold meetings and perform other union functions on company time. Thus, the well-financed Socialists retained their lead in urban union membership. Frei could have seriously undercut this lead by instituting profit-sharing plans that Christian Democratic thinkers had been writing about for decades. He put little real effort into this project, however.

Instead, Frei sought to get control of labor by taking over the most important functions of unions. Frei felt that the government should set wage ceilings, determine minimum working conditions, and represent labor before management. During his presidential campaign, Frei promised to give workers annual cost-of-living increases to protect them from inflation. The Chilean legislature exceeded each of his salary increase proposals, however, making Frei less impressive to workers.

Like subsidizing families or schools, this sort of government largess simply makes laborers wards of the state. This is what Catholic social thought tries to prevent. If Frei thought that this was tolerable during a Christian Democratic administration, he should have given some thought to the future. Pinochet would have had more difficulty repressing independent unions than ones tied to political parties.

Some Christian Democrats wanted to infiltrate the Socialist and Communist labor unions or find ways to work with their leaders and perhaps bring them into the Christian Democratic fold. Again, this misses the point. Catholic social thought insists that union strength comes from independence. Any attempt to link unions with a political party, or with the state, undermines labor leaders who will respond to the desires of workers, rather than those of politicians.

While defended as a pragmatic policy given the preponderance of leftists in the labor movement, this waffling and attempted collaboration only cost the Christian Democrats labor votes they received in the 1964 election. Disappointed workers left the party in droves to vote for the more coherent and committed Salvador Allende in 1970.

In Venezuela, Copei members believed in 1946 that the proper government role in protecting labor rights involved things like inspecting working places and providing methods of conciliation and arbitration for labor and management. The party also upheld the right to a family wage.[46] Under the Pérez Jiménez dictatorship, Copei formed its own labor confederation, the Confederation of Autonomous Unions of Venezuela (CODESA). Copei also defended CODESA's right to independence against government harassment.

Acción Democrática still dominated Venezuelan organized labor in 1958, and Copei sacrificed its chance to make genuine inroads into this dominance. During the 1958 negotiations with AD, Caldera agreed to dissolve Copei's trade union federation in return for guaranteed seats on the executive committee of a "united" national union federation. He also ceded the right to try for the presidency of this confederation, choosing a guarantee of a Copei secretary-general.[47] After this devastating agreement, Copei's own labor confederation declined in importance.

Caldera may have made what he considered to be a pragmatic decision to reduce AD's labor strength, but the effect was to accept a second-place status in the labor movement and for the foreseeable future give up any chance to improve that position. Even more important, Caldera's agreement denied Venezuelan workers the right to choose the leadership of their national union and prevented the appearance of labor unions independent of government.

El Salvador's Christian Democrats have had less success than their counterparts elsewhere in gaining union support. Again, they did not provide workers with a coherent and attractive alternative to the promises and political clout of existing unions tied to other political parties.

Christian Democratic theorist Roberto Lara Velasco insisted in 1961 that workers were as much investors in a business as stockholders and as such deserved a share of the company's profits and a decent living.[48] In their 1966 presidential campaign, the Christian Democrats "declared their primary goal to be full employment at dignified wage levels." The economic growth necessary to make this a reality, according to the party, should be provided "by fostering industrial development and national production in general." Like many early Christian Democratic statements, it was closely in line with Catholic social thought.

By the 1980s, El Salvador's Christian Democrats had resorted to the familiar formula of imitating, or trying to outbid, their leftist rivals for labor support. They accepted the statist proposition that labor rights and benefits come from the state. In 1989, the Christian Democrats' presidential candidate, Fidel Chávez Mena, promised to create hundreds of thousands of new jobs during his administration.

Ecuador's Febres Cordero, like Frei, tried to purchase the loyalty of organized labor with pay increases. Christian Democratic President Hurtado had opposed a 1979 proposal to double the minimum wage. His supposedly more conservative successor, for his part, boasted in 1987 that he had raised salaries by more than the rate of inflation and raised the minimum wage four times.

Some months earlier, however, Febres's labor minister announced that a 1987 salary increase was "out of the question when the country faces an anguishing emergency and economic crisis."[49] The predictable union disappointment with this announcement shows the danger in inducing labor to rely too heavily on government largess. To buy loyalty is to imply a willingness to keep on paying for it. When the money runs out, so does the loyalty.

Laborers sometimes benefit from Christian Democratic neglect. In Peru, the Christian Democrats were latecomers to the process of union organization. In the 1950s, a union federation committed to Catholic social thought appeared and immediately declared its independence from the Christian Democratic Party. Consistent with Catholic social thought, union leaders retained their independence even from a related political party.

The value of this independence became clear in 1959 when a Christian Democratic labor minister helped to organize and support embryonic rural labor unions while also promoting their independence. In 1962, a new labor minister, who was hostile to Catholic organizations, took over. The independent labor unions sustained themselves without a government patron.

CONCLUSION

The temptation to run people's lives, from a perceived position of greater wisdom, and for their own good, motivated many of the actions of Latin America's Christian Democrats. Near the end of his term, Eduardo Frei decided that the best way to hold down rising beef prices in Chile was to institute ten "beef-less" days per month. The notion of encouraging greater beef production did not occur to him. This scheme admittedly represents the extreme of Christian Democratic social engineering, and Frei soon dropped it. However, it shows how easy it is to go from telling people how to spend their money to telling them how to manage other aspects of their lives.

Frei at one point withdrew government advertising from a Santiago newspaper that was critical of him. Because the government had already taken over many economic functions and thus provided a higher percentage of the paper's total advertising business, Frei's leverage over the paper was greater. It was also successful, as the paper's editorial slant changed.

Latin America's Christian Democrats were motivated by the fear of large corporations that could act independently and to the detriment of the common good. They shared this fear with the authors of Catholic social thought. Christian Democrats have tried to implement Catholic social thought on business, however, while ignoring Catholic social thought on the state. The popes believed that both had to exist, even though they were not enamored of either. Reducing the power of large corporations need not mean a radical and permanent increase in state economic power. It could mean using existing political and economic levers to encourage the formation of more businesses.

Such a policy has several positive effects. First, it increases the choices of workers and consumers who are looking for employers and vendors. Second, if more domestic businesses appear, then the economy is genuinely nationalized. Third, even if only foreigners create new businesses, a greater number and variety of foreign investors make harmful collusion more difficult. Fourth, more businesses tend to spur diversification of the economy, which is something that the Christian Democrats said they favored.

In addition to these positive economic effects, a policy of encouraging multiplication of capitalist enterprises has the endorsement of Catholic social thought. In spite of all these advantages, Christian Democrats have invariably discouraged the appearance of new, small businesses. In fact, except during a short period in the term of Febres Cordero, Christian Democrats have driven most entrepreneurial talent in their countries underground.

The growth of the illegal underground economy, which some analysts call the informal economy, is a significant social and political development in Latin America. In Chapters 7 and 8, we will see that this growing informal sector, and the parties that have begun to speak for it, have defeated the Christian Democrats in elections in Peru and Guatemala. In the process, the Christian Democrats' rivals have supplanted them as the bearers of Catholic social thought.

NOTES

1. Leonard Gross, *The Last, Best Hope: Eduardo Frei and Chilean Democracy* (New York: Random House, 1967), p. 128.

2. Ramiro Rivera, *El pensamiento de León Febres Cordero* (Quito: Ediciones Culturales, 1986), p. 60.

3. "Change in Chile: What It Means to U.S. Business," *U.S. News and World Report*, 26 April 1965, pp. 84–85.

4. John D. Martz, "Ecuador: the Right Takes Command," *Current History* 84, 499 (1985): 69.

5. Quito, "Voz de los Andes," 15 September 1987 (from Foreign Broadcast Infor-

mation Service, Latin America *Daily Report*, hereinafter FBIS, 18 September 1987, pp. 27–29).

6. "Reaganomics in Quito," *Forbes*, 3 June 1985, p. 222.

7. Donald Herman, *Christian Democracy in Venezuela* (Chapel Hill: University of North Carolina Press, 1980), p. 13.

8. Rafael Caldera, "The Christian Democratic Idea," *America*, 7 April 1962, p. 14.

9. Winfield Burggraff, "Oil and Caribbean Influence: The Role of Venezuela," in Richard Millet, ed., *The Restless Caribbean: Changing Patterns of International Relations* (New York: Praeger Publishers, 1979), p. 195.

10. Robert Bond, "Venezuela's Role in International Affairs," in Robert Bond, ed., *Contemporary Venezuela and Its Role in International Affairs* (New York: New York University Press, 1977), p. 228.

11. John D. Martz, "Venezuelan Foreign Policy toward Latin America," in Bond, p. 158.

12. Burggraff, p. 196.

13. Ibid., p. 197.

14. John D. Martz, "The Crisis in Venezuelan Democracy," *Current History* 83, 490 (1984): 73.

15. Williams, p. 119.

16. Eduardo Frei, *Latin America: The Hopeful Option* (Maryknoll, N.Y.: Orbis Books, 1978), p. 126.

17. *Wall Street Journal*, 6 August 1969, p. 23.

18. Quoted in Heinz Sontag and Rafael de la Cruz, "The State and Industrialization in Venezuela," *Latin American Perspective* 12, 4 (1987): 95–96.

19. Rafael Caldera, "The Christian Democratic Idea," *America*, 7 April 1962, p. 14.

20. Charles Ameringer, "The Foreign Policy of Venezuelan Democracy," in John D. Martz, ed., *Venezuela: The Democratic Experience* (New York: Praeger Publishers, 1977), p. 349.

21. Alfredo Peña, *Conversaciones con Luis Herrera Campins* (Caracas: Editorial Ateneo de Caracas, 1978), p. 91.

22. René Salgado, "Economic Pressure Groups and Policy-Making in Venezuela: The Case of FEDECAMERAS Reconsidered," *Latin American Research Review* 22, 3 (1987): 94–95.

23. Ibid.

24. Ibid., p. 331.

25. *Andean Report*, 28 July 1988, p. 7.

26. David Schodt, *Ecuador: An Andean Enigma* (Boulder, Colo.: Westview Press, 1987), p. 147.

27. Rivera, p. 139.

28. Quito, "Voz de los Andes," 15 September 1987 (FBIS, 18 September 1987, p. 27).

29. Schodt, p. 162.

30. Michael Holliman, "Ecuador's Free Market Experiment Takes Wrong Turn," *Wall Street Journal*, 8 April 1988, p. 17.

31. Figures from the *Europa World Yearbook*, 1988, 1989, and 1990 editions.

32. Guatemala City, Domestic Service, 20 March 1987 (FBIS, 25 March 1987, p. P16).

33. Guatemala City, *El Gráfico*, 20 December 1987, p. 3 (FBIS, 28 December 1987, p. 8).

34. *Wall Street Journal*, 12 April 1967, p. 1.

35. Eduardo Frei Montalva, "Paternalism, Pluralism and Christian Democratic Reform Movements in Latin America," in William V. D'Antonio and Frederick B. Pike, eds., *Religion, Revolution and Reform: New Forces for Change in Latin America* (New York, Praeger Publishers, 1964), p. 32.

36. Williams, p. 100.

37. *Wall Street Journal*, 11 April 1986, p. 27.

38. Quito, "Voz de los Andes," 15 September 1987. (FBIS, 18 September 1987, p. 27).

39. Guatemala City, Radio TV, 17 August 1987 (FBIS, 24 August 1987, pp. G1-4).

40. Mexico City, *Notimex*, 31 May 1990 (FBIS, 4 June 1990, p. 5).

41. Martz, "Crisis," p. 75.

42. Robert J. Looney, "Venezuela's Economic Crisis: Origins and Successes in Stabilization," *Journal of Social, Political and Economic Studies* 11, 3 (1986): 336.

43. *Andean Report*, 28 July 1988, p. 7.

44. *Andean Report*, 2 March 1989, p. 2.

45. Frei, p. 60.

46. Gehard Cartáy Ramírez, *Política y partidos modernos en Venezuela* (Caracas: Ediciones Centauro, 1983), p. 93.

47. Cecilia M. Valente, *The Political, Economic and Labor Climate in Venezuela* (Philadelphia: University of Pennsylvania Press, 1979), p. 183.

48. Stephen Webre, *José Napoleón Duarte and the Christian Democratic Party in Salvadoran Politics, 1960-1972* (Baton Rouge: University of Louisiana Press, 1979), p. 62.

49. Quito, "Voz de los Andes," 18 March 1987 (FBIS, 24 March 1987 p. G3).

III

Latin American Christian Democracy and Neoliberalism

7

Christian Democracy and Neoliberalism: Central America

Christian Democrats in Latin America faced a series of elections in 1989–1990. To varying degrees, economic issues were important in all these elections. In some, the Christian Democrats opposed candidates who advocated free market economic policies. Because these reformers support an updated version of nineteenth-century laissez-faire, they are called neoliberals.

Neoliberalism presented Christian Democracy with a new economic and political challenge. Until the end of the 1980s, Latin America's Christian Democrats had mainly opposed Social Democrats or other enthusiasts of state economic power. The challenge of the next decade, however, will be to counter the attractiveness of neoliberal economic change. To understand the trials that faced Christian Democracy as it campaigned in 1989–1990, we must understand the conditions that spurred the growth in neoliberalism's popularity, the neoliberal movement itself, and its relationship to Catholic social thought. We can then move to an analysis of the elections themselves, first in Central America and second, in Chapter 8, in South America.

THE LEGACY OF STATISM

By the end of World War II, a large degree of state control over the economy was a fact of life in most of Latin America. Changes since the war, until

very recently, have only marginally changed the level of government interference in the national economies, or they have changed the identity of the
beneficiaries. By the start of the 1980s, Latin American states, both those
governed by democracies and those under dictatorships, featured statist
economies. Most had managed and subsidized credit. All had large and
growing state sectors as well as government monopolies of many goods and
services. Governments retained control over most of the continent's mineral
resources.

Throughout the twentieth century, the overwhelming economic, political,
and social reality in Latin America has been poverty, usually accompanied
by enormous gaps between rich and poor people. Many analysts, most
notably those of the dependency school, held that Latin America's reliance
on the export of primary products and the influence of foreign MNCs were
largely responsible for this poverty and economic polarization. Among other
things, the dependency analysts recommended insulating developing economies from the reputedly baleful effects of contact with the global capitalist
economy.

Such insular policies tended toward greater state control over the economy. States that adopted a policy of import substitution, for example, raised
tariff levels to protect fledgling industries from "unfair" foreign competition.
In some cases, governments accompanied tariffs with quotas and other regulatory regimes that not only served to raise prices and limit choices to consumers but also increased state control over the national economy.

The dependency school also taught that banning or limiting foreign direct
investment imposed regulations to ensure that such investment remained
under state control. One of the central purposes of the Andean Pact was to
tightly regulate foreign investment. Such policies had the economic effect of
under state control. One of the central purposes of the Andean Pact was to
tightly regulate foreign investment. Such policies had the economic effect of
ensuring that only the richest MNCs could overcome the barriers placed in
front of foreign investment. Here again, dependency recommended increasing government power.[1]

The dependency theorists were not alone in their determination to increase
state intervention in the economies of Latin America. As we have seen, Latin
America's Christian Democrats pursued a number of policies that, intentionally or not, vastly increased the power of states to determine the economic
activities of their citizens. Christian Democratic family policy created wards
of the state, dependent on government largess to survive and prosper. Christian Democrats, with few exceptions, tried to tie schools, charities, and other
independent social groups to government as well.

Christian Democratic land reform sought to create rural cooperatives that
were the product of government action, answerable to government officials,
and, if possible, partisan recruiting grounds for the Christian Democrats in
government. Far from extending rural landowning, it extended government

power into the countryside to a remarkable and almost unprecedented extent. Similarly, Christian Democratic efforts at nationalization, another policy suggested by the dependency school, similarly extended state power by attacking not only foreign-owned businesses but also indigenous businesses.

In addition, Christian Democrats manipulated exchange rates and imposed or continued heavy taxes and tariffs. They blocked independent capital investment, both foreign and domestic. Even in the field of labor, Christian Democratic governments sought not so much to protect workers, or to empower them and their unions, but to extend their own power over the unions through the extension of state power. The pattern repeats itself in every area of economic policy in which the continent's Christian Democrats took an interest.

Defenders of Christian Democracy could point out that most of their economic policies were not any different that those of their political rivals. In some cases, the Christian Democrats were somewhat less enthusiastic about increased state economic power than their main political rivals. In no such case, however, was the difference any more than a dispute over the speed with which statism should be imposed.

Herein lies the tragedy of Christian Democracy in Latin America. Christian Democracy was never meant to be just another political party or movement. The founders of Latin America's Christian Democratic parties wanted to renovate their countries' political systems, not just to get their share of power from them. For these early idealists, dedicated to the social thought of the Catholic Church, Christian Democracy was a chance to overcome the traditional patterns of Latin American politics that had served the continent so badly since independence. Their transformation into a political movement only marginally distinguishable from many of their political rivals is striking.

Catholic social thought accepts, and even promotes, capitalist elements such as risk taking, investment for profit, and the direction of energy and ingenuity toward greater productivity. It supports the enormous individual economic liberty that a capitalist system allows. The authors of Catholic social thought also denounce too much economic decision making by the state and fear a state-led monopoly of economic goods more than a private monopoly. Catholic social thought, in addition, acknowledges the possibility that a state enterprise can be perverted to private gain.

Both capitalism and statism are insufficient to meet human needs, according to Catholic social thought. Both productivity and equitable distribution, the respective goals of capitalism and socialism, are oriented solely toward the material needs of humanity. Both ignore spiritual needs, which are far more important. Since both capitalism and socialism are materialistic, the Church rejects both.

The story does not end there, however. Since choices have to be made in this world, Catholic social thought analyzes capitalism and socialism and determines that since capitalism is more respectful of the autonomy of persons, it is, to that extent, preferable to socialism. Pure capitalism, however, also becomes destructive of this autonomy if wealth becomes concentrated in too few hands. Worst of all is concentrating wealth in only one hand, the state's. Statism can only go so far in preventing capitalism's abuses, and it brings its own set of problems.

The real answer is to develop a moral capitalist system. This would retain capitalism's positive features, such as the encouragement of productivity and creativity, while inducing people to put aside selfishness and greed.

Small capitalist enterprises are more likely to produce these positive effects than large ones. Small capitalist enterprises feature closer links among owners, managers, and workers. New capitalists are less likely to forget their social obligations and are more likely to desire to help others, even if these are only in their own extended family. States should rebuff the inevitable blandishments of large businesses for government favoritism in the form of tariffs or regulations that make market entry more difficult for newcomers.

The more capitalists a country has, the more they will all have to compete with one another. If price fixing is a problem, an influx of new suppliers will address it. If low wages are a problem, an influx of new employers will supply upward pressure on wages. If some capitalists act abominably, consumers can choose to take their custom to others.

Catholic social thought also advocates government funding for basic social programs, and a tax system that requires the rich to pay a higher percentage of their income than the poor. The popes created, in short, a well-developed and comprehensive policy for dealing with capitalism. With capitalism seemingly headed for demise in the 1960s and 1970s, this part of Catholic social thought did not seem important to Christian Democrats. The challenges of the 1980s and 1990s, however, were different.

The Christian Democrats' loss of their ideological roots left them completely unable to take advantage of the most significant political and social change in Latin America in the last 50 years. A trend toward liberal economics began in the 1970s and caught fire as the 1980s drew to a close. The evidence from recent elections in Central and South America compellingly suggests that Latin American electorates are willing to support policies of less government intervention in economic matters. They are not, however, confident enough in the free market to support pure capitalism.

The evidence suggests that parties that offer an essentially free market direction, but with some modifications in the capitalist prescription, received the warmest reception in recent Latin American elections. Catholic social thought, combining as it does a suspicion of the state and an unwillingness to allow capitalists free reign, represents a promising political position in Latin America.

Had they retained their identity with Catholic social thought, Latin America's Christian Democrats could have offered a continent weary of statism an alternative to the sometimes brutal capitalism offered by statism's opponents. In Chapters 7 and 8, I shall examine recent elections in El Salvador, Guatemala, Costa Rica, Chile, and Peru. In not one of these cases did a party espousing the principles of Catholic social thought lose.

Christian Democrats in Chile adopted Catholic social thought and won their election. In Costa Rica, a Christian Democratic candidate made only passing references to Catholic social thought and nearly lost. In El Salvador, Christian Democrats clung to statism and were defeated.

In Guatemala, Christian Democrats lost because they were too statist; whereas in Peru, they lost because they were too purely liberal. In neither case did the Christian Democrats present Catholic social thought to the voters. Instead, the Catholic social banner was picked up by others. For Christian Democrats, this is the most embarrassing trend of all.

NEOLIBERALISM IN LATIN AMERICA

By 1980, the effects of Latin America's statist policies were becoming more and more obvious. Inflation was worsening, tax bases were shrinking, foreign investment was evaporating, and domestic investment was stagnating. Overlaying all these problems and providing impetus for reform was the continent's growing external debt. One by one, Latin American leaders began to search for an alternative to state economic control.

The current wave of neoliberal economics first came to Latin America by dictate. The military regime of Chile's Augusto Pinochet invited a number of U.S.-trained economists to Chile in the 1970s to dismantle the substantial Chilean state economic apparatus. Because of their ties to the economics department at a university in that city, these economic reformers were dubbed the "Chicago boys." Their policy suggestions included making large cuts in government spending, lowering taxes and tariffs, privatizing state enterprises, radically deregulating economic decisions, welcoming foreign investment, freely floating exchange rates, attacking the power of organized labor, promoting profit sharing, expanding business ownership (usually in the form of shares of stock), and eliminating government subsidies, even for basic foodstuffs.

Because of the connection with the Pinochet regime, some observers have drawn a close connection between economic liberalism and dictatorship. The Pinochet regime, however, was unique among bureaucratic-authoritarian regimes in Latin America because it did not increase state economic power. Even the purportedly capitalist military dictatorship in Brazil retained many state enterprises and severely limited the access of most Brazilians to market economic activity. More to the point, however, Chile was not the only government in Latin America to experiment with a freer economy as the 1980s progressed.

In 1985, the civilian regime of Bolivia enacted liberal economic measures that were at least as radical as those undertaken in Chile.[2] In Ecuador, León

Febres Cordero was making some halting steps toward less state intervention in the economy. Even if his actual effect was not great, Febres talked constantly about the need for liberal reform. He was soon joined by others.

As 1991 began, statism was in decline not only in Chile and Bolivia but also in Brazil (under a civilian regime), Guatemala, El Salvador, Nicaragua, Peru, Venezuela, Argentina, and even Mexico. In Bolivia, Argentina, Venezuela, and Mexico, liberal reforms were enacted by political parties and leaders who had previously championed statism.

It is not possible to examine in detail the exact nature of all these neoliberal reforms or even to go into great depth about their causes and effects. What recent experience does show, and what even this brief summary suggests, is that there is a strong trend toward less state economic intervention in Latin America in the 1990s.[3] Whether this trend is good or bad for Latin America is disputable. That such a trend exists is not.

Reversing state economic intervention is often painful. It involves cutting subsidies, which raises the price of basic goods. It involves mass layoffs of government employees, often with little or no social safety net. It involves cutting tariffs, which hurts domestic producers.

What makes this political pain sustainable is that statism did not increase general wealth and also did not eliminate greed and selfishness. In much of Latin America, public enterprises remained private in their attitudes and orientation. Managers of state enterprises looked out for themselves, their friends, or their party. They were not, for the most part, the judicious, evenhanded, public-spirited experts that statist theory promises.

Those who have changed from statist to antistatist positions, including Carlos Saul Menem of Argentina, Victor Paz Estenssoro of Bolivia, Carlos Andrés Pérez of Venezuela, and Carlos Salinas de Gortari of Mexico, have presented the state economic apparatus as an oligarchy opposed to the interests of the nation as a whole.

Christian Democracy was seemingly taken by surprise by neoliberalism. Its party leaders have not taken full advantage of this trend toward government on the basis of Catholic social thought. Only in Chile did a Christian Democratic party present Catholic social thought. It was rewarded with victory. Other Christian Democrats have clung to statism. That other parties have taken up their discarded mantle is the strongest evidence that the Christian Democrats overlooked a stunning opportunity to become the continent's most important political movement.

EL SALVADOR: CLINGING TO STATISM

Christian Democracy underwent a series of electoral tests in Central America in 1989 and 1990. The first of these came in El Salvador in March 1989 as the Christian Democratic Party (PDC) tried to retain its position as the country's leading political party. Party leaders realized this would be difficult after the legislative and municipal elections of March 1988 went to ARENA (the National Republican Alliance), a right-wing coalition. Under different leaders, ARENA had been challenging the Christian Democratic dominance of Salvadoran politics since 1980.

Two issues dominated the 1989 campaign: the economy and the war against the guerrillas. Much of the early discussion of the former was eclipsed when the guerrillas' political front offered to cooperate with the political process in return for a six-month postponement of the election and the enfranchisement of Salvadorans living abroad. Although El Salvador held its elections on schedule, the war issue remained paramount.

Nevertheless, economic issues did receive a hearing. ARENA lost no time in attacking the Christian Democrats' policies regarding land reform, nationalization of banks and export trading, and its other statist measures. It also successfully tied the issue of state economic power to the issue of corruption. Its new majority in the Legislative Assembly allowed ARENA to oversee many of the Christian Democrats' financial transactions.

The ARENA overseers had little difficulty finding examples of corruption on the part of PDC officials. Early in 1988, ARENA accused PDC president José Napoleón Duarte's son of corruption. This revelation was largely responsible for the Christian Democrats' loss of the mayoralty of San Salvador, which had been a party preserve for years. It also pointed up a specific instance of public office being used for private gain.

The PDC's 1988 candidate was particularly handicapped in refuting the charges of statism and corruption that ARENA found so effective. Fidel Chávez Mena had been a member of Duarte's inner circle for years, and after Duarte became president in 1984, he raised Chávez to the senior post of planning minister over the strenuous objections of some less statist members of the PDC.[4] Again with Duarte's help, he became the party's 1989 standard-bearer.

Under these circumstances, it would have been difficult for Chávez to effectively separate himself from the statist policies of the outgoing administration. Nevertheless, the PDC tried to present their candidates as somewhat separate from the party. This, the PDC hoped, would blunt some of the charges of corruption. They also made some concessions to the free market.

At the same time, however, Chávez promised to create 160,000 new rural jobs and to enact the long-abandoned Phase 2 of the 1980 land reform plan. Phase 2 would have divided the most productive cash crop farms in El Salvador into subsistence plots and, by all accounts, would have played havoc with the country's agricultural production.[5] It also would have meant even greater state power over the agricultural sector.

The PDC's candidate, in other words, injected some antistatist rhetoric into an overwhelmingly statist campaign. This inconsistency had the effect of repelling both those who wanted more state intervention in the economy and those who wanted less. Both were able to find more coherent spokespersons for their cause in other parties. Chávez's campaign strategy is just one more failed attempt by a Christian Democrat to win votes by diluting his party's message.

For its part, ARENA promised to shrink the powerful economic state the Christian Democrats had created. The party promised to undo just about all the PDC's economic policies. They pledged to begin by privatizing the nation's banking system and by dismantling the coffee marketing board. They also said they would not try to undo the land reform that had already taken place. Indeed, they would move expeditiously to distribute full legal titles to peasants on government co-ops.

The alliance was aided by its choice of candidate. Alfredo Cristiani, having defeated the forces of Roberto D'Aubuisson for the party leadership, presented a less violent and more urbane image to Salvadoran voters. He also contrasted himself, a relative outsider to the political process, to Chávez, a long-time insider. Cristiani was free from any taint of corruption.

When the results came in on March 19, 1989, they revealed a devastating defeat for the Christian Democrats. They did place second in the balloting with 36 percent, but ARENA carried 54 percent and avoided a runoff election. The PDC's total was less than half of its 1984 second-round vote. The National Conciliation Party, another conservative party, took third place with 4 percent, barely ahead of the Democratic Convergence, a coalition representing the guerrillas.

It is impossible to gauge the electoral effectiveness of Catholic social thought based on the 1989 results. Except for Cristiani's stated desire to increase social spending and for the commitment to further disseminate land ownership, ARENA did not offer a program even close to Catholic social thought. It was much closer to pure neoliberalism, which has not been successful in head-to-head electoral meetings with Catholic social thought elsewhere.

At the same time, the Christian Democrats also did not offer Catholic social thought. On balance, Cristiani's liberalism was somewhat closer to the Church's economic and social thought than the increased statism of Chávez. The loser in 1989 was the statism of the Christian Democrats. The Salvadoran Christian Democrats continue their decline. In the March 1991 municipal and legislative elections, they garnered only 28 percent of the vote. Yet the party shows no signs of returning to its antistatist roots in Catholic social thought.

GUATEMALA: FORFEITING CATHOLIC SOCIAL THOUGHT

Christian Democrats in Guatemala not only failed to present Catholic social thought but also allowed a rival party to appropriate its major themes. Guatemala held presidential elections on November 11, 1990. Christian Democratic President Vinicio Cerezo could not succeed himself, but since the Guatemalan Christian Democratic Party, the DCG, had done so much to bring a semblance of democracy to Guatemala, many people thought it would be rewarded with another five years in power.

In the last 18 months of his term, however, Cerezo fell victim to the temptation to use government economic power for private political ends. During the first three and one-half years as president, Cerezo had followed some vaguely free market policies and sought to reduce the economic power of the Guatemalan state. His tactics changed, however, as the election approached. Quasi-capitalism gave way to populist statism as the DCG shamelessly tried to buy votes from Guatemalans. In the process, the party ignored the strictures of Catholic social thought, only to see them taken up by a rival party consisting largely of non-Catholics.

The DCG commitment to reduce state economic power had never been strong. Even in 1985, they promised rigid price controls, housing for the poor, higher wages, and more jobs, with all these benefits to be guaranteed by government action. Public spending rose by 75 percent over that of the military government, and the Christian Democrats placed strict controls on the exchange rate market, on wages, and even on exports, which they subjected to a new tax.[6]

Cerezo reacted to the inflation that his original policies caused with cuts in government spending, reform of the exchange rate regime, tax reform and the antistatist rhetoric examined in Chapter 6. Even if driven to it by circumstances, Cerezo adopted the rhetoric of personal responsibility, productivity, and skepticism of state power that animates Catholic social thought. Had he and his party retained even a tactical commitment to these policies, the 1990 election might have gone differently.

Cerezo concluded, however, that Catholic social thought would cost his party votes. His actions indicate he believed that patronage, clientism, increased social spending, and other methods to tie Guatemalans to the Guatemalan state would also tie them to his party. That Guatemalans might respond positively to someone exhorting them to make sacrifices, act morally, and remember that economic gain is secondary to ethical rectitude, seemed not to occur to him.

In a speech to the nation in January 1988, Cerezo promised salary increases, more jobs, more roads, and more social services. He announced in August that his government had decided to increase its gas subsidies. He added that "we [the state] will ensure supply at reasonable prices by watching overproduction and by guaranteeing certain prices for producers so that they can increase production with greater investment."[7]

One year later, with the election even closer, Cerezo went beyond control of the gasoline market to control over other markets as well. His government announced a 500-day plan to establish government stores in which subsidized items would be available to eligible purchasers. Leaving aside the enormous amount of public spending necessary to offer such subsidies, the increase in state economic power is considerable. To decide the identity of eligible purchasers is to virtually determine a person's economic future. The possibilities for misuse, inefficiency, and corruption are myriad, and thus they point up the reasons why Catholic social thought is so suspicious of state power. The DCG's political rivals used the corruption issue to great effect during the 1990 campaign.

About the only limitation on government economic power that Cerezo seemed willing to accept was the establishment of "free" trading zones in which customs duties would be lower or lifted altogether. Besides being somewhat vague, the program seemed designed to benefit importers, particularly foreigners, more than Guatemalans. Given that the plan was coupled with the stated desire for foreign investment and an unwillingness to lower export taxes, many Guatemalans concluded that Cerezo was providing relief from statism only for foreigners.

Guatemala's economic situation heading into the 1990 campaign was terrible. Not all of this is the fault of the DCG, since they had no control over the international economic system, which was sliding into recession in 1990, nor over the destructive guerrilla war that sapped both government and private resources. Where the Christian Democrats did have control, however, their efforts had, among other things, led to an explosion of inflation at the start of 1990. The Guatemalan Statistics Office admitted that inflation in the last week of December 1989 was 18.5 percent. The office pointed out that before Cerezo's latest economic measures had been adopted, the worst weekly inflation had been 10.4 percent.[8]

The 1990 Christian Democratic Campaign

According to one analysis, at the start of 1989 it looked as though the DCG would easily defeat any opposition. It was the country's largest single party. Its opponents seemed divided and more intent on carping at one another than offering any coherent alternative to the DCG program, as vague and contradictory as this was. Opposition parties spent much of their time arguing over the inclusion of former military dictator Efraín Ríos Montt, while the DCG stayed above this fray and quietly provided social services and subsidies. In addition, its five years in power had given the DCG a patronage organization rivaled by none of the other parties.

Despite these advantages, there were disquieting signs. The Christian Democrats lost the 1988 municipal elections to the liberal National Center Union (UCN), in spite of the latter's complete lack of a patronage network. In addition, the DCG underwent bitter infighting to determine just who the 1990 standard bearer would be. The rivals were René de León Schlotter and Alfonso Cabrera Hidalgo. De León fought with the Cerezo faction, which backed Cabrera, arguing that under Cerezo the party had lost its reformist zeal and had become too pragmatic. He also charged that corruption stained the DCG, and that corruption was a natural outgrowth of political "pragmatism."

Although Cabrera eventually won the nomination, de León's charges stuck and hurt the party's chances. Cabrera's close identification with President Cerezo, and thus with his economic policies, were also a factor in the party's very poor showing. Cabrera was a long-time personal friend of the president and had been his foreign minister.

De León, for his part, ran on his own for president. Leftist members of the DCG linked up with the Democratic Socialist Party to form an anti-Cabrera alliance. Cabrera, they said, had moved too far to the right.[9] Espousing an unabashedly statist and leftist version of Christian Democracy, this electoral coalition, called the National Opposition Front (FNO), ended up with less than 4 percent of the vote.[10]

As the election approached, the Christian Democrats lost hope of scoring a first-round victory but were confident of coming in first or second and using the advantages of incumbency all the more effectively in the runoff. The DCG sedulously avoided talking about the principles of Catholic social thought during the campaign. They stressed instead issues such as competence, experience, access to foreign aid from Washington, and their record of providing goods and services during the previous five years. They attempted to take full credit for Guatemala's transition to democracy, and they repeatedly attempted to tie opponents to Ríos Montt.

The DCG succeeded in proving that while Catholic social thought may not guarantee electoral success, ignoring it leads a Christian Democratic party to electoral failure. In the case of the DCG, this failure was almost complete. When the first-round results came in, the DCG not only failed to gain the plurality it had hoped for but did not even make it into the second round. The Christian Democrats finished third, well behind the free market UCN and the Solidarity Action Movement (MAS), which was made up largely of Evangelical Protestants. In fact, another right-of-center party, the National Advance Party (PAN), nearly deprived the ruling party of the third-place slot.

Parties that advocated even more statism than the DCG fared very poorly in the balloting. Besides a clear rejection of the Christian Democratic Party, the November first round was an equally clear rejection of statist economic and political policies. Three of the top four positions went to parties that advocated a smaller and economically weaker state. Had the DCG not been able to depend on the votes of government employees and those who voted to retain their state handouts, the news on election day would have been even worse.

The Parties in the Runoff Campaign

The connection between the principles of Catholic social thought and political success in Latin America became even clearer in Guatemala's runoff campaign. Both contenders promised to reduce the state sector and to be far friendlier to capital investment than the Christian Democrats had been. As the campaign progressed, however, it became increasingly clear that the almost pure free market message of the UCN's Jorge Carpio Nicolle was losing its attraction. Guatemalans opted instead for the less orthodox approach of the MAS's José Serrano Elías.

The UCN presented a platform of pure capitalism to the Guatemalan electorate in the first- and second-round campaigns. The party chose Manuel Ayau, a famous free market analyst from the conservative Francisco Marroquín University, as vice-presidential candidate. Other than the endorsement of some labor groups upset with Cerezo, the party did little to soften its insistence on a harsh austerity program.

Carpio was unable to persuade a majority of Guatemalans that he was capable of carrying out such an austerity program, even with the help of Dr. Ayau. In a debate involving most of the major candidates, held before the first-round balloting, Carpio seemed unable to say why he thought Guatemala should cut taxes. His later "clarification," that he was talking about reducing tariffs, did little to correct the feeling that he was plunging into economic orthodoxy without fully understanding its implications. Of greater concern was his determination to pursue capitalism regardless of its social costs.

That Carpio's UCN took first place in the first round shows the attractiveness of antistatism to Guatemalan voters, even when presented by a candidate who does not enjoy their complete confidence. The UCN's first-round balloting had to be a disappointment, however, since its members had expected to be further ahead, and at one time even entertained hopes of avoiding a runoff altogether. As it was, UCN candidates repeated their impressive 1988 performance on the local level.

On January 6, 1991, José Serrano, the MAS Evangelist candidate, received over 60 percent of the votes in the runoff election. Like Alberto Fujimori of Peru, Serrano got the votes of most of Guatemala's growing, and very politically active, Protestant movement. But unlike Fujimori, he is not a stranger to the national political scene.

Serrano and his running mate, a well-known businessman, emphasized reducing the power of the Guatemalan state, especially in economic matters. Like the UCN and PAN, the party stressed reduced government spending, a friendlier atmosphere for business, austerity in the form of reduced or eliminated government finances, and moderately lower taxes and tariffs.

This essentially free market approach was enough to get the MAS near the top when the first-round votes were counted. Had they only repeated the platforms of the other conservative parties, however, it is unlikely that Serrano would have won the runoff. Many analysts attribute his runoff victory to the high turnout among Evangelicals.[11] This explanation is insufficient. First, the Evangelical churches themselves do not claim that more than one-quarter of all Guatemalans have left the Catholic Church. Even had Serrano gotten all the votes of the Evangelicals, it would not have been near a majority. Second, although Carpio injected religion into the campaign in the last days, it was not a major issue in the runoff.

To say that Serrano won because of the Evangelicals is to beg the question of why they voted for him. As important, it does nothing to answer why so many Catholics gave him their votes. The answer to these questions lies in Serrano's proximity to Catholic social thought.

Serrano was adamant about stressing the importance of expanding business opportunities in Guatemala. He wanted the capitalist system of Guatemala to be open to newcomers. He was particularly determined to allow the growing number of Guatemalans in the informal sector of the economy to prosper. These small capitalists, because of their deep-seated suspicion of the state and because of the high levels of social solidarity that analysts have found in informal communities, form the most promising new constituency for a political platform based on Catholic social thought.

In Guatemala, the 1990 election saw the mantle of Catholic social thought picked up by a non-Catholic. Only Serrano seemed to understand the importance of fragmenting the capitalist class, both to make it work better and to protect society from its rougher edges. Only Serrano offered concrete ideas on how to go about this. The main plank of his economic platform was a program of loans to small businesses and to independent rural cooperatives.[12] Such a program promised to achieve capitalist dispersion while boosting independent social groups in the country.

More important to the program's appeal, however, was its moral content. Here the connection with Catholic social thought is even stronger. Serrano's MAS promised clean, and thus effective, government. The party promised to perform government's essential functions more efficiently, ceasing extraneous or unjustified activities. To abandon some activities, the MAS had to persuade Guatemalans not to expect so much from the state but, rather, to depend more on themselves, their families, and their independent social groups.

A large part of the Evangelical appeal in Latin America has been its emphasis on personal morality and personal responsibility. In the economic sphere, Serrano and his supporters reminded listeners that vices such as drinking, gambling, or womanizing meant that they and their families would have less money for personal improvement. The MAS promised to provide the opportunities to use money wisely and profitably. It would be up to Guatemalans, however, to accumulate the savings to seize these opportunities.

Finally, Serrano and the other Evangelicals reminded the people of Guatemala that economic well-being, even in their impoverished land, was secondary to the eternal salvation of souls. (Christian Democrats in Latin America had once talked the same way.) The message struck a chord with Guatemalans and induced them to choose the economic morality of Serrano over the economic orthodoxy of Carpio.

In Chapter 8, we will see another example of a non-Christian Democrat, backed by Evangelicals and espousing a version of Catholic social thought, besting a candidate who represented pure capitalism. Even if Christian Democrats have come to doubt the potency of their original message, some of their opponents have no doubts whatever.

COSTA RICA: REPEATING EARLIER MISTAKES

Latin America's newest Christian Democratic president is Rafael Ángel Calderón Fournier of the Social Christian Unity Party (PUSC) of Costa Rica. His election on February 4, 1990, ended eight years of rule by the social democratic National Liberation Party (PLN).

Calderón's sizable victory came in part because of his outward commitment to some of the principles of Catholic social thought and in part because of his partial endorsement of elements of neoliberal economics. However, most analysts agree that his election had more to do with circumstances having nothing to do with him. Many voters recalled the contributions of his father, for whom the younger Calderón was named. Calderón reminded voters of his father's 1940–1944 presidency and sought to exploit his name recognition. In addition, Costa Ricans traditionally deny their political parties lengthy runs in office. Since the PLN had held power for eight years, there was a widespread desire for change.

Calderón offered little change in his campaign, and so he diluted his mandate. Despite his characterization by one North American journal as "right wing," there was little to choose between Calderón and Carlos Manuel Castillo, the PLN candidate.[13] Calderón's campaign statements veered from pro-statist to antistatist, depending on his audience. He included just enough references to elements of Catholic social thought, and just enough references to his father, to distinguish himself from his opponent. His statements since election have been every bit as inconsistent.

The PUSC and the 1990 Campaign

Rafael Calderón, Sr., helped to establish democracy in Costa Rica in the 1940s. By providing a more or less loyal opposition to the PLN of José (Don Pepe) Figueres, he allowed Costa Rica's long-running democratic experiment to get underway. His four-year term was marked by extensive social and labor legislation, as well as by Costa Rica's first government housing plan. As far as it goes, this is generally consistent with Catholic social thought and quite progressive for Central America in the 1940s. But his administration was also marked by what one author called "unusual administrative ineptitude, corruption and electoral fraud."[14]

Reminding voters of his father's contributions, Calderón, Jr., could not help but remind them of his ineptness and corruption as well. A suspicion that the PLN was also corrupt, however, helped Calderón's 1990 campaign. The strategy of pointing to PLN corruption had worked before for the PUSC. Rodrigo Caranzo Odio, the PUSC's successful 1978 presidential candidate, charged the ruling party with rampant corruption and suggested that the PLN had accepted bribes to allow Robert Vesco, the fugitive financier, to live in Costa Rica.[15]

Calderón's 1990 campaign was marked by equivocation toward statism, liberal economics, and Catholic social thought. With a good chance of getting elected in any event, given Costa Ricans' preference for alternation in government, the Christian Democrats could have used the 1990 election to explain and display the movement's original ideology.

Such a campaign strategy would have ensured discussion of important economic issues and provided the PUSC with a clear mandate for action, even if a more ideological campaign might have meant a slightly smaller majority. The nomination of Calderón, and his campaign of reminiscences, indicated a more defensive posture and a desire to let the propensity for alternation take its course without upsetting anyone.

During the campaign, Calderón occasionally referred to elements of Catholic social thought, though he rarely used the term himself. Describing himself as a "center-leftist," he said that his "priority task" was to restore "social equilibrium." Beyond blaming the PLN, he failed to mention what had caused the disequilibrium. Equally confusing were his statements on state agencies. Leaning toward neoliberal economics, he promised to continue the outgoing administration's policy of privatizing some state agencies. Those that remained in government hands, he promised, would be made to run more efficiently. In the same speech, he also promised that there would be no mass layoffs of government employees. He never explained how he planned to find buyers for overstaffed state agencies.[16]

As election day approached, polls showed that the PUSC lead over the PLN was in double figures. Much of this support, significantly, came from outside San José. In areas where there were many government workers, Calderón's support was weak. This caused Calderón to abandon some of the antistatist rhetoric he had used earlier and to try to attract those who favored a large state as well. He succeeded only in diluting the support he had gained earlier. His lead in the polls shrank to 5 percent, and his victory, with 52 percent of the vote, was shorn of much meaning.

Like many Latin American Christian Democrats, Calderón had gained popularity when he talked about reducing the state, protecting civil society, and generally taking a stance opposite that of his Social Democratic rival. He then backed away from these positions and instead repeated the common Christian Democratic mistake of seeking votes through imitation. This sort of "pragmatism" rarely works. Had it not been the PUSC's "turn" in office,

Calderón would probably have been badly defeated. Indeed, the 1986 PUSC candidate, who followed the same strategy of pragmatic imitation, was badly defeated.

Calderón in Office

Even before Calderón took his oath of office, it was plain that his administration would have difficulty acting in a resolute and determined manner. As his cabinet began to take shape, it was divided between those who favored continued state intervention in the economy and those who opposed it. Vice-President Germán Serrano, Minister of Planning Helio Fallas, and Minister of Labor Erick Thompson supported a larger state and, at the least, planned to defend existing state economic power.

On the other hand, Minister of Finance Thelmo Vargas and Jorge Guardia, president of the Central Bank, favored a reduced state and hoped to implement serious privatization once Calderón was inaugurated. Guardia was a prominent member of the National Association of Economic Development, which favored economic liberalization and a substantially weaker state.

The great question during the transition period was which side of his administration would Calderón favor in his policy decisions. Calderón's statements gave no indication of his direction. Soon after the election, for example, he promised to "pay attention to the plight of 120,000 Costa Ricans who lack adequate housing." Somewhat later, he spoke of the importance of having economic growth, development, and "good economic indicators." But it was equally important, he added, to "promote the fair distribution of wealth so that it will be shared by all."[17]

Calderón's inaugural address, given on May 8, 1990, demonstrated more clearly than ever how indeterminate his economic policy ideas were. It was a speech that had something for everyone and gave no indication that Calderón would do anything more than react to economic events as they occurred. He began by recalling his father, who had given Costa Rica a labor code and government housing programs.

He then insisted that he viewed private enterprise as the "motor of development." "I believe," he continued in a vague reference to Catholic social thought, "in free enterprise with a social responsibility." He added, "Man must not be at the service of the state, but the state at the service of man." The twentieth century, the new president said, again faintly echoing Catholic social thought, "has proven to us that an almighty, bureaucratic and inefficient state makes development impossible, and it undermines the creativity and freedom of communities and people."[18]

Calderón said that he would work closely with the private sector, establishing an alliance between it and the state. The private sector should be freed from some government interference, since "the history of the past century has proven that a private sector constrained by limitations and regulations leads first to social polarization and later to class struggle." To ensure that capitalist enterprises did not become too concentrated, Calderón promised to create "thousands of small-scale businesses, many of them related to tourism."

With all of this probusiness, procapitalism and antistatist rhetoric, Calderón made it clear that he had not forgotten the pro-statist elements in his cabinet either. In a significant transitional paragraph, he said, "We believe in a state that guides, regulates and promotes development, not in a state that smothers, replaces and hampers private initiative."

Besides leaving the impression that the one kind of state can exist without the other, Calderón was also warning businesses that if they did not contribute to his administration's notions of development, they could depend upon being smothered, replaced, and hampered. That Calderón's trust of the free market was limited was clear in his statement that Costa Rica "cannot build a future clinging to a liberalism of the last century that promotes the single-minded doctrine of laissez-faire."

Calderón hoped to invest the Costa Rican state with increased economic power. In his inaugural address, he called for a constitutional amendment that would allow the government to control the inflation rate. He envisioned a "fatherland in which no youth is deprived of the opportunity to study and to have a job."

Thus, his reduced state would continue to provide housing, education, jobs, and a low inflation rate while not creating a bureaucratic or inefficient state that would constrain or smother private enterprise. Calderón evidently believes that a government can deliver on these promises and somehow remain less threatening to business and to civil society when in the hands of a Christian Democrat. Here again he has repeated a common Christian Democratic error.

In May 1990, Calderón announced his New Economic Policy. Like his inaugural address, the announcement included the rhetoric of neoliberalism and Catholic social thought, along with policies that violated both by increasing state economic power. Calderón proposed decentralization of public services and a reduction in the bureaucracy. Fifty percent of the state's vacant jobs would remain vacant, he promised, and his administration would transfer additional government employees to the private sector.

The PUSC president committed himself to a $70 million reduction in the official budget. He hoped to accomplish this by cutting subsidies on fuel, telephone, and water. At the same time, he pledged to stimulate exports and "adjust" some tariff rates to allow more imports. He raised other tariffs. Also while cutting the budget, Calderón submitted "social promotion measures" to the nation, which would reduce the cost of adjustment to lower-income groups. In effect, Calderón meant to replace the subsidies whose elimination was supposed to produce budgetary savings.[19]

The real purpose of the New Economic Policy, though, was to impose tax increases. Calderón announced a number of steps to improve tax collection, partly by initiating a program of tax withholding, with businesses performing the collecting chores. In addition, he discontinued tax exemptions on a number of staples. Also part of the package were increases of up to 43 percent in fees for government services.[20]

The New Economic Policy raised consumption taxes from 10 percent to 13 percent, which meant a 30–65 percent tax hike for professionals, workers, and retirees, depending on their annual income. This part of the program was so unpopular that Calderón was forced to back away from it. In July, he announced that the 13 percent rate was only temporary. It would drop by 1 percent each year, returning to 10 percent in 1994 (which, he did not add, is an election year.)[21]

On August 17, 1990, Calderón made yet another unsuccessful attempt to clarify his contradictory economic policy. In a lengthy address on his first 100 days in office, he told Costa Ricans of an impending budget deficit crisis and how he planned to forestall it. Echoing other Christian Democrats who have placed economic and regulatory burdens on their entrepreneurs, he began by complaining of a lack of incentive in the productive centers, especially the farming sector. To deal with this, he said, "we plan to reform the Costa Rican state. We are going to transfer enterprises . . . to the private sector."

As he had on previous occasions, Calderón mentioned some policies that bore a resemblance to those recommended by the authors of Catholic social thought. "I want to firmly reiterate," he said, "that I want to create the necessary conditions so that an increasingly large number of workers own their enterprises." He added later, "I have ordered social compensation programs destined to, with great solidarity, help pay for the basic needs of our most impoverished families."[22]

Part of this solidarity program was a free housing bonus to lower-class families and increased spending on primary-care and nutrition centers, as well as on school dining halls. Catholic social thought approves of social spending, but Calderón, like many other Christian Democrats, did not stop there. He went on to announce the formation of the Institute for the Family, which would "protect family unity and gradually promote it to attain higher standards of living." This policy turns Catholic social thought on its head. The family does not require protection by government; it requires protection from government. Changes in the tax code to favor families would have been much more efficient and much more in line with Catholic social thought than a new government agency.

Calderón did announce the creation of a customs free zone, which he expected to produce $100 million in exports in 1990 alone and create 17,000 new jobs by 1995.[23] It is significant that Calderón had such high hopes for a program that did little to remove tariff and export tax barriers. He did not conclude that even less statism would result in even greater returns.

Instead, in a speech that was supposed to be on the impending budget crisis, Calderón announced a new food bonus and free housing bonus program. In a speech in which he criticized businesses for their lack of incentive, he levied an additional 1 percent tax on company assets, made foreign exchange more expensive, and imposed an additional 5 percent tariff on raw materials and semifinished products.

Some Early Results of Calderón's Policies

The Christian Democratic president of Costa Rica has repeated almost all the mistakes that earlier Christian Democratic presidents have made. He has abandoned Catholic social thought, except as an occasional, and increasingly transparent, rhetorical tool. He has increased state economic power and then wondered aloud why the country's productive sector was not producing. He has attempted to "protect" independent social groups by creating new government bureaucracies. He has lost an opportunity to experiment with some liberal economic policies and to demonstrate how a uniquely Christian party would steer a course between too much statism and too much capitalism.

Calderón's economic statements have been confusing and contradictory. If the divisions in his cabinet are the cause, then he has failed to provide leadership. To the extent that divisions in the cabinet reflect divisions in the party, the necessity for leadership is even greater. Calderón is fast ensuring that his administration will be just another interregnum between PLN presidents.

Costa Ricans, who elected Calderón by a margin that polls showed was shrinking fast, have continued to lose faith in his leadership. After Calderón's first 100 days in office, only 34 percent of one sample thought he was doing a good or a very good job. Some 39 percent thought he had made almost no difference at all in the country's economic direction.[24]

By February 1991, the country was no longer so indifferent. Sixty-four percent of Costa Ricans thought the country was worse off than it was one year earlier. While 38 percent thought that they were worse off themselves, 55 percent thought that the country would be worse off one year in the future. Four months later, the same percentage thought that things would be worse in two years.[25]

The economic results have been no more encouraging than the political results. Between 1989 and 1991, economic growth has slowed from 5.5 percent to a projected 2 percent in 1991. Inflation remains high, and the balance of payments is showing enough of a deficit to force Costa Rica to seek help from the World Bank. In February 1991 there was word that Costa Rica may have some exploitable oil fields. The excitement from this news was tempered, however, with the government's announcement, before any oil was actually drilled, that there would be high taxes and high royalties awaiting any company that did extract it.

CONCLUSION

Recent experience in Central America shows that statism is no longer attractive as a political philosophy. In elections from one end of the isthmus to the other, parties committed to some form of antistatism won. Although noneconomic factors in some elections may not allow a firm conclusion that opposing statism invariably leads to victory, the evidence is more than sufficient to conclude that statism carries no guarantees either.

Central America's recent elections show that pure neoliberalism also has a limited appeal to Latin American voters. In contests in which openly and unabashedly liberal candidates faced opponents espousing the principles of Catholic social thought, they have lost. Catholic social thought is thus a potent electoral weapon against both statism and liberalism. In the next chapter, we will see the strength of Catholic social thought in Chile and Peru.

NOTES

1. The literature on *dependencia* is extensive and includes many more policy suggestions that the ones I have mentioned here. This discussion is not meant to be comprehensive; rather, it is meant to demonstrate the number and variety of regimes that advocated greater state economic power in Latin America. For dependency, see F. H. Cardoso and E. Faletto, *Dependency and Development in Latin America* (Berkeley, Calif.: University of California Press, 1978); Ronald H. Chilcote and Joel C. Edelstein, *Latin America: The Struggle with Dependency and Beyond* (Cambridge, Mass.: Schenkman, 1974); and James Petras, *Politics and Social Structure in Latin America* (New York, N.Y.: Fawcett, 1968).

2. For more information, see my "New Economic Policy of Victor Paz Estenssoro: Implementation and Aftermath," paper presented to the 17th International Congress of the Latin American Studies Association, Washington, D.C., April 7, 1991.

3. For further discussion of neoliberalism in Latin America, and for a critical view of the trend, see Joseph R. Ramos, *Neoconservative Economics in the Southern Cone of Latin America* (Baltimore, Md.: Johns Hopkins University Press, 1986). For a more specific and more sympathetic view, see Jeffrey Sachs, "The Bolivian Hyperinflation and Stabilization," *American Economic Review*, no. 77 (May 1987): 279–83. A balanced view, and one of particular importance because of its treatment of the divisions in the business class regarding neoliberalism, is provided by Catherine M. Conaghan, James M. Malloy, and Luis A. Abugattas, "Business and the 'Boys': The Politics of Neoliberalism in the Central Andes," *Latin American Research Review* 25, 2 (1990): 3–30.

4. Max Manwaring and Court Prisk, eds., *El Salvador at War: An Oral History of Conflict from the 1979 Insurrection to the Present* (Washington, D.C.: National Defense University Press, 1988), p. 203.

5. San Salvador, Canal Doce, 3 March 1989 (Foreign Broadcast Information Service, Latin America *Daily Report*, hereinafter FBIS, 7 March 1989).

6. *Wall Street Journal*, 6 June 1986, p. 25.

7. Guatemala City, Domestic Service, 13 August 1988 (FBIS, 15 August 1988, pp. 8–11). January statement from ACAN, 4 January 1988 (FBIS, 7 January 1988, p. 13).

8. Guatemala City, *El Gráfico*, 17 February 1990, p. 3 (FBIS, 29 March 1990, p. 26).

9. Guatemala City, Radio Nuevo Mundo, 16 November 1989 (FBIS, 27 November 1989, p. 25).

10. Frederico Estevez and Eva Loser, "CSIS Latin American Election Study Series: The 1990 Guatemalan Elections" (Washington, D.C.: Center for Strategic and International Studies, 1990), p. 5.

11. Both *Time* and *Newsweek* made this connection, as did other, more thoughtful analyses.

12. *Christian Century*, 20 February 1991, pp. 189–90. This Protestant magazine has followed Serrano's political career for some time.

13. Vicki Kemper, "Exporting Politics," *Common Cause Magazine*, January-February 1990, pp. 20–23.

14. James Busey, "The Presidents of Costa Rica," *The Americas*, 18, 1 (1961): 69.

15. Mitchell A. Seligson and Edward N. Muller, "Democratic Stability and Economic Crisis: Costa Rica, 1978–1983," *International Studies Quarterly* 31, 3 (1987): 301–26.

16. Panama City, ACAN, 3 February 1990 (FBIS, 5 February 1990, p. 19).

17. Latin American Regional Reports, *Central America and the Caribbean*, 29 March 1990, p. 3.

18. San José, Radio Reloj, 8 May 1990 (FBIS, 9 May 1990, pp. 16–20).

19. Panama City, ACAN, 31 May 1990 (FBIS, 31 May 1990, p. 4).

20. Mexico City, *Notimex*, 31 May 1990 (FBIS, 4 June 1990, p.5).

21. San José, *La Nación*, 30 July 1990, p. 5A (FBIS, 7 August 1990, p. 10).

22. San José, Radio Reloj, 17 August 1990 (FBIS, 20 August 1990, pp. 10–12).

23. San José, *La República*, 19 August 1990, p. 2A (FBIS, 11 October 1990, p. 20).

24. San José, *La Nación*, 12 August 1990, p. 5A (FBIS, 11 October 1990, pp. 18–20).

25. Latin America Regional Reports, *Weekly Report*, 5 February 1991, pp. 9–10, and 27 June 1991, p. 12.

8

Christian Democracy and Neoliberalism: South America

Christian Democracy in South America faced two crucial tests in 1989 and 1990. In Chile, the first free elections since March 1973 took place as the military government reluctantly returned power to civilians. The Chilean Christian Democratic Party (PDC) recovered from its doldrums of the 1970s and early 1980s to lead the victorious coalition. Much of their electoral appeal was due to their embrace of Catholic social thought.

In Peru, the Popular Christian Party (PPC) became a partner in a coalition headed by Mario Vargas Llosa, a political outsider who offered Peruvians classical liberal economic policies. The reasons for his loss, and the role that the PPC played in the 1990 campaign, also show the importance, and the enduring value, of a commitment to Catholic social thought. The experiences of the Christian Democratic parties of these two states present two possible futures for the movement.

CHILE: CATHOLIC SOCIAL THOUGHT REDISCOVERED

Christian Democracy under the Military Government

When Chile's military overthrew Salvador Allende in September 1973, many PDC members were more relieved than outraged. Allende's disastrous economic policies and repressive political actions were still present before them, and the severe repression of the Pinochet years had not yet started. As it did, the Christian Democrats moved into opposition.

At first, however, the PDC was reasonably friendly to the military. The leadership of the PDC was determined to give the new government a chance to prove itself worthy of its support. The party had taken the same stand toward Allende after his surprise 1970 victory. The Christian Democrats did not expect military rule to last long. Like most Chilean civilians, they thought that the military would be in power for no more than two or three years.

Former president Eduardo Frei offered what he called "patriotic" support to the army in "its task of reconstruction." For both the army and the PDC, this included the "purification" of the political arena and the "restoration of the country's social health." Although the junta barred Christian Democrats from political positions, it did offer the civilian parties, including the Christian Democrats, technical posts in the administration. Many PDC members accepted.[1]

The honeymoon did not last long, however. By late 1974, the junta turned its repressive machinery against Christian Democratic targets. Following the shameful example of Allende and Frei himself, Augusto Pinochet attacked the independent press, including the PDC newspaper, by withdrawing government advertising contracts. The Christian Democratic radio station was also shut down, and the junta began arresting leading Christian Democratic spokesmen and rank and file. In early 1975, the PDC started calling Pinochet a Fascist.

In the 1980s, the attitude of the PDC toward the military seemed to fluctuate according to the latter's economic success. In 1980, for example, in the prosperity that preceded the terrible 1981 recession, 80 percent of the delegates at a PDC plenum declared that they preferred life under the junta to life under Allende. This is faint praise, to be sure, but it is also an acknowledgment of the junta's economic achievements.

Christian Democratic trade unionists, for their part, led the fight for outright opposition to the junta and cosponsored illegal May Day celebrations in 1977 and 1978. They worked closely with the Socialist and Communist parties on these events. The first labor group to emerge from the chaos following the coup was the Catholic-inspired Group of Ten. The Ten were mostly moderate, Christian Democratic union leaders. They followed Catholic social thought and rejected recent Christian Democratic practice by insisting on their independence, on free collective bargaining, and on a minimum of state interference.

In 1980, Pinochet presented Chileans with a new constitution that, among other things, allowed Pinochet to remain in power until the end of the twentieth century and gave him substantial government power even after that. The PDC worked hard to have the constitution rejected. Their work included cooperation with the Chilean Communist Party. Whereas most civilian politicians were shocked that the 1980 constitution received so many votes, the Christian Democrats were not. They knew better than their political rivals just how much their support had dwindled.

Andrés Zalvidar, the PDC party president, denounced the 1980 plebescite as fraudulent, and the party contemplated joining the left in violent opposition. The regime promptly exiled him.

Christian Democrats, and other political forces, got an unexpected boost from the economic reversals that occurred just after the constitutional vote. Christian Democrats of all classes rejected the classical economic policies imposed by the Pinochet government. Andrés Zalvidar, finance minister under Eduardo Frei, was a particularly strong critic of the "Chicago boys." As late as 1987, Christian Democratic leader Ramón Brianes declared, "Our country has been handed to foreign powers through the renegotiation of the foreign debt, the norms that guide our foreign trade and, most of all, the sale of state-owned enterprises."[2]

Opposition to Pinochet broadened and deepened in the early 1980s. New PDC president Gabriel Valdés, Frei's foreign minister, was critical of Pinochet and open to collaboration with all but the nondemocratic left. The arrest of Valdés in June 1983 galvanized this opposition and led to a series of pan-banging demonstrations in Santiago, similar to the ones that plagued Allende. In August 1983, the PDC, along with the Radical Party, the Republican Right Party, the Social Democrats, and the Socialists, helped found the Democratic Alliance (AD).

The AD began talking with the government about democratization but soon found that Pinochet was skillful in exploiting the differences and disagreements among the AD members. He was also not shy about making these disagreements public, decreasing further the Chileans' esteem for politicians. At the same time, the talks helped to legitimize the Pinochet regime. Seeing that the junta was gaining more from the discussions than its opponents, the PDC recommended suspending the fruitless dialogue in October.

Since the Christian Democrats had insisted upon a hegemonic position in the AD and had staked so much of their reputation on its success, they suffered the most from its failure. They faced an electorate that did not trust them in power as much as it hated Pinochet's political repression. The PDC would have to change radically to regain Chileans' affections.

Part of this change came in 1985 as the PDC signed the National Accord for the Full Transition to Democracy with ten other political parties. In a grudging concession to the new economic realities that Pinochet had created, the accord accepted full respect for private property as one of its principles. The PDC rejected recent Christian Democratic practice and moved back toward Catholic social thought.

In the second half of the decade, as the regime's economic policies began to bear fruit and, more importantly, property and business ownership became more widespread, Christian Democrats faced a dilemma. On the one hand, accepting the economic measures of the regime, even in vague, partial terms, would seem to dilute their opposition. It would also mean turning their backs on the anticapitalist policies of the Frei administration.

On the other hand, the very economic liberalization that Pinochet oversaw was leading to demands for greater political liberalization. If the Christian Democrats could represent those demands, they could emerge from the military era stronger than any other party. Thus, in August 1987 PDC leader Sergio Molina gave a newspaper interview praising the Pinochet economic program while criticizing the political repression.

The PDC also resolved the issue of cooperation with leftist parties. After the October 1986 assassination attempt on Pinochet, party president Valdés stated that there would be "no kind of pact with the Communist Party or with any sector that espouses the path of arms or terrorism." With this statement Valdés assuaged the mistrust that still surrounded the PDC.

The debate over economic policy continued, however. For some PDC members, including Valdés, the idea of embracing any part of capitalism was repellent. On August 3, 1987, after an exhausting eight-month process, the party defeated the leftist Valdés faction and removed him as president. The new party president was Patricio Aylwin Azocar, who had been Senate president in September 1973 and was a fierce critic of Allende.

Aylwin's first political test was the scheduled 1988 plebiscite to determine whether or not Pinochet could run for an eight-year term as constitutional president. The general had won the 1980 constitutional plebiscite by presenting the opposition as squabbling incompetents thirsting to take away the economic gains of the Pinochet era. Aylwin calculated that only by assuring voters that return to civilian rule would not endanger their farms, their businesses, or their shares of stock could the opposition hope to defeat Pinochet.

At the same time, to merely repeat the junta's economic formulas would not provide any reason for a change. In differentiating himself from Pinochet, Aylwin has consistently moved toward Catholic social thought. Its criticisms of capitalism became Aylwin's, and he also adopted its suspicion of the state and its reliance on civil society.

The October 1988 plebiscite was a devastating defeat for Pinochet, and it set the stage for general elections on December 14, 1989. After trying unsuccessfully to get the other members of the junta to support him as a candidate, Pinochet withdrew. Seventeen opposition parties combined to form the Concertación and agreed on PDC president Aylwin as their candidate.

Backing the Junta's Economic Policies

Much of the difficulty that Christian Democrats have had, in Latin America and in Europe, stems from their efforts to please their leftist opposition. In Chile this policy had allowed Pinochet to link the PDC with the Allende years. Many PDC members insisted on a left-leaning policy anyway, to wash away the stain of early collaboration with the regime. Aylwin's policy was less reactive. He staked out his own political ground and invited other parties to come along. Although he made some minimal concessions to keep the Concertación together, he stopped trying to please the left and concentrated on attracting voters.

In its last years, the Pinochet government had privatized many state holdings. Most shares in state companies went to Chilean smallholders, rather than to large foreign buyers. The determination of these new owners' to remain owners made it expedient for Aylwin to accept the broad outlines of the regime's economic policies.

Popular capitalism, as its backers called it, was becoming genuinely popular in Chile. A December 1989 poll found that employers stood just below doctors and professors in public esteem, and above men of culture, priests, and artists. Employers ranked well above politicians. Sixty percent of Chileans preferred private employers to public employers.[3]

Aylwin moved to reassure the capitalists. "We are going to maintain," he insisted, "an open, competitive economy. We are going to keep stimulating the reinvestment of capital. We are going to keep in place inducements for investment."[4] He acknowledged the achievements of the Pinochet government, citing the opening to foreign trade, the diversification and expansion of Chilean exports, and the restriction of inflation to reasonable levels.[5]

Aylwin promised to continue privatizing state firms, to diversify exports even further, and to continue to limit public spending. He would not attack the independence of the Central Bank, the freedom of investment, or the right to private property. He even pledged not to try land reform anywhere in the country. Aylwin assured foreign investors that he would not significantly change the rules governing their activity, nor would he attempt to maintain an unrealistic exchange rate.

Alejandro Foxley, who became Aylwin's finance minister, told the Interamerican Development Bank that the new government's priorities would be economic stability, low inflation, and a balanced budget. Only after these things were achieved would Aylwin undertake major social programs.

Aylwin maintained his commitment to some neoliberal economic policies after his election. In a speech to workers on May Day 1990, he declared that redistribution was less important than growth. Growth requires productivity, which requires efficient businesses and efficient workers. Social programs are not, he insisted, worth the risk of unemployment, inflation, and instability. These economic reverses hurt workers more than anyone and are the surest route back to dictatorship.[6]

Businesses seemed to accept Aylwin's assurances by planning major investment expansion in the 1990s. Manuel Feliu, president of the Confederation of Production and Commerce, stated that presidential elections in Chile no longer meant investment lethargy. Businesspeople insisted, however, that there be no major changes in the "rules of the game."

Aylwin and Catholic Social Thought

Unlike his counterparts in Central America, Aylwin adhered to the principles of Catholic social thought during both his campaign and his first days as president. He struck a balance between the economic neoliberalism of the Pinochet regime and the old statism of the PDC that had failed so often to attract votes. Aylwin accepted the sanctity of private property, sought to increase the number of Chilean entrepreneurs, but limited the earlier regime's privatization policy. He also promised more social spending, respect for independent social groups and businesses, and political subsidiarity.

Aylwin worked hard to distinguish himself from Pinochet and from his actual opponent, former finance minister Hernán Buchi Buc, who was closely identified with the economic plans of the "Chicago boys." Aylwin was greatly assisted in this effort by Buchi's sudden populism as the campaign progressed. Buchi offered some of the prescriptions that were so popular with Christian Democrats in the 1960s and 1970s.

Buchi's economic program included "subsidiary assistance" for the private sector, which many took to mean preferential treatment for some businesses. He also announced a goal of a million new jobs in four years and greater job security. Reviving an old Christian Democratic favorite, he even promised 100,000 new housing units per year during his presidency.

Aylwin steered between failed populism and lock-step adherence to free market economics. He was assisted by the so-called Cieplan monks, named for the Cieplan Institute at Santiago's Catholic University. The institute had been critical of Pinochet's economic orthodoxy.

Aylwin moved quickly to dampen the expectations of social groups expecting major changes quickly. Rather than turning these social groups into clients, as his predecessors had, he warned them against selfishness and shortsightedness. Most importantly, he told them not to expect from government everything they wanted. Aylwin asked Chileans to ask themselves what they could do to put the country on the path to progress.

Government would play a part in the economy, however. Aylwin promised to inaugurate certain social programs for poor Chileans. To do this, it would be necessary to raise taxes. Aylwin kept his eyes on his goal of balancing growth with distribution. Although income taxes had to rise, the PDC proposed a small rise. The largest rise would be from 29 percent to 45 percent for the top 10 percent income bracket.

Corporate taxes, starting from a low level, would increase to 15–20 percent of income. Aylwin brushed aside the complaints of businesspeople who pointed out that this was nearly a 100 percent increase in the tax rate. He compared his proposed 20 percent rate with the 35–60 percent corporate tax rate in most developed countries. He also insisted that businesses had plenty of time to prepare for the increase. Perhaps most significantly, he quoted Pope John Paul II, who said that solidarity meant not just the creation of new businesses but also the financial contribution of those who earn more to those who earn less.[7]

The Concertación platform proposed not only a rise in corporate taxes but also the removal of tax breaks for selected businesses, an old mainstay of Christian Democratic business policy. Aylwin's coalition also promised to retain incentives for reinvestment of profits. Under Pinochet, reinvested profits were exempt from taxes.

In his inaugural address, Aylwin revealed the tightrope under his feet. He told Chile: "We need to grow if we want to overcome poverty. This requires that we stimulate savings, investment, creative initiative and the entrepreneurial spirit. Government must reconcile the spirit of social justice and the legitimate requirement to satisfy essential needs."[8]

In an interview just after taking office, Aylwin said that the current system did not take into account social needs. His government would, he promised, provide for social needs like jobs, housing, health, and education. None of these ambitions, however, required him to increase state economic power, as so many other Christian Democratic administrations had done.

Aylwin also signaled his intention to avoid overvaluing Chilean currency or, indeed, manipulating the exchange rate at all. A Central Bank announcement soon after Aylwin's inauguration, made with Aylwin's blessing, said that while the official exchange rate would remain, an informal, but legal, exchange market would exist alongside it. Only a few financial operations would require access to the official rate; most transactions could use the informal rate. At the same time, the legal status of the informal market would help to prevent the government from overvaluing the local currency.

Aylwin's policy on privatization radically differed from that of the Pinochet era. Speaking at the May Day rally, Aylwin said: "Some sectors of our economy — which belong to the entire nation — were the target of a [Pinochet] policy that deliberately sought to destroy the state apparatus and the national wealth, seeking to transfer it to private hands for ridiculous prices."

Aylwin appointed one of the more leftist members of the coalition to head Corfo, the state holding company. In November 1990, the company announced its new privatization policy. Service companies would remain wholly in state hands. Energy-providing companies would be partially privatized, but the state would retain a 51 percent interest. The shipping and port authorities, both of which needed major capital inputs, would be put on the block.

In addition, the Aylwin government announced it would not use privatization to finance the budget. The government's budget changes, including more social programs, were permanent, and funding them with one-time privatization income would be unfair and unwise, according to Budget Director José Pablo Arellano.

Aylwin adhered closely to Catholic social thought in this regard. While retaining possession, or at least control, of several vital or strategic companies, he shied away from acquiring more for the state. He also accepted private participation in some companies and recognized that capital inputs were important. There is nothing to indicate that he will expand state economic power.

Aylwin abandoned Pinochet's labor policies and replaced them with policies drawn from Catholic social thought. His first act was to assure labor unions that they had full legal sanction and that the days of repression were over. He hastened to warn labor unions, however, about expecting too much too soon. Aylwin was determined to avoid the errors of the civilian leaders in Peru and Argentina. After overthrowing military governments, both had rushed to improve wages and social services, only to find fiscal deficits and inflation forcing them into deep recessions.[9] These, he insisted, threatened the democracy for which they had all worked. The unions were receptive to his long-term commitment to democracy. After telling one union audience not to expect any substantial change for 18 months, Aylwin received a standing ovation.[10]

The unions might also have been applauding Aylwin's evident commitment to union independence, which Catholic social thought champions and recent Christian Democratic practice had compromised. Aylwin told the May Day crowd: "We do not want to impose rules. To the extent possible, we would like such rules to be the result of fair accords between interested parties."

He referred to an April 28 labor-business accord, in which labor and management had, without resorting to government intervention, worked out new rules for bargaining and representation. The accord showed, Aylwin said, that people were aware that the improvement of the situation of workers "is inevitably linked with the success of enterprises and with the development of the economy."

Labor unions did not desire more government intervention. They had no desire to become wards of the state, as earlier Christian Democratic governments had insisted. Rather, their leaders believed that the state should limit itself to providing unemployment insurance to workers displaced by improvements in technology. Again demonstrating a positive reluctance to increase state economic power, the Aylwin government suggested that the private sector fund such insurance, not the state.

Aylwin's platform called for an increase in labor-intensive industries, a minimum wage, mandatory union dues, and collective bargaining by geographic area, rather than by firm. He also revived the Catholic social goal of self-management of enterprises through profit sharing.

Owners did not welcome all these changes. Area bargaining, for example, was anathema. Seeing the way the tide was turning, however, the larger business confederations suggested bargaining by industry or by economic sector, both of which would be more manageable than geographic area.

Labor and business also contended over union dues for nonmembers, although compromise was reached here also. The Aylwin government announced an agreement, reached by the parties themselves, through which nonunion workers would pay lower union dues, which were reserved for specific activities. Business owners also sought to make union formation easier by simplifying the rules and reducing the numbers of employees required to start a new union. Labor and the Aylwin government responded cautiously to this proposal, fearing that owners were trying to fragment existing unions.

Severance pay was another issue on which Aylwin persuaded the two sides to compromise. Under Pinochet, fired workers were entitled to one month's wages for each year of employment, to a maximum of five years. Unions wanted the limit removed, and the Concertación had promised this in its campaign statement. The PDC-led government finally decided that the costs of removing the limit were prohibitive, and it recommended a ten-year limit.

Having placed a good deal of confidence in the private sector, Aylwin showed that he was also conscious of the attempts made by private owners to avoid competition. Aylwin has consistently sought to make the private enterprise system work more efficiently and more humanely. Where collusion was a problem, he addressed it with more competition, consistent with Catholic social thought.

He began by taking on the powerful Santiago bus cartels. The private bus lines of the capital had effectively insulated themselves from competition and produced only poor transportation and pollution. Rather than taking over the bus lines, as earlier Christian Democratic governments would have done, Aylwin moved to ease market entry for newcomers while providing incentives to put older, and dirtier, buses off the streets. He also offered incentives to move buses to the provinces, which needed them more than Santiago's overcrowded streets.[11] Aylwin suggested tolls on major streets to fight congestion.

The PDC's social agenda included more spending on health, housing, and family allowances. Catholic social thought tolerates slower and less efficient economic growth to achieve these goals. Aylwin also promised debt relief for poor Chileans with laws limiting their mortgage payments to a percentage of income and spreading out the debt as necessary. To help prevent permanent indebtedness, the PDC added incentives for paying debts early.

Aylwin also promised the democratization of city halls, with the election of mayors and aldermen, consistent with the Catholic social precept of subsidiarity. This policy reduces the power of the central government, something that Christian Democrats have avoided until very recently.

Results: Can Aylwin Succeed?

The December 1989 election was a smashing victory for the Concertación. Buchi's misguided and belated populism, plus the assurance that they could vote for a Pinochet opponent and yet retain the desired features of the Pinochet regime, persuaded Chileans to vote for Aylwin in large numbers. Besides the presidency, the PDC-led coalition also won a 72–48 seat majority in the lower house of the national legislature.

Aylwin faces opposition in the Senate, however, where eight appointed senators give his opponents a three-seat edge. Even in the lower house, Aylwin lacks the votes to change the constitution or to pass measures requiring large majorities. Much of this opposition represents businesspeople unwilling to compete and hoping for special relationships with the state. This political pressure will make it more difficult for Aylwin to remain on his course.

Aylwin also faces potential opposition within his own coalition. His ministers of education and economy and his government general secretary are Socialists who may become impatient with Aylwin's reluctance to increase state power. Ironically, this potential leftist opposition could join forces with the senators who represent businesses that desire more government favoritism.

Aylwin's political success so far is directly related to his commitment to Catholic social thought. This faithfulness has allowed him, so far, to balance the rising expectations of Chile's new popular capitalist class with the long-checked hopes of poorer Chileans. Continued economic growth is vital to keeping these two constituencies supportive. Two full years into his term, Aylwin continued to foster both economic growth and to moderately increase social spending.[12]

Of the factors that Aylwin can control, the level of government economic intervention will have the greatest impact on this growth. If the economy falters, the temptation to use statism to stave off political opposition will be strong. It would, however, mean abandoning Catholic social thought, as well as major parts of the Aylwin coalition. Aylwin has both an ideological and a political motive to avoid this.

PERU: CATHOLIC SOCIAL THOUGHT ABANDONED

Peru's Popular Christian Party

Christian Democracy in Peru started in the 1950s and was originally disposed to work with APRA, the American Popular Revolutionary Alliance, under its founder, Víctor Haya de la Torre. As the 1960s approached, the party disdained the gradualism of Haya and moved radically leftward under Héctor Cornejo Chávez. It came in a poor fourth in the 1962 election.

Although Cornejo Chávez had been very critical of him during the campaign, President-elect Fernando Belaúnde Terry, of the Popular Alliance Party (AP), accepted the Christian Democrats into a coalition and offered them cabinet posts. Belaúnde's agriculture minister was Enrique Torres Llosa, who was active in fighting for agrarian reform. The Christian Democrats left Belaúnde's government in 1967, charging that he was too friendly to capitalists.

The decision to quit the government exposed a long-simmering division between leftists and centrists in the Christian Democratic party. Luis Bedoya Reyes, a centrist, took many of his followers out of the party in February 1967 and founded the Popular Christian Party (PPC). Bedoya could not abide Cornejo Chávez's "structural revolution" in which the state would plan, promote, and coordinate the sectors of production.

The PPC became a forceful advocate of free enterprise and of reduced restrictions on foreign and domestic investment. Typically for a Christian Democratic party out of power, the PPC followed Catholic social thought rather closely. They were rewarded with a large share of the votes in 1978 legislative elections. In the 1980 presidential race, however, they declined to seek election on their own, joining instead with Belaúnde's AP and offering essentially the same platform as the AP.

During the presidency of APRA's Alan García (1985–1990), the PPC became a more and more strident critic of the government. The issue that would focus their opposition and determine their future political fortunes occurred in 1987.

García's Bank Nationalization Plan

To some observers, García's 1987 plan to nationalize the country's banking industry was nothing more than a reasonable plan to get control of the Peruvian economy. García himself justified it on these grounds. Foreign banks, however, were exempt from the policy. Its targets were domestic operations, control of which would also give the government effective control over almost all of Peru's business transactions.

Reaction to the plan was immediate and vehement. The PPC instantly opposed the nationalization, although their brother Christian Democrats in El Salvador had done something similar seven years earlier. Party deputy Enrique Elías Laranza, for example, called the nationalization plan unconstitutional, unconscionable, and "a step backwards for democracy."[13] The issue seemed destined to galvanize a population weary of García's economic missteps, and PPC leaders probably hoped the issue would catapult them to leadership of the opposition.

It very well could have but for the appearance of Mario Vargas Llosa on the political scene. The internationally known writer had eschewed partisan politics, though his novels frequently had political overtones. Like many Latin American intellectuals, he was once a Marxist. Disillusioned with the repression in Cuba and inspired by Poland's Solidarity movement, however, he abandoned Marxism by the mid-1980s. He emerged in 1987 to lead opposition to the bank takeover. Largely as a result of his efforts, García had to abandon the plan. Even then, Vargas Llosa seemed to lead reluctantly, saying he would rather be in his study.

Close beside Vargas Llosa was Hernando deSoto, author of *El Otro Sendero* and popular antistatist economist. DeSoto discovered the political potential of Peru's informal economy, and he hoped that Vargas Llosa would adopt this sector as his political base. DeSoto and Vargas Llosa parted company in 1987, however, due in large part to the latter's insistence on pure neoliberalism. As suspicious of state economic power as any of the authors of Catholic social thought, deSoto also shared some of their objections to pure capitalism.

The Formation of Fredemo

Vargas Llosa's victory over García's plan prompted Luis Bedoya and Fernando Belaúnde to merge their parties with the Liberty Movement, which Vargas Llosa had founded to oppose the bank policy. Their goal was to use Vargas Llosa's personality, famous name, and his reputation for honesty and independence to defeat APRA in the 1990 election and prevent what they feared would be Peru's economic meltdown. A successful coalition would, of course, also bring them to power.

On January 30, 1988, Belaúnde, Bedoya, and Vargas Llosa agreed to form the Democratic Front (Fredemo). After 14 months of close collaboration, they registered jointly for the November 1989 municipal elections. Their more important goal, as everyone knew, was the April 1990 presidential balloting.

The coalition partners did not always get along well, however. On June 21, 1989, Vargas Llosa resigned from the party leadership in a disagreement over joint lists for the November municipal elections. The issue was important, and it reveals a vital clue toward explaining Vargas Llosa's later presidential defeat.

If the three parties in Fredemo offered separate candidates for local offices, Vargas Llosa, as the party's presidential aspirant, would have to stay neutral. This would mean months of virtual silence at a time when Vargas Llosa wanted to proclaim his free market gospel to the country. When his partners relented, he returned to the fray and campaigned in earnest.

Peruvians rewarded Fredemo for its forthright antistatist stance with large gains in the municipal voting. Its only substantial loss came in Lima, whose mayoralty it lost to Ricardo Belmont, an independent conservative. Both the wins and the loss were harbingers. When Fredemo was identified with the social and economic ideas of deSoto, and with the informal market, it won large gains. Fredemo had lost much of this identity by April 1990, and even more in the disastrous runoff.

The Lima race also showed that Peruvians wanted a change, but they mistrusted traditional politicians to give it to them. They preferred newcomers and independents. To win, Fredemo would have to emphasize its belief in popular capitalism and maintain its independence from Peru's insider political system. It did not.

Fredemo and Catholic Social Thought

The new party's philosophy had some important elements in common with Catholic social thought. Its leaders distrusted the state to repair the dangers of capitalism. Speaking about the news media in 1990, Vargas Llosa acknowledged that private media outlets are subject to powerful interests, but he added that state control was a cure worse than the disease.[14]

In an earlier interview, he underlined his suspicion of the state. He said: "In a country like Peru, where democracy is still weak, if the government has great economic power it will use it in order to consolidate and maintain its own power. . . . The state in Peru belongs not to the citizens, but to the government."[15]

During the campaign, he added that economic democracy must find its center in the consumer or the producer, certainly not in the bureaucrat.[16] He deplored the fact that so many democratic governments had started preaching state intervention and state usurpation of initiative.

Vargas Llosa's statements on privatization also seemed consistent with Catholic social thought. He would achieve privatization, he said, through a controlled sale of stock that would give preference to workers and employees. He added, however, that such sales would not entail any dismissals. For Peru's overloaded state agencies, this meant there would be no buyers. Catholic social thought does not guarantee jobs to state workers, especially if their inefficiency threatens the entire enterprise.

Vargas Llosa wanted to begin a system of profit sharing in the private sector. He defended incentive programs to allow workers to purchase stock. He also promised "genuine union democracy," a goal consistent with Catholic social thought.

Vargas Llosa maintained an outward commitment to the multiplication of capital enterprises. Fredemo's planning chief, Luis Bustamente Belaúnde, told a business daily in March 1990 that a Fredemo government would offer financing to small-scale, labor-intensive projects in urban neighborhoods and in the country. These projects would develop independently, at local initiative. The government would favor projects that increased wages before buying more materials or sophisticated equipment.

Economic Neoliberalism

Vargas Llosa's proposals are consistent with Catholic social thought, and had he continued to speak in this vein, his election would have been certain. (Indeed, it was certain until late in the campaign.) The Fredemo candidate, however, added elements of neoliberalism that emphasized its most harsh individualism, the very element the popes had criticized in their encyclicals.

In some cases, Vargas Llosa's free market policies did not conflict with Catholic social thought. For example, he promised to cut the number of taxes from over 100 to 10. He promised to eliminate exemptions and rationalize the corporate tax to spur reinvestment. At the same time, he hoped to increase the tax burden from 4 percent to 15 percent of GDP. His tariff policy was equally benign. Fredemo promised to reduce both the number and level of tariffs drastically, allowing them to fall quickly to 15–20 percent. Peru would also have a single market exchange rate under Fredemo, Vargas Llosa pledged.

On other matters, Vargas Llosa's capitalism seemed unnecessarily harsh and strayed from the Catholic social precept that, in some cases, relieving human suffering is more important than strict economic efficiency. For example, Vargas Llosa promised to reduce Peru's escalating inflation rate, which was over 1 million percent for the García administration, to 10 percent per year. He admitted, and even seemed to take pride in the fact that this would be horribly recessionary and painful.

Adding to the pain was Fredemo's plan to free the prices of all publicly provided goods and services and to lift price controls on all other goods and services. This is sound economics. Getting the government out of the price-setting business is good Catholic social thought. Weaning a society off statism, however, takes time if it is not to cause great disruption. Vargas Llosa was singularly unwilling to give Peru any time. Similarly, he promised to privatize all state companies, without exception, even those in strategic sectors that were turning a profit.

In the countryside, Vargas Llosa was committed to offering those who worked the land a permanent deed, but without temporary credit support or exchange rate protection that would allow new landowners to accumulate capital. He seemed intent on promoting his policies of extreme economic individualism at any cost. Many Peruvians concluded from this statement that Fredemo intended to create conditions that would allow reconsolidation of land. Although good economics, this is inconsistent with Catholic social thought, which discourages consolidation in any part of the economy.

Workers and Management

A campaign based on Catholic social thought would have recruited Peruvian workers, especially workers in the informal market, into a crusade against the entrenched privilege of favored businesses. This would have required a balance of free market economics and social programs. It is a delicate balance, but Aylwin's experience shows that skill and a commitment to Catholic social thought make it possible. Vargas Llosa, for his part, managed to alienate both the businesspeople and the workers, while offering almost nothing to the informals and other small businesspeople who make up Christian Democracy's most promising new constituency.

As the campaign progressed, Vargas Llosa became more emphatic in his statements on eliminating monopolies and other "mercantilist" elements from the economy. Peru's wealthy businesspeople, accustomed to shopping for special privileges when new governments come to power, became nervous. Fredemo policies split the business class into traditional and nontraditional exporters. The former wanted their protection continued; the latter wanted a level playing field. It was the traditional exporters who had the greater political clout, however.

Vargas Llosa might have overcome all these obstacles had he tried to mobilize and galvanize Peru's large and growing informal sector. These Peruvians had numbers, energy, and no political patron in 1989–1990. They seemed tailor-made for Fredemo's needs. Vargas Llosa praised them numerous times during the campaign and did promise to lighten the regulatory burden that forced many people into the informal market in the first place.

He did little to excite their support, however. One of his only proposals directly related to them was his determination to register them so they could start paying taxes. His recessionary measures seemed calculated to increase vastly the numbers of informals, hardly a boon to those already in that market. Vargas Llosa evidently concluded that informals were as enthusiastic about individualistic neoliberalism as he was. Informals see capitalism at its harshest, and they desire some protection from its rougher edges.

Part of Fredemo's economic plan was the firing of 500,000 state employees. In addition, Vargas Llosa planned to extend the grounds for just dismissal, threatening job security even further. Fredemo promised to allow exceptions to the just dismissal rule for those in seasonable employment, for young people, and for those in new businesses. Job security, Vargas Llosa pointed out early on, was inconsistent with rapid economic growth.

For Catholic social thinkers, this inconsistency means that economic growth will have to be slower. For Vargas Llosa, it meant adding half a million people to the unemployment rolls. (This policy cost him the support of Poland's Lech Walesa.) While Catholic social thought has no patience with bureaucrats who do not work, neither does it tolerate starvation in the name of growth. Vargas Llosa presented the ideas in the same cold, calculating tone that he used for all his most painful ideas.

After his loss, Vargas Llosa admitted that his lack of "feelings, solidarity and compassion" was a mistake. Still, he betrayed little knowledge that there was more to his loss than style. He said in a November 1990 retrospective: "In the future, the [political] battle will not be between socialism and capitalism but between populism — the politics of Yeltsin and Walesa — and classical liberalism. Populism is terribly appealing but destructive because it sacrifices the future for the present."[17]

CAUSES OF VARGAS LLOSA'S DEFEAT

Vargas Llosa was handicapped by the decision of Peru's ruling state oligarchy to combine against him in the runoff election. Immediately after the first-round results came in, both the ruling APRA and the United Left (IU) signaled that they would recommend voting for Alberto Fujimori of Cambio 90 or, more precisely, against Vargas Llosa, in the second round.

After Vargas Llosa lost the runoff, outgoing president Alan García hailed Vargas Llosa's defeat as a rejection of the free market policies he represented. The right, García maintained, had suffered an enormous defeat. García all but announced his intention to run for reelection in 1995.

The defeat of the Fredemo coalition was not a defeat for the right. It was certainly not a defeat for Catholic social thought, in spite of the fact that the PPC was perhaps the major victim of the defeat. There were numerous reasons for Vargas Llosa's defeat, the most important of which was the embrace of Catholic social thought by his opponent.

Vacillation in the Runoff

One trait that Vargas Llosa did share with Christian Democrats was the tendency to retreat from principled stands to pragmatic compromises during times of political stress. After barely finishing with a plurality in the April 1990 general election and being forced into a runoff, Vargas Llosa's first instinct was to quit and return to Europe. Persuaded by his opponent to stay in the race, he tempered many of his positions, thereby confusing those whom he did not repel.

In a crucial debate one week before the runoff, Vargas Llosa insisted that he did not propose shock treatment for the Peruvian economy, even though he had said during the campaign that this was exactly what Peru needed and that only he could administer it. While his proposals stayed the same, he ceased to call them shock treatment. This cosmetic change fooled no one.

He also backed off on his promise of mass layoffs, saying that he would merely demand greater efficiency from workers. For those who were laid off, he promised that small enterprises would provide all the assistance they needed. Eventually, he claimed that only the wealthy would suffer from his economic stabilization program, not the poor.

One of Vargas Llosa's most puzzling reversals was on inflation, the heart of his economic program. After promising to reduce inflation to 10 percent, regardless of the recessionary cost, he announced in January 1990 that his first action would be a massive infusion of currency into circulation. This, he said, would enable the government to dispose of its domestic debt, which the outgoing García regime was accumulating rapidly.

He did not mention that the resulting burst of inflation, coming on top of Peru's prevailing five-digit rate, would also mean the destruction of most of the savings in the country. It would be particularly damaging to small investors, and devastating to informals, who had to keep most of their assets in cash. Vargas Llosa's opponents were quick to highlight these dangers.

Except for the last one, Vargas Llosa's policy reverses were moves toward Catholic social thought. One of the troubles with last-minute changes in policy, however, is that even when they are correct, they are often unbelievable and so politically counterproductive. Peruvians simply did not trust Vargas Llosa to implement the policies they wanted.

Tactical Mistakes

Vargas Llosa was simply not a good campaigner. He had enormous difficulty with the comparatively easy task of remaining in Peru during the electoral contest. In the fall of 1989, for example, he suddenly left for a four-week trip to Asia to study the neoliberal policies of that region's newly industrialized states. His absence from Peru at this crucial time hurt him. In February 1990, only weeks from the balloting, he went to visit Brazilian President Fernando Collor de Mello. He not only lost more time but acted like a visiting head of state, giving the impression that the election was already won.

His campaign style was also flawed. Although justifiably fearful of Peru's Shining Path guerrillas, Vargas Llosa seemed oddly reluctant to actually meet voters, preferring either television or short rallies on short notice. He traveled by private jet, which became a target for his political enemies.

Squandering the Status of an "Outsider"

More important than tactical errors was Vargas Llosa's failure to make use of his status as a political outsider. Peruvians held traditional politicians, and existing political parties, in low esteem in 1989–1990, and one of the reasons for Vargas Llosa's early success was his independence from these mistrusted parties.

Joining with the AP and the PPC, however, detracted from his original appeal as an independent. (It did not do the PPC any good either.) As the runoff campaign progressed, Vargas Llosa's opponent repeatedly emphasized Vargas Llosa's links with Peru's professional politicians. Vargas Llosa made Fujimori's task easier by stating, in October 1989, "If there is someone who believes in the political parties in Peru, it is I, despite the fact that I am very independent."[18]

His proclamations of independence might have worked had he not had to run against someone even more obviously a political outsider than he was. As it was, his opponent was Alberto Fujimori, a former talk show host with a wide audience in the countryside. He was unknown to Peru's political elites and received almost no mention in early analyses of the campaign.

For a time, he also seemed invisible to most Peruvians. A poll in January 1990 did not even include his name, and even by March he had gained the support of only 9 percent of the sample.[19] On April 8, however, he received 30 percent of the votes to Vargas Llosa's 33 percent.

Fujimori emphasized his independence during the runoff campaign and insistently reminded voters of Vargas Llosa's links with the AP and PPC. In the televised debate on April 3, he mentioned these links on ten separate occasions.

FUJIMORI AND CATHOLIC SOCIAL THOUGHT

Fujimori's victory was not a rejection of free market economics. As the following discussion will show, his platform was very similar to Vargas Llosa's. They shared a commitment to the free market and were almost indistinguishable on other issues as well.

To explain why Vargas Llosa lost, however, is not to explain why Fujimori won. Fujimori differed from Vargas Llosa on some economic policies. He was less extreme in his language, less committed to pure capitalist orthodoxy, and more sensitive to the immediate needs of a society addicted to government intervention. More significantly, Fujimori's policies were consistently closer to Catholic social thought. The victory of Fujimori is yet another proof of the electoral potential of this philosophy.

The Peruvian people themselves were strongly committed to less government intervention in the economy in 1990. In a March poll on economic questions sponsored by the probusiness *Comercio*, 54.4 percent of the sample agreed that there should be less state intervention in the economy. Over 90 percent wanted less bureaucratization. In addition, 53.8 percent favored privatization of state companies, and 75 percent believed that foreign investment was necessary and salutatory.[20]

Fujimori promised less state intervention in financial policy. He proposed the creation of a new currency that would not only be allowed to fluctuate freely, according to market pressures, but would be pegged one to one with the U.S. dollar. In his April 3 debate with Vargas Llosa, Fujimori maintained that Cambio 90 would guarantee all forms of property.

He even suggested, as deSoto had, that security of property was the only long-term solution to Peru's corrosive drug trade. Substituting other crops for coca, he insisted, was possible only when peasants in the countryside held true and undisputed title to their land. Only then would they make the investments necessary to make other crops more profitable than coca.

In his debate with Vargas Llosa, Fujimori himself acknowledged that Fredemo and Cambio 90 had many objectives in common, but he reminded viewers that they differed on methods. These differences place Fujimori, intentionally or not, consistently in line with Catholic social thought.

Catholic social thought suggests gradual solutions that do not make the existing situation worse. Thus, Fujimori took issue with Vargas Llosa on controlling inflation. While Vargas Llosa promised to plunge the country into a deep recession to cut inflation to 10 percent, Fujimori promised to release prices gradually and compassionately. Hyperinflation is socially corrosive, he agreed, but so was unemployment.

Fujimori also recommended a slow and cautious course on privatization. Whereas Vargas Llosa demanded the immediate privatization of all state companies, Fujimori suggested privatizing most of them (230 of 240), while forcing the others to operate more efficiently. He would retain the state oil and gas monopoly, he said, while inviting foreign investors as partners. Fujimori pointed out the illogic of Vargas Llosa's demand that state companies be immediately privatized without firing any of the workers. Large payrolls were what was making the state companies a drain on state resources. Under those conditions, the only buyers would be speculators or fools.

It would be better, Fujimori contended, first to make the gradual changes necessary to make the state companies run more efficiently, then seek buyers. This would also be more humane to the state employees. Those who refused to work for their pay would be let go, but not all at once and only for cause.

Fujimori drew closest to Catholic social thought in his proposals to support and create small businesses. Like Vargas Llosa, Fujimori promised to streamline Peru's Byzantine tax system, but his plan added incentives for small-scale agriculture and mining. A Cambio 90 vice-presidential candidate proposed to exempt from taxes all companies with transactions of less than U.S.$800,000 per year.[21]

Fujimori told Peru: "I understand the small and medium producer, and they know that I will defend them." He also told listeners, not entirely accurately, that Vargas Llosa's supporters, and the people on the Fredemo candidate list, were all big businesspeople. Cambio 90, on the other hand, had small businesspeople on its list, and many informals. There were no informals with Fredemo, he said.

Fujimori also reminded listeners that his parents had immigrated to Peru from Japan and had actually been in the informal market. Fujimori had worked in this demanding environment himself. The contrast between him and the wealthy and cosmopolitan Vargas Llosa must have been striking.

Vargas Llosa's weak defense was to link himself with deSoto. Most Peruvians must have been aware that the two had parted company some time before. The issue that separated them was, significantly, Vargas Llosa's refusal to temper his free market formulas with Catholic social precepts. DeSoto's commitment to this philosophy goes back to his early days as a leader of the Arequipa branch of the PPC.

Fujimori had other beliefs in common with Catholic social thought. While Vargas Llosa variously suggested doing away with public education and guaranteeing it through the university level, Fujimori promised that his education system would have a flexible and simplified curricular structure that could be diversified in accordance with the geographic, ethnic, and cultural characteristics of students.

Had Fujimori been completely in step with Catholic social thought, he would have emphasized the primary role of the family in education. However, his commitment to local diversity at least represents a tendency toward subsidiarity in education. Fujimori favored devolving power to the regions in other matters as well.

Finally, although he had a good deal of support from Protestant Evangelicals, Fujimori is a practicing Catholic. He contrasted his faith with Vargas Llosa's agnosticism on a number of occasions. To the deeply religious people of Peru, the contrast only emphasized the gulf between them and the cosmopolitan sophisticate who ran against Fujimori.

President Fujimori, however, has learned just how difficult it is to implement the balanced and nuanced strictures of Catholic social thought. Many Latin American Christian Democrats encountered the same challenge and responded by moving toward greater state intervention. Fujimori, for his part, has moved toward the harsher neoliberalism that he had promised to avoid.

To fight inflation, and to balance the budget, he removed subsidies, suddenly and immediately, sending prices up 200 percent to 3,000 percent overnight. Within a week of this shock, and within a month of his inauguration, he allowed another large rise in public service rates. For all his talk of protecting the informals, he immediately levied a sales tax on all purchases, forcing the informals into the tax system. He also levied what he said would be a short, one-time 10 percent tax on exports.

When Fujimori took office, the National Administrative Institute said that there were 738,000 Peruvians on the state payroll. Independent estimates showed that 1.0 million of the 7.2 million people in Peru's active economy worked for the government. Fujimori the candidate bitterly attacked Vargas Llosa's promise to remove 500,000 of these employees. Once in office himself, he moved to fire 400,000.[22]

The central thrust of Fujimori's economic message was his promise to protect small business. After his first two months in office, an independent businessman claimed that Fujimori's price and tax policies put 7,000 small-and medium-sized companies out of business.[23] The effect of these policies on the informal market was even more devastating.[24]

If Catholic social thought is difficult for ardent supporters to implement, it is impossible for those not fully committed to it to do so. The proper bearers of the Catholic social message in Peru should be the Popular Christian Party. The 1990 campaign represents a tragically lost opportunity for this party, as well as for Christian Democracy in Latin America. It almost offsets the Aylwin victory in Chile.

Like so many Christian Democratic parties before them, the PPC lost its nerve at a crucial moment. The enormous early attractiveness of Mario

Vargas Llosa seemingly hypnotized the party into an ill-fated coalition. Vargas Llosa had nothing to offer the PPC except his name and his independence. The baggage that he brought along, including his atheism, his estrangement from Hernando deSoto, and his unswerving commitment to a free market, was damaging.

It turned out to be a poor bargain for the PPC, but this was predictable from the start. They could have provided everything that Vargas Llosa had going for him, with none of the negatives. The Fujimori victory proved that a famous name was not a necessary element of victory. The PPC could have nominated a new face and emphasized that except for a few ministries under Belaúnde in the 1960s, they had never been in government. Thus they could have campaigned as outsiders also. Most importantly, they could have spread the message of Catholic social thought, which had so much to do with Fujimori's victory.

CONCLUSION

Christian Democracy must abandon its nonideological "pragmatism" or face its demise. Since 1978, as formal democracy has returned to Latin America, the continent has held 36 presidential elections. Christian Democratic parties competed in 19 of these elections. In only seven were they victorious. No Latin American Christian Democratic party has ever successfully sought reelection. When Christian Democrats have won, their victory can, in all but one instance (Ecuador 1984), be traced to their support for Catholic social thought.

The Aylwin victory points up the attractiveness of Catholic social thought. Through the long years of the Pinochet dictatorship, Chileans consistently voted for the one option that promised the closest approach to Catholic social thought. In 1980, with opposition parties leaning heavily toward the left, they endorsed Pinochet's constitution.

In 1988, with the Christian Democrats having rediscovered their Catholic social roots, Pinochet was soundly rejected. In 1989, with the junta's favored candidate veering toward populism and state favoritism for insiders, Chileans endorsed the Concertación, in which economic policies consistent with Catholic social thought were dominant.

If Christian Democracy has a future in Latin America, it lies in this rediscovery. Although challenging in its implementation, Catholic social thought has the advantages of coherence, consistency, and compassion. It is friendly enough to the free market to benefit from the current popularity of economic orthodoxy in Latin America. It can also present itself as the best qualified, and the most gentle, guide to societies trying to travel the painful path from state-guided economies to free economies.

Statism corrodes the very talents, attitudes, and abilities that make a free economy productive and humane. These include self-reliance, self-discipline, and self-sacrifice. When government makes all the economic decisions, or at least all the important ones, people come to expect government officials to see to their needs, and they come to depend upon government. As the newly liberated republics of Eastern Europe and the former Soviet Union are learning, capitalistic attitudes cannot be reinstilled overnight. Statism has dominated Latin America far longer than Eastern Europe.

The challenge is even greater, however. The self-oriented characteristics of the successful capitalist must coexist with empathy, charity, and social solidarity. Punishment for the lazy must coexist with help for the indigent. The accumulation of profits must remain a means to an end, not an end in itself. Consumer sovereignty cannot become consumerism, or the system loses clemency.

Catholic social thought offers the best chance of reconciling these tensions. It will not be easy. All the time that Latin America's Christian Democrats spent denying their roots and reconciling themselves to the seemingly unstoppable growth of the state was so much wasted time. It has left them ill prepared for the neoliberal politics of the 1990s, for which Catholic social thought was always prepared.

Christian Democrats still ignore opportunities to represent their natural constituency, the informals. In Venezuela, the leftist AD has already moved to claim this sector for its own, under the eyes of the Christian Democratic Copei. Catholic social thought, dismissed by many, including many Christian Democrats, as hopelessly medieval, anticipated the economic conditions of the 1990s almost perfectly. As the Church marks the centennial of *Rerum Novarum*, the encyclical that started it all, events transpire to prove its continuing importance.

NOTES

1. For an excellent treatment of the party under Pinochet, see Michael Fleet, *The Rise and Fall of Chilean Christian Democracy* (Princeton, N.J.: Princeton University Press, 1985).

2. Santiago, Radio Chilena, 12 March 1987 (Foreign Broadcast Information Service, Latin America *Daily Report*, hereinafter FBIS, 18 March 1987, pp. E4–5).

3. Santiago, *El Mercurio*, 10 December 1989, p. 12 (FBIS, 11 January 1990, p. 41).

4. *World Press Review*, May 1990, p. 52.

5. Santiago, *Ercilla*, 11 October 1989, p. 6 (FBIS, 16 November 1989, p. 45).

6. Santiago, Domestic Service, 1 May 1990 (FBIS, 3 May 1990, pp. 32–36).

7. Santiago, *El Mercurio*, 17 December 1989, pp. 1D–2D (FBIS, 24 January 1990, pp. 54–60).

8. Santiago, Domestic Service, 12 March 1990 (FBIS, 13 March 1990, pp. 34–37).

9. Pamela Constable and Arturo Valenzuela, "Chile's Return to Democracy," *Foreign Affairs* 68, 2 (1989): 182.

10. Latin America Regional Reports, *Weekly Report*, 15 February 1990, p. 8.

11. Latin America Regional Reports, *Weekly Report*, 6 September 1990, p. 9.

12. *New York Times*, 30 April 1992, p. A3.

13. Lima, Panamericana TV, 13 August 1987 (FBIS, 19 August 1987, pp. R10–15).

14. Mario Vargas Llosa, "A Cultural Battle," *Unesco Courier*, September 1990, p. 45.

15. Mario Vargas Llosa, "Privatizing Peru," *New Perspectives Quarterly* Fall 1989, p. 40.

16. Lima, *El Comercio*, 3 December 1989, p. 4a (FBIS, 5 January 1990, pp. 69–71).

17. *U.S. News and World Report*, 5 November 1990, p. 15.

18. Lima, *Caretas*, 30 October 1989, pp. 30–35 (FBIS, 16 December 1989, p. 32).

19. Latin America Regional Reports, *Weekly Report*, 29 March 1990, p. 11.

20. Lima, *El Comercio*, 23 March 1990 (FBIS, 10 April 1990, pp. 37–38).

21. Latin America Regional Reports, *Weekly Report*, 31 May 1990, p. 3.

22. Latin America Regional Reports, *Weekly Report*, 17 January 1991, p. 3.

23. Latin America Regional Reports, *Andean Group*, 11 October 1990, p. 2.

24. Fujimori's harsh economic policies, however, were not a major factor in the April 1992 auto-coup, even though they had generated significant opposition. The central issue behind Fujimori's seizure of power was the question of how to deal with the Shining Path guerrillas.

» «

Selected Bibliography

BOOKS

Alexander, Robert J. *Latin American Political Parties*. New York: Praeger Publishers, 1973.

Almond, Gabriel, and Powell, G. Bingham, Jr., eds. *Comparative Politics Today*. Glenview, Ill.: Scott, Foresman, 1988.

Armstrong, Robert, and Shenk, Janet. *El Salvador: the Face of Revolution*. Boston: South End Press, 1982.

Baloyra, Enrique, and Martz, John D. *Electoral Mobilization and Public Opinion*. Chapel Hill: University of North Carolina Press, 1976.

Bond, Robert, ed. *Contemporary Venezuela and its Role in International Affairs*. New York: New York University Press, 1977.

Borregales, Germán. *Copei hoy: Una negación*. Caracas: Ediciones Garrido, 1968.

Cartáy Ramírez, Gerhard. *Política y partidos modernos en Venezuela*. Caracas: Ediciones Centauro, 1983.

Chaufen, Alejandro A. *Christians for Freedom: Late-Scholastic Economics*. San Francisco: Ignatius Press, 1986.

deKadt, Emanuel. *Catholic Radicals in Brazil*. London: Oxford University Press, 1970.

Delgado, Oscar, ed. *Reformas agrarias en la América Latina*. Mexico City: Fondo de Cultura Económica, 1965.

deSoto, Hernando. *The Other Path: The Invisible Revolution in the Third World*, trans. June Abbott. New York: Harper and Row, 1988.

Einaudi, Mario, and Goguel, François. *Christian Democracy in Italy and France*. Notre Dame, Ind.: University of Notre Dame Press, 1952.

Fitzmaurice, John. *The Politics of Belgium: Crisis and Compromise in a Plural Society*. New York: St. Martin's Press, 1983.

Flannery, Austin P. *Documents of Vatican II.* Grand Rapids, Mich.: William B. Eerdmans Publishing Co., 1975.

Fleet, Michael. *The Rise and Fall of Chilean Christian Democracy.* Princeton, N.J.: Princeton University Press, 1985.

Fogarty, Michael P. *Christian Democracy in Western Europe, 1982–1953.* Notre Dame, Ind.: University of Notre Dame Press, 1957.

Frei Montalva, Eduardo. *Latin America: the Hopeful Option.* Maryknoll, N.Y.: Orbis Books, 1978.

———. *The Mandate of History and Chile's Future.* Athens, Ohio: Center for International Studies, Papers in International Studies, Latin America Series, no. 1, 1977.

Ghose, Ajit Kumar. *Agrarian Reform in Contemporary Developing Countries.* London: Croon Helm, 1983.

Gross, Leonard. *The Last, Best Hope: Eduardo Frei and Chilean Democracy.* New York: Random House, 1967.

Herman, Donald L. *Christian Democracy in Venezuela.* Chapel Hill: University of North Carolina Press, 1980.

Hurtado, Osvaldo. *Political Power in Ecuador.* Translated by Nick D. Mills, Jr. Albuquerque: University of New Mexico Press, 1980.

Irving, R. E. M. *The Christian Democratic Parties of Western Europe.* London: George Allen & Unwin, 1979.

———. *Christian Democracy in France.* London: George Allen & Unwin, 1973.

Jorrín, Miguel, and Martz, John D. *Latin American Political Thought and Ideology.* Chapel Hill: University of North Carolina Press, 1970.

King, Russell. *Land Reform: A World Survey.* Boulder, Colo.: Westview Press, 1977.

Kirchner, Emil. *Liberal Parties in Western Europe.* Cambridge: Cambridge University Press, 1988.

Leo XIII, Pope. *The Great Encyclical Letters of Pope Leo XIII.* New York: Benzinger Brothers, 1903.

Lijphart, Arend. *Democracy in Plural Societies.* New Haven, Conn.: Yale University Press, 1977.

Lynch, Edward A. *Religion and Politics in Latin America: Liberation Theology and Christian Democracy.* New York: Praeger, 1991.

Manwaring, Max G., and Prisk, Court, eds. *El Salvador at War: An Oral History of Conflict from the 1979 Insurrection to the Present.* Washington, D.C.: National Defense University Press, 1988.

Maritain, Jacques. *Freedom in the Modern World.* New York: Charles Scribner's Sons, 1936.

———. *Man and the State.* Chicago: University of Chicago Press, 1951.

Martz, John D., ed. *Venezuela: The Democratic Experience.* New York: Praeger Publishers, 1977.

Millet, Richard, ed. *The Restless Caribbean: Changing Patterns of International Relations.* New York: Praeger Publishers, 1979.

Morgan, Roger, and Silvestri, Stephano. *Moderates and Conservatives in Western Europe: Political Parties, the European Community and the Atlantic Alliance.* London: Heinemann, 1982.

Padrón, Paciano, ed. *Copei: Documentos fundamentales, 1946.* Caracas: Ediciones Centauro, 1981.

Peña, Alfredo. *Conversaciones con Luis Herrera Campins*. Caracas: Editorial Ateneo de Caracas, 1978.

Pius XI, Pope. *Sixteen Encyclicals of Pope Pius XI*. Washington, D.C.: National Catholic Welfare Conference, 1938.

Powell, John Duncan. *Political Mobilization of the Venezuelan Peasant*. Cambridge, Mass.: Harvard University Press, 1971.

Powelson, John P., and Stock, Richard. *The Peasant Betrayed: Agriculture and Land Reform in the Third World*. Boston: Oelgeschlager, Gunn and Hain, 1987.

Prosterman, Roy L., and Riedinger, Jeffrey M. *Land Reform and Democratic Development*. Baltimore: Johns Hopkins University Press, 1987.

Rivera, Ramiro. *El pensamiento de León Febres Cordero*. Quito: Ediciones Culturales, 1986.

Schmitter, Philippe C. *Interest Conflict and Political Change in Brazil*. Stanford, Calif.: Stanford University Press, 1971.

Schodt, David W. *Ecuador: An Andean Enigma*. Boulder, Colo.: Westview Press, 1987.

Schrems, John J. *Principles of Politics*. Englewood Cliffs, N.J.: Prentice Hall, 1986.

Stepan, Alfred J. *The State and Society: Peru in Comparative Perspective*. Princeton, N.J.: Princeton University Press, 1977.

Sturzo, Luigi. *Church and State*. New York: Longmans, Green and Co., 1939.

——. *Italy and the Coming World*. New York: Roy Publishers, 1945.

——. *Politics and Morality*. Translated by Barbara Barclay Cater. London: Burn, Oates and Washbourne, 1938.

Téfel, Reinaldo Antonio. *El infierno de los pobres: Diagnóstico sociológico de los barrios marginales de Managua*. Managua: Ediciones el Pez y el Serpiente, 1972.

Thiesenhusen, William C., ed. *Searching for Land Reform in Latin America*. Boston: Unwin Hyman, 1989.

Warriner, Doreen. *Land Reform in Principle and in Practice*. Oxford: Oxford University Press, 1969.

Webre, Stephen. *José Napoleón Duarte and the Christian Democratic Party in Salvadoran Politics, 1960–1972*. Baton Rouge: University of Louisiana Press, 1979.

Williams, Edward J. *Latin American Christian Democratic Parties*. Knoxville: University of Tennessee Press, 1967.

Yzermans, Vincent A. *All Things in Christ: Encyclicals and Selected Documents of Saint Pius X*. Westminster, MD: The Newman Press, 1954.

Zuckerman, Alan S. *The Politics of Faction: Christian Democratic Rule in Italy*. New Haven, Conn.: Yale University Press, 1979.

ARTICLES

Bizzarro, Salvatore. "Rigidity and Restraint in Chile." *Current History* 74, 434 (1978): 66–69, 83.

Caldera, Rafael. "The Christian Democratic Idea." *America*, no. 7 (April 1962): 14–15.

Christian Democratic Review. Various issues.

Collier, David. "Overview of the Bureaucratic-Authoritarian Model," in Collier,

David., ed. *The New Authoritarianism in Latin America.* Princeton, N.J.: Princeton University Press, 1979: 19–32.

Constable, Pamela, and Valenzuela, Arturo. "Chile's Return to Democracy." *Foreign Affairs* 68, 2 (1989): 169–187.

Falcoff, Mark. "Eduardo Frei Montalva, 1911–1982." *Review of Politics* 44, 3 (1982): 323–327.

Fitzmaurice, John, and Van den Berghe, Guido. "The Belgian General Election of 1985." *Electoral Studies* 5, 1, (1986): 73–83.

Frei, Eduardo. "The Second Latin American Revolution." *Foreign Affairs* 50, 1 (1971): 83–96.

Latin America Regional Reports. *Andean Report; Southern Cone Report; Weekly Report.* Various issues.

Martz, John D. "The Crisis of Venezuelan Democracy." *Current History* 83, 487 (1984): 73–77, 89.

———. "Ecuador: The Right Takes Command." *Current History* 84, 499 (1985): 69–72, 84–85.

O'Donnell, Guillermo. "Tensions in the Bureaucratic-Authoritarian State and the Question of Democracy." In Collier, David, ed. *The New Authoritarianism in Latin America,* 285–318. Princeton, N.J.: Princeton University Press, 1979.

Pridham, Geoffrey. "The Italian Christian Democrats after Moro: Crisis or Compromise?" *West European Politics* 2,1 (1979): 69–88.

Rudd, Chris. "The Aftermath of Heysel: The 1985 Belgian Election." *West European Politics* 9, 2 (April 1986): 282–288.

Salgado, René. "Economic Pressure Groups and Policy Making in Venezuela: The Case of FEDECAMERAS Reconsidered." *Latin American Research Review* 22, 3 (1987): 91–106.

Thoumi, Francisco E. "The Hidden Logic of 'Irrational' Economic Policies in Ecuador." *Journal of InterAmerican Studies and World Affairs* 32, 2 (1990): 43–68.

Thoman, Victor E. "The Informal Sector in Latin America: Fifteen Years Later." In Turnham, David, Salome, Bernard, and Schwartz, Antoine, eds. *The Informal Sector Revisited,* 93–110. Paris: Organization for Economic Cooperation and Development, 1990.

Vargas Llosa, Mario. "A Cultural Battle." *Unesco Courier,* September 1990, pp. 44–45.

———. "Privatizing Peru." *New Perspectives Quarterly,* 6, 3 (Fall 1989): 38–41.

PAPAL DOCUMENTS

John XXIII, Pope. *Mater et Magistra* (Christianity and Social Progress). 15 May 1961.

———. *Pacem in Terris* (Peace on Earth). 11 April 1963.

John Paul II, Pope. *Laborem Exercens* (On Human Labor). 15 May 1981.

———. *Sollicitudo Rei Socialis* (Of Social Concerns). 30 December 1987.

———. *Centesimus Annus* (On the Hundredth Anniversary). 15 May 1991.

Leo XIII, Pope. *Graves de Communi* (Christian Democracy). 18 January 1901.

———. *Humanum Genus* (Freemasonry). 20 April 1884.

———. *Immortale Dei* (The Christian Constitution of States). 1 November 1885.

———. *Inscrutabili Dei* (On the Evils Affecting Modern Society). 21 April 1878.

——. *Quod Apostolici Muneris* (Socialism, Communism, Nihilism). 28 December 1878.

Paul VI, Pope. *Octogesima Adveniens* (On the Coming Eightieth). 14 May 1971.

——. *Populorum Progressio* (On the Development of Peoples). 26 March 1967.

Pius X, Pope. *Il Fermo Proposito* (Letter to Italian Bishops). 11 June 1905.

Pius XI, Pope. *Divini Redemptoris* (On Atheistic Communism). 19 March 1937.

——. *Mit brennender Sorge* (Letter to the German Bishops). 14 March 1937.

——. *Non abbiamo bisogno* (On Catholic Action). 29 June 1931.

——. *Quadragessimo Anno* (On Social Reconstruction). 15 May 1931.

Pius XII, Pope. *On the Function of the State in the Modern World.* 20 October 1939.

Index

ABOUT THE AUTHOR

EDWARD A. LYNCH is Assistant Professor of Political Science at Hollins College in Virginia. He is the author of *Religion and Politics in Latin America* (Praeger, 1991).